BY THE SAME AUTHOR

EVELYN WAUGH

A
LITTLE ORDER

a selection from his journalism
edited by Donat Gallagher

LITTLE, BROWN AND COMPANY   BOSTON   TORONTO

FIRST AMERICAN EDITION

Library of Congress Cataloging in Publication Data

Waugh, Evelyn, 1903–1966.
  A little order.

  I. Gallagher, Donat. II. Title.
PR6045.A97L5 1980   824'.912   80-23116
ISBN 0-316-92633-7

Acknowledgements

I am indebted to the Estate of Evelyn Waugh and to A. D. Peters & Co.,
Ltd. for permission to quote unpublished material; to the Humanities
Research Center of the University of Texas, Austin, USA, for permission
to consult the Evelyn Waugh Collection and make use of many other
splendid facilities; to the courteous and efficient staff of HRC for many
kindnesses; and to Mrs Joan Engris of the Library of James Cook University, Townsville, Australia, for much valuable assistance. How hard it
is to find words of gratitude beyond the stereotyped formalities: when
I say that half the work that has gone into compiling this book is my
wife's I am stating a simple fact.

MV

CONTENTS

"To introduce a little order into this chaos."
Matthew Arnold

"He said it with a facetious intonation . . . he said it as though it were a joke, but in his heart he believed he was speaking the simple truth."

Put Out More Flags

BIBLIOGRAPHICAL NOTE

No complete bibliography of Evelyn Waugh's journalism has yet been published. Three sources list almost everything of interest :

1.   Robert Murray Davis, *et al.*, *Evelyn Waugh: A Checklist of Primary and Secondary Material* (Troy, New York : Whitston Publishing Company, 1972).
2.   Thomas Gribble, "Some New Waugh Bibliography", *Evelyn Waugh Newsletter*, Autumn 1972, pp. 8–9.
3.   Alain Blayac, "Evelyn Waugh : A Supplementary Bibliography", *The Book Collector* (London), Spring 1976, pp. 53–62.

INTRODUCTION

Waugh drew a distinction (which does not apply to his novels) between writing "for money" and writing "for intelligent people" (14 June 1956).[1] He was far too daemonic to observe it closely. In 1962, after a lifetime as a professional writer, a routine newspaper article on British Guiana could "go stale" on him. Furthermore, while he was never too proud to attempt to suit editors' tastes, he was too much governed by conviction, by anger, by a sense of the absurd, to tailor his work at will to their requirements. Consequently, even his most frankly mercenary journalism is likely to contain glimmers of real interest : what he wrote "for money" cannot possibly be discounted *en bloc*.

Nevertheless, Waugh did make this distinction and it decisively influenced his choice of subject and manner. Broadly, what he wrote, and how he wrote, depended on how much money he had. And since he scolded the 1959 *Dictionary of National Biography* for giving too much space in its entries on authors to "personal impressions", and too little to details of education, social circle, and earnings, I intend to avoid his posthumous wrath by approaching his journalism through "basic information" about his professional career.

On 1st March 1927 Waugh wrote in his diary : "I have been trying to do something about getting a job and am tired and discouraged . . . It seems to me the time has arrived to set about being a man of letters." As "Myself . . ."* puts it, rejected by the blacking factory, David Copperfield-in-reverse was "reduced to the family trade of writing". It was not until the war made him look at life in a new way that, as he relates in "Fan-Fare"*, he abandoned hope of becoming a "man of the world" and devoted himself to his art as "an end in itself". He also had a cause to espouse – the Roman Catholic faith.

[1]A. D. Peters & Co were Evelyn Waugh's literary agents from 1928 until his death. Since the late A. D. Peters quickly became Waugh's friend and intimate business adviser as well as his agent, the correspondence between Waugh and the Peters firm is full of interest. Lodged at the Humanities Research Center, University of Texas, Austin, USA, none of it has been published. All quotations of letters in this book are from the file in HRC. Dates are enclosed in brackets.
* Articles marked with an asterisk are included in this collection. See list of contents, p. v.

Both talent and family background made professional writing an obvious choice. Waugh wrote and drew successfully from a very early age, and in the preface to his "nursery novel" could complain only of difficulties arising from surroundings that were "entirely literary". He showed precocious literary abilities at his private and public schools and Oxford. Given the decision to become a writer, every portent was hopeful. His first book, *Rossetti*, won respectful reviews. In 1928 *Decline and Fall* achieved some success and notoriety. "The value of writing books," he says in "Myself . . ."*, is that "it gives one a market for articles." Newspapers began to use the *enfant terrible*'s work. Waugh put himself in the capable hands of A. D. Peters & Co, the firm of literary agents with whom he remained until his death. From that time onwards he earned his whole living by his pen. His career in journalism falls into three stages.

The first stage extends from 1928 to 1945. Waugh's situation during this period is summed up in a letter to Peters : "Please fix up anything that will earn me anything even cricket criticism or mothers' welfare notes" (12 Nov. 1928). He was almost always short of money. At first, as he had no income from any other source than writing, and as *Decline and Fall* sold slowly, he was genuinely poor. After *Vile Bodies* became a best seller in 1930, bringing with it lucrative newspaper and glossy magazine commissions, he earned on average two thousand pounds a year, seven hundred pounds coming from journalism. A hyper-active social life, however, kept him, as he put it, "starving". The result was that, unless he were working on a novel, or travelling, or temporarily in funds, he was eager for any highly paid work he could get. His journalism therefore tended to be written to order for editors who wanted stories or articles "in Mr Waugh's usual vein".

In "Literature : the Way to Fame" he succinctly expresses another consideration : "the reviews don't matter, the important thing is to make people talk". In *Labels* he elaborates :

> So you have to spend half your leisure in writing articles for the papers; the editors buy these because people buy your books, and people buy your books because they see your articles in the papers. (p. 2)

Waugh made enterprising use of Lady Eleanor Smith, Tom Driberg, and other friendly gossip columnists "to make people talk". Some of the elements in his journalism can be put down to professional self-advertisement.

Most of Waugh's articles appeared in the *Daily Mail* and *Harper's Bazaar* (then advertised as "the most luxurious fashion magazine in the world"), the *Harper's* pieces often being reprinted in the United States. Their usual subject was the world of fashion : clothes, parties, gambling, night life, the Season, holiday resorts . . . As a rule, they opposed some new craze from the viewpoint of one who could see through both the absurdity of the fashion and the prudery of the Mrs Grundys who opposed it, e.g. "This Sun-bathing Business".* The manner was lively, not unlike

Shaw at his most "energetically egotistical" : writing to Peters Waugh called it "forcefulness" (27 Nov. 1928).

It should be added that Waugh did not find society topics unworthy of him. On the contrary, he had a keen, and eccentrically deep, interest in food, clothes, wine and amusements, which he invested with an importance comparable to the mystique Hemingway found in sport. What seriousness there is arises from determination to uphold "qualitative standards", the lack of which is deplored in "The War and the Younger Generation"*; and from a policy of militant intolerance, which forbade condoning the second rate.

In bulk, general reviewing competes with society articles during this early period. Waugh had his own page for six months in the *Graphic* during 1930, and again for six months in *Night and Day* during 1937. He reviewed frequently for the *Spectator* and the *Observer*, and occasionally for many other papers, most notably the Roman Catholic *Tablet* after it changed hands in the late thirties : "There are still things which are worth fighting *against*."

During the thirties newspapers often called on novelists for "challenging" articles on subjects such as "Is There an After Life?" Waugh scorned the genre : the "average sophisticated novelist" did not "take propaganda seriously" but "sat down to earn his weekly guineas from the penny daily in a mood of apology".[2] But being too much in need of money to resist completely, he wrote several lively articles on such subjects as censorship, marriage and divorce, and one on Wilberforce pointing out some of the advantages of slavery. Five articles on Youth are the most interesting of these pieces, because they reveal important affinities Waugh shared with his generation, and an intensely critical attitude towards the modern period. Little straightforwardly serious journalism occurs at this time. Two essays, on Ronald Firbank* and Palladian architecture ("A Call to the Orders"*), are of considerable importance. A few letters to editors (on Edmund Campion, Abyssinia, and Fascism) and reviews of books on political and religious topics reveal clear, firm convictions.

A second stage of Waugh's career began in 1945 when *Brideshead Revisited* sold 600,000 copies. Bringing him new popularity, and an international reputation as a "Catholic novelist", it created opportunities for journalism in which financial considerations were not paramount. In the army Waugh had suffered the double humiliation of finding himself unemployable as an officer and being compelled to resign from his Brigade. Moreover, the outcome of the fighting was utterly disillusioning. The changes brought about by these private and public tragedies can be read in "Fan-Fare"* and other pieces : Waugh finally put aside hope of a non-literary career, and conspicuously withdrew from the "new dark age" that was "the modern world"; positively, he devoted himself wholeheartedly to writing and to religion for the first time. A minor circumstance was the Labour Party's winning office when post-war conditions were still hard.

---

[2] Review of *Assorted Articles*, by D. H. Lawrence, *Graphic*, 31 May 1930, p. 476.

All of these factors led Waugh to reverse his attitudes to journalism. He now avoided purely commercial work, but promoted his new interests. Thus, refusing an offer of regular work on the *Evening Standard,* he left the way open for short articles "when the subject particularly excites me" (12 Nov. 1947). Of his article opposing President Tito's visit to England he wrote : "The price is not important provided I could be as truthful as I liked in the words I liked" (19 Nov. 1952). Always pleased "to spend January and February in the sun at someone else's expense", he now eagerly sought work involving trips to Scandinavia, America, Palestine, Goa, and elsewhere, as a means of escaping "occupied" England. A connection with *Life* magazine formed through friendship with Randolph Churchill and the Luces made travel easier for a time.

Waugh's style altered. Essays marked by a rich vocabulary, more elaborate sentences, and deliberate cadence took the place of "forceful" articles. The new style reflected Waugh's advice to read a page of Ruskin a day, and his determination to counteract the plain or "drab" prose style that was then fashionable, part of the "flight from magnificence" lamented in "Literary Style in England and America"*.

The subject on which Waugh chose to write most often was Roman Catholicism. To this must be added that he frequently introduced religious considerations into secular articles with disconcerting explicitness. "The American Epoch in the Catholic Church"*, "The Plight of the Holy Places", and "Death in Hollywood" in *Life,* "Mgr. Ronald Knox"* in *Horizon,* "Saint Francis Xavier's Bones" in *Esquire,* combine a religious theme with Waugh's most formal style, and, to his mind at least, mark the high point of his journalism. Smaller essays, reviews, and letters to editors more closely mirrored his personal response to a religion which admits of wide diversity among its members. The more important religious pieces appeared both in England (in the *Tablet* and the *Month*) and in America (in *Life* and *Commonweal*); most were translated into the major European languages.

His non-religious journalism, though relatively infrequent in the post-war years, was far from insignificant. Two widely admired articles on Scandinavia were aptly titled "Dreary Paradise" in America. "Why Hollywood is a Term of Disparagement"* prompted a reply from Sir Alexander Korda, and a crop of letters in support of Waugh.

An outstanding event of this period was "Our Guest of Dishonour"* which appeared on the front page of the *Sunday Express* attacking President Tito's state visit to England. Waugh's principal objections to the visit were that Tito was being represented as an ally, when in fact he had been a treacherous enemy, and as a liberal, when he was a doctrinaire Marxist persecuting the Catholic Church in a way of which the public was kept ignorant. Moved by the plight of his fellow Catholics when he had served in Croatia in 1945, Waugh had written reports to the Vatican and the Foreign Office and letters to *The Times* on their behalf. Now in 1952–53 he followed his article with letters, interviews, and talks, culminating in an address to a large meeting in Glasgow organized by the Catholic Truth Society. He failed to prevent the visit, but succeeded in provoking an uproar. It is instructive that he later refused tempting requests for similar performances. When invited to attack Kruschev and Bulganin's visit to England, he offered to explain instead why there was nothing unchivalrous in eating with *open* enemies (2 March 1956).

There is no clear dividing line between the second and third stages of Waugh's journalistic career; a new situation simply emerged as the money earned by *Brideshead* dwindled. Waugh grew modest. Once he had shrugged off criticism and abused the editor who made it. Now he had misgivings: "I am not much good at writing articles", he said before a trip to Rhodesia, "but if anyone is interested I might try" (5 Jan. 1958). Fearing an end to his creative powers, he had also become reluctant to waste time on journalism:

> I think while I have any capacity left for original work I ought to avoid hack work. As soon as Knox is done I must start a novel and get it done while I have inventive strength left. . . . I shall have to live and support my children for many years. *Then* I shall need any job that can be done by experience in the trade of writing. (18 April 1958)

But by December 1959 he was writing to Peters: "I shall be very hard up soon. Please give anxious thought to my future."

Ironically, by achieving notoriety as a snob and reactionary he had now become more valuable to newspapers than ever before. To comprehend this it must be understood that he was pre-eminently an author whose art was in his life as well as his writing. From the late forties onwards, in creating a style of living opposed to that of the "modern world" and the "classless society", he was fashioning a "little independent system of order" ("Fan-Fare"*), which served to rebuke the times as much as what he wrote. "Anything Wrong with Priestley?"* explains that Waugh sought "to live like a gentleman". His "Victorianized" house strikingly embodied admiration for "the immediate past" and rejection of contemporary taste. *Wine in Peace and War* (1947) advocated a return to the "Arcadian Age" of "leisurely entertaining and profuse expenditure", and the pursuit of luxury as an ideal (p. 76). Waugh followed his own advice: "Luxury not lionization is the thing . . ." he wrote when arranging a trip to Hollywood (3 Oct. 1946). Many came to regard him as an awesome perfectionist; "One could hear the ghost of Evelyn Waugh snorting . . ." says a critique of a central Texas restaurant. Most were outraged by his flaunting of class distinction.

Bizarre pronouncements on politics and religion contributed to Waugh's notoriety. The Mugwump* deplored the Crown's adopting that "hazardous means of choosing advisers: popular election". The belligerent Papist declared in the "Foreword" to *William Weston* that "for her fullest development England needed a third conquest, by Philip of Spain".

In the roles he had created for himself, Super-Snob, Connoisseur-impossible-to-please, and Tory-for-whom-*The-Times*-was-too-Red, newspapers welcomed Waugh. They were uninterested in his less bizarre opinions. The situation is well illustrated by the history of two articles "Return to Eldorado" and "Manners and Morals". In 1961 the *Daily Mail* commissioned Waugh to visit British Guiana, then approaching independence, to write five articles. His diaries record diligent investigation of the situation. The *Mail* happily accepted his first article, a gently satirical piece about pleasure-cruising in the Caribbean; but it made so many difficulties about his serious account of the country that Waugh had to give this to the *Sunday Times*, and work off his debt to the *Mail* by reviewing the *Pan Book of Etiquette*. Pleased with the arrangement, the *Mail* instructed Waugh to be as "hard-hitting" as he liked. The result was "Manners and Morals", in which Waugh told the English that they were becoming a race of "slatterns and louts", and English women that they were dirty :

> There were never more bathrooms in England than there are today and never so many dirty necks and fingernails . . . countless (girls) should be sent to bed supperless.

The paper which welcomed this sort of thing paid Waugh for an article on religion for its Philosophers' Club, and for another on *Lady Chatterley's Lover*, but would print neither.

Of several newspaper pieces of the period, "I See Nothing But Boredom . . . Everywhere"* (1959), a forecast of what the next ten years would bring, is the most self-revelatory. Waugh was not the least nervous about a nuclear holocaust; what he feared was "boredom" arising from the drab uniformity of everything. An article on Monte Carlo is the most significant. Waugh admired Monte Carlo because he regarded it as "the prime achievement of pre-1914 sweetness of life". His question, "Why can we not have a casino at the end of every pier?" is a fantastication of one of his deeply held convictions, that the modern world should return to "the immediate past" to re-learn the art of living well. An article on Venice, "Sinking, Shadowed and Sad"*, best expresses Waugh's attraction to beauty and "decorum".

In spite of discouragements, Waugh published a considerable amount of serious work in this final period. It is important to understand that he was, as Andrew Sinclair says, "the most perfect observer of English social gradations in this century"[3] because his acute observation of social rank plays a much larger part in his novels and short stories than does plain snobbery. A contribution to the U and non-U debate, which reveals intense interest in the English class system, is the most noteworthy example. Other important pieces from this time dealing with art, literature, and politics have been reprinted in this book.

Inevitably Waugh was asked to deal with Catholic subjects in the popular press. He responded with urbane articles on Popes Pius XII and John XXIII, which hinted disapproval of papal policies. In 1962 he startled England with "The Same Again, Please", a spontaneous attack on changes in the Church contemplated by the Second Vatican Council. Waugh had

---

[3] *The Last of the Best: The Aristocracy of Europe in the Twentieth Century*, London, 1969, p. 233.

an arguable case, a talent for attracting attention and admirable consistency at a time when many Catholics were disavowing the opinions of a lifetime. He followed this article with a long series of letters. Although widely separated from most conservatives in moral and cultural outlook, he became established as England's "leading ecclesiastical die-hard". Was this such an improbable end for the former *enfant terrible*? Waugh had begun his career as a spokesman for the Youngest Generation, insinuating into the conventional bombast of Youth attacking Age criticism of his seniors for "pretending to be young" (i.e. for following modern fashions) and for failing to uphold "the standards of civilization". At the close of his life he rebuked the Bishops of the Catholic Church, not excluding the Bishop of Rome, for their failure to defend the traditions entrusted to them.

Had he lived, would Waugh have collected his journalism? What pieces should be reprinted in a brief anthology? What claims to attention does this work of his have? The questions are closely connected. *The Holy Places*, of course, already includes "The Defence of the Holy Places" and "St. Helena Empress"*. Waugh also planned a *Book of Pilgrimages* comprising existing pieces, and new articles on Lenin's tomb and Salt Lake City. When selling weightier essays, such as "The American Epoch in the Catholic Church"* and the introductions to the "Saki" and Galsworthy novels,* Waugh explicitly reserved rights for a "future book of collected essays" (14 Nov. 1946, 23 Oct. 1953). Furthermore, he permitted various pieces to be anthologized, although he was apt on these occasions, as Peters warned an editor, "to rewrite, subtract, and add quite extensively" (9 Jan. 1956). The expansion and "polishing" undergone by "Death in Hollywood" (*Life*) before its reappearance as "Half in Love With Easeful Death"* (*Tablet*) is an indication of what would have happened to many magazine pieces before they appeared in a book. On the other hand Waugh was cynical about much of his commercial work. "Here is some balls for . . ." sums up his attitude towards a number of pieces. He once described his early newspaper work as "beastly little articles" (2 Aug. 1950). It is quite certain that he would never have consented to its being reprinted while he was alive.

In compiling this anthology, I have taken little account of Waugh's condemnation of his early work. Given his classical standards of judgment, and his famous preference for his late over his early novels, it is perfectly intelligible, though few readers will share it. Those who consider the early novels superior to the later will almost certainly enjoy the "beastly little articles" more than the "essays". The majority will probably find that each category has its own virtues. The aim of this selection is to provide a conspectus of Waughism; of the opinions, attitudes, interests, and styles most representative of the full range of his journalism.

D.G.

I

Myself . . .

Some of the pieces in this chapter are directly autobiographical, some are lightly fantasticated personal experience (e.g. "Literature"), some state important policies and attitudes, others deal in a self-revealing way with topics close to Waugh (e.g. the post-Great-War generation and Oxford), while "People Who Want to Sue Me", which is about "putting people into books", is a piece of almost pure bluff. Everything illustrates the career of the "public" Evelyn Waugh.

The Youngest Generation

During the last few years, a new generation has grown up; between them and the young men of 1912 lies the great gulf of the war. What will they stand for and what are they going to do?

The men of Rupert Brooke's generation are broken. Narcissus-like, they stood for an instant amazedly aware of their own beauty; the war, which old men made, has left them tired and embittered. What will the young men of 1922 be?

They will be, above all things, clear-sighted, they will have no use for phrases or shadows. In the nineteenth century the old men saw visions and the young men dreamed dreams. The youngest generation are going to be very hard and analytical and unsympathetic, but they are going to aim at things as they are and they will not call their aim 'Truth'.

And because they are clear-sighted, they will not be revolutionaries and they will not be poets and they will not be mystics; there will be much that they will lose, but all that they have will be real.

And they will be reticent too, the youngest generation. The young men of the nineties subsisted upon emotion and their poetry and their painting thrills with it. They poured out their souls like water and their tears with pride; middle-aged observers will find it hard to see the soul in the youngest generation.

But they will have – and this is their justification – a very full sense of humour, which will keep them from 'the commission of all sins, or nearly all, save those that are worth committing.' They will watch themselves with, probably, a greater egotism, than did the young men of the nineties, but it will be with a cynical smile and often with a laugh.

It is a queer world which the old men have left them and they will have few ideals and illusions to console them when they 'get to feeling old.' They will not be a happy generation.

Editorial, *Lancing College Magazine*, December 1921, p. 5.

Oxford and the Next War

A LETTER OF EXHORTATION FROM AN UNDERGRADUATE TO A FRIEND ABROAD

Dear Bill,

It occurs to me that I have allowed almost the whole term to go by without writing to you. This was disgraceful. My only excuse can be your utter remoteness and the complete heart-breaking dreariness of everyone and everything in Oxford.

You did well to go down. I can think of nothing which has happened this term which could at all interest you. All your friends have behaved more or less abominably to each other, as they used in your time, and have fallen into various degrees of ill favour with the authorities. The Proctors have been peculiarly aggressive this term. You probably saw, or will have seen before you get this, that they banned our 1840 Exhibition without any sort of reason. They seem to be determined that we shall not enjoy ourselves. The other day I was walking home with a pickaxe which I borrowed to complete the costume of 'the Conservative Working Man' for a fancy dress party, when I was stopped by a bowler-hatted servant and brought to the Proctors, who told me that it was not seemly to carry workmen's tools about. I wonder if it was just snobbery or ill-nature, or whether he was afraid of being attacked.

The Union has been sadder than ever and has just been celebrating a centenary. I do think it is time that something was done to stop the thing. You cannot imagine what the debates have been like this term, with Scaife setting a tone of arrogant mediocrity and people like de Gruchy trying to clear things up. They have elected Gerald Gardiner President this term – do you remember him? A tall man with a jerky voice who is generally writing things in the O.U.D.S.

The O.U.D.S., by the way, have shown themselves in no way as contemptuous of the Press as Scaife. I have never seen anything like the amount of comment and praise which Gyles' simple little performance of 'Hamlet' roused in the London papers. It was a thoroughly good amateur show; that is to say, everyone knew his part tolerably well, and the lights didn't go out or the curtains catch fire, or the wigs come off, or anything like that, but all the fuss in Fleet Street was utterly silly. It is a pity that all these editors and reporters treat Oxford so seriously. They even, some of them, swallowed poor Jim Fagan's lame little excuses about 'infinity' for his very commonplace 'geometry and curtains.'

The Bicester have had to close down owing to foot-and-mouth disease, but that doesn't affect a poor man like myself. There has been quite enough to exasperate us all without that.

You know, Bill, what we want is another war. I become more and more convinced of that every day.

These tiresome historians always find causes for their wars in national expansion and trade rivalry and religion and such things. I don't know about these because, as you know, I am never up in time to read the newspapers, but I gather from those who do that things are pretty unsettled. What seems to me more important is that we have a great body of young men of all sorts of education just longing for another general disturbance. We all had the fortune to be brought up in easy familiarity with bombs and casualty lists and bad bread and all the things young men used to be warned about, and we know exactly how bearable and unbearable they are.

We also know that when there is a war the fighting people at least have moments of really intense enjoyment and really intense misery – both things which one wants at our age. As far as I can see, there is just no chance of any of us being able to earn a living, or at least a living decent enough to allow of any sort of excitement or depravity. Here we are with bills, over-fastidious tastes, and a completely hopeless future. What can we do but to long for a war or a revolution?

If on your travels you meet any traitors who want to levy war against the king, or kings who want to overthrow representative institutions, or fanatics who want to convert people by the sword to some ghastly religion, or jolly adventurers who want to kill all the Mormons or check the Yellow Peril, or restore the Hapsburgs or the Stuarts, or invade America in the cause of alcohol or China in the cause of opium, or France in the cause of Sabbatarianism, or the Vatican in the cause of compulsory vaccination, please tell them, him or her that we can raise a very jolly platoon of gentlemen-adventurers for them in Oxford if they, he or she will pay us handsomely and give us a good chance of a speedy death.

What a long letter, Bill!

Yours,

Evelyn.

Take Your Home Into Your Own Hands!

I do not know who started the idea of "good taste." I strongly suspect that D.O.R.A.* had a younger brother who went to art classes at an evening polytechnic, and that it all began with him.

Certainly no one worried much about it in the eighteenth century, when people who were rich enough put cupids all over their ceilings, and built fireplaces in a style happily based on a combination of Greek, Chinese and French Gothic. Nor, I think, did it much concern our grandparents who went on accumulating the grossest kinds of bric-à-brac in superb disregard of all that Mr Ruskin was saying in his clever books. But quite lately, with the advent of all the other worries which gave that hunted look to Mr Strube's "Little Man", came the plague of "good taste".

One has only to look around today at the bleak little parlours of the suburbs and the still bleaker great drawing rooms of Belgrave-square to see the havoc it has caused. Some terrific voice from behind the bar seems to have said "Time, gentlemen, please," and forthwith every one began carrying away her dearest possessions to the lumber-room or sending them down to a very chilly reception in the servants' hall.

In some mysterious way, for which I strongly suspect my fellow journalists in the Home Pages are largely responsible, everybody seems to have been bullied into an inferiority complex about their own homes.

In Victorian times people were terrified of being thought poor, and starved themselves in order to clothe a second footman.

Nowadays we are all desperately poor and quite boastful about it, but I have yet to find anyone but myself who still says with absolute complacency "I don't know much about art, but I do know what I like." I say that about three times a day and it always has the profoundly shocking effect that I hoped for.

Look around your own drawing room. Where is the firescreen with the family coat-of-arms worked in coloured wools by your Aunt Agatha?

And why is that horrible earthenware pot, which someone else's Aunt Agatha made in a suburb of Brighton, sitting so coldly on the mantelpiece? And do you really find it comfortable to read by that triangular lamp

Daily Express, 16 January 1929, p. 5.
* Defence of the Realm Act.

shade which throws all the light on the ceiling? And where is the stuffed parrot?

Have you made all these changes because you really like them or because someone has been at you about "good taste"?

It may be that you really do like them, but it seems odd that Colonel Brown's wife who disagrees with you about politics and religion and how to bring up her daughters should see eye to eye with you on this point. And the vicar's drawing room is exactly like yours, although you could never bear the vicar; and so is the doctor's wife's, who they say, drinks far more than is good for her, and wears such extraordinary hats.

If by some odd coincidence you really do heartily agree with your neighbour's taste in house decoration, well and good; but if she likes to fill her window with arts-and-crafts pottery bowls of crocuses, and you like aspidistras better, just fill your house with aspidistras till it looks like a conservatory, and if you like Benares brass pots, put them in those, and if you like bamboo stands, put them on them.

By all means hide the tiger's head which your Uncle George shot in India, if it keeps you awake at night, but if you like it, don't be bullied into putting it away by Mrs Brown who lives next door. March round with your umbrella and tell her that her hunting prints and Staffordshire pottery are "middle-class" or "bad taste."

And if you see sarcastic glances being cast on the family photograph album or the cup you won at the cycling gymkhana or at the tinted photograph of the Acropolis or the Landseer engravings, just you say very decisively, "I don't know much about art, but I do know what I lilke"; then they will see that they are beaten, and Mrs Brown will say to the vicar's wife that it is so sad that you have no taste, and the vicar's wife will say to the doctor's wife that it really only shows what sort of people you are, but all three will envy you at heart and even perhaps, one by one, bring out from the attics a few of the things they really like.

Too Young at Forty

YOUTH CALLS TO THE PETER PANS OF MIDDLE-AGE WHO BLOCK THE WAY

Every ten years or so an unaccountable wave of feeling seems to engulf the British Public and awaken them to the fact that there is a "Younger

Generation". I do not know why this should be so, because, of course, people are born and grow up daily, and not in decades; it is, however, one of the many odd idiosyncrasies of the public mind that its recognition of the ordinary facts of growth should invariably take the form of sudden and indiscriminate booms in Youth. At the beginning of this century we had the Reforming Boom – Fabianism and feminism hand-in-hand; then there was the Merrie England Boom – folk dancing and beer drinking eyeing each other askance; the last, or Conquering Hero Boom, at the end of the war, was stupendous and almost in proportion to the four years' slump in everything worth while which preceded it.

Ten years ago everyone was agog for youth – young Bishops, young Headmasters, young Professors, young Poets, young advertising managers. It was all very nice, and, of course, they deserved it, but I hope that I shall not be thought ungrateful to the men who defended me when I was a helpless schoolboy in the O.T.C. if I mention the fact that once again *there is a younger generation.*

Things have not been particularly easy for those of us who have grown up in the last ten years. In former years a young man or woman setting out on his career saw his progress marked out in a gentle gradation of seniority. It may have been slow, but it *was* progress. At the head of everything tottered "the old man"; his second in command, a few years his junior, waited respectfully to take his place; another sharp winter and everyone would get a rise; a few more fogs, perhaps a railway accident or an epidemic, and another death would move the procession a step nearer its goal; success waited on succession.

But to-day things are very different. In business, in the professions, in art, in the public services the way is blocked by the phalanx of the Indestructible Forties. A fine, healthy lot, these ex-captains and majors work by day, dance by night, golf on Sundays, nothing is too much for them, and nothing is going to move them for another 30 years. How they laugh and slap their thighs and hoot the horns of their little two seater cars. I don't suppose that I shall be heard at all when I diffidently whisper that *there is a younger generation.*

And yet I think I see signs that another boom in youth is coming, though it is going to be quite different from all its predecessors. Always before it has been the younger generation asserting the fact that they have grown up; to-day the more modest claim of my generation is that we are young.

Our seniors cannot have it every way; they really must begin to grow up a little. They must cure themselves of the arrested development that seems to afflict them. In the Church we see tough old clergymen expounding the exploded heresies of the Dark Ages under the name of "Modern" Churchmen. Cézanne died long before we were born and still his imitators proclaim their paintings as "Modern" Art. In Society indefatigable maiden ladies of Chelsea and Mayfair, dyspeptic noblemen and bald old wits still caper in the public eye as "the Bright Young People." There are the Peter Pans of Bloomsbury, the skittish old critics who will not grow up, who must always be in the movement. Is there no one who will gently remind them of their silver hairs and explain to them, patiently and tactfully, that *there is a younger generation*?

A healthy system of classification has divided prominent people in three classes; from birth to the age of forty they are spoken of as "young and brilliant"; from forty to sixty they are "distinguished"; from sixty to death "veteran." Surely it is time that the pre-war *enfants terribles* became a little more circumspect in their demeanour, a little more thoughtful in their public utterances, a little more "distinguished"?

"But," I shall be asked, "if these plump old soldiers whom we have so long looked upon as 'modern' are not the younger generation, what is this younger generation like?" In reply I can mention five writers all known already to a considerable public who seem to me to sum up the aspirations and prejudices of my generation. These are, first, Mr Harold Acton, poet and novelist; Mr Robert Byron, the art critic; Mr Christopher Hollis, the Catholic apologist; Mr Peter Quennell, poet and literary critic; and Mr Adrian Stokes, philosopher. Each of these writers has already published more than one work and it is in them that the spirit of my generation can be read. They are all diverse in interests and method, but they have the unifying quality of Youth in them and in the other less articulate members of my generation.

I see certain common tendencies which may be called the Spirit of the Age. One is a tendency to be bored with the problems of Sex and Socialism, which so vexed our seniors; another is the horror of the "ye olde" picturesque, folk dancing, art-and-crafty relaxations of our seniors; another is a disposition to regard very seriously mystical experience and the more disciplined forms of religion; another is a complete freedom from any kind of prudery, from either the Victorian facility of being shocked or the Edwardian will to shock; and, lastly, we all have the earnest wish that people will soon realise that *there is a younger generation*.

Careers for Our Sons: Literature
THE WAY TO FAME

There is a great deal to be said for the Arts. For one thing they offer the only career in which commercial failure is not necessarily discreditable. Shabbiness of appearance and irregularity of life are not only forgiven to the artist but expected. Art offers scope for profound and prolonged laziness, and in the event of success gives rewards quite out of proportion to industry.

Of all the Arts the one most to be recommended to the young beginner is literature. Painting is messy; music is noisy, and the applied arts and crafts all require a certain amount of skill. But writing is clean, quiet, and can be done anywhere at any time by anyone. All you need is some ink, a piece of paper, a pen and some vague knowledge of spelling. Even the last is not essential if you employ a competent typist.

All you have to do is to write "Chapter One" at the head of your paper and from then onwards for better or worse you are an author. Many people never get any further than that.

The best sort of book to start with is biography. If you want to make a success of it, choose as a subject someone very famous who has had plenty of books written about him quite recently. Many young writers make the mistake of choosing some forgotten Caroline clergyman or eighteenth century traveller.

They become deeply interested in their subject, spend dreary days in the British Museum Reading Room, and write a graceful, carefully documented work.

But is it a success? No. The reason being, that either the editor has never heard of your clergyman or traveller, and therefore does not take the trouble to have the book reviewed at all, or else it falls into the hands of someone who has himself been attracted by the same character, knows as much about him as you do and rather thought of writing the book himself. In which case he will jump on all the inevitable inaccuracies with terrific severity.

On the other hand, if you choose someone like Disraeli or Shakespeare

Passing Show, 2 February 1929, p. 16.

or the elder Pitt, you can be quite certain of what is called a "respectful hearing."

That means that all the famous critics who write weekly articles in learned journals see in your book a pleasant opportunity for once more printing their nicely turned opinions about Disraeli or Pitt, or whoever you have chosen. Every time a life of anyone really famous is published, they bring out the same old article they wrote when they were taking Schools at Oxford.

It is two easy columns for them and if they are at all amiable at heart they will show their gratitude by prefacing their essays with some little allusion to your book. "A new author, coming to his task with youthful exuberance but mature judgment," they will write "has once again raised the perennially engrossing problem of the elder Pitt."

You will not make very much money by this first book but you will collect a whole list of kindly comments which your publisher will be able to print on the back of the wrapper of your next. This should be a novel, preferably a mildly shocking one. Your biography has made you a "man of letters" and established your integrity of purpose. Librarians who see that distinguished critics have spoken respectfully of your work will be slow to ban it.

The reviews matter very little in the case of a novel. The important thing is to make people talk about it. You can do this by forcing your way into the newspapers in some other way. Attempt to swim the Channel; get unjustly arrested in a public park; disappear. There are innumerable means of attracting public notice.

Even a severe accident in a gale should be enough to secure you a commission for a series of articles on "the Church" or some such topic.

From then onwards your fame is secure. Your advice will be enlisted over the telephone upon questions of public moment; photographers will offer you complimentary sittings, you will be inundated with letters from the wives of starving clergymen offering to do your typing for you if you will buy them a typewriter and a correspondence course. You will be asked to lecture in America and give expert advice in courts of law, and restaurants bribe you to stage seductions there in your next book.

Finally, at the end of a happy and full life, you can look forward to a knighthood, a Civil List pension and a funeral in Westminster Abbey, if only you play your cards successfully at the beginning.

The War and the Younger Generation

One of the oddest results of the Great War is the vigour and accuracy which it has lent to the catch-phrases of the Ibsenite movement. Until ten years ago it was nonsense to talk in any general way about "The Younger Generation." Youth and age merged together in a gentle and unbroken gradation; even in single families the paradoxes of fecundity by which aunts were not infrequently born after their own nephews and nieces tended to weaken the arbitrary distinctions of the genealogical tree. But in the social subsidence that resulted from the War a double cleft appeared in the life of Europe, dividing it into three perfectly distinct classes between whom none but the most superficial sympathy can ever exist. There is (a) the wistful generation who grew up and formed their opinions before the War and who were too old for military service; (b) the stunted and mutilated generation who fought; and (c) the younger generation.

Every accident of environment contributed to make of this latter generation the undiscriminating and ineffectual people we lament to-day. For their elders, the War was either a shocking negation of all they had represented, or a reckless, rather thrilling, plunge into abnormality. For the younger generation it was simply the atmosphere of their adolescence. Darkened streets, food rations, the impending dread of the War Office telegram, hysterical outbursts of hate and sentiment, untrustworthy sources of information and the consequent rumours and scares; these were the circumstances which War-time children observed as universal and presumed to be normal. The air raids, for the vast majority of children, were rather amusing events, when servants appeared in improbable night clothes and everyone drank Bovril in the basement; the real and lasting injury was caused, not by danger, but by the pervading sense of inadequacy. Everything was a "substitute" for something else, and there was barely enough even of that. The consequence is a generation of whom nine hundred and fifty in every thousand are totally lacking in any sense of qualitative value. It is absurd to blame them if, after being nurtured on margarine and "honey sugar," they turn instinctively to the second-rate in art and life.

The only thing which could have saved these unfortunate children was the imposition by rigid discipline, as soon as it became possible, of the standards of civilization. This was still possible in 1918 when the young schoolmasters came back to their work. Unfortunately, a very great number, probably the more influential and intelligent among them, came with their own faith sadly shaken in those very standards which, avowedly, they had fought to preserve. They returned with a jolly tolerance of everything that seemed "modern." Every effort was made to encourage the children at the Public Schools to "think for themselves." When they should have been whipped and taught Greek paradigms, they were set arguing about birth control and nationalization. Their crude little opinions were treated with respect. Preachers in the school chapel week after week entrusted the future to their hands. It is hardly surprising that they were Bolshevik at eighteen and bored at twenty.

The muscles which encounter the most resistance in daily routine are those which become most highly developed and adapted. It is thus that the restraint of a traditional culture tempers and directs creative impulses. Freedom produces sterility. There was nothing left for the younger generation to rebel against, except the widest conceptions of mere decency. Accordingly it was against these that it turned. The result in many cases is the perverse and aimless dissipation chronicled daily by the gossip-writer of the Press.

What young man to-day, for example, in choosing a career, ever considers for one moment whether, by its nature, any job is better worth doing than any other? There was once a prevailing opinion that "the professions," which performed beneficial services to the community, were more becoming to a man of culture than "trades" in which he simply sold things for more than he gave. To-day that prejudice is suppressed and shop-keeping has become a polite hobby.

There seem signs, however, that a small group of young men and women are breaking away from their generation and striving to regain the sense of values that should have been instinctive to them. If this is so, there may yet be something done by this crazy and sterile generation. But it is too early at present to discern more than the vaguest hope.

People Who Want to Sue Me

I suppose that a novelist's life is not more full of embarrassments than anybody else's. There is no art or profession, except possibly higher mathematics, which one can practise without exposing oneself to amateur criticism and interference.

A novelist's trade, however, is the only one in which his acquaintances insist on coming right into the workshop and playing with the tools.

One of the most mischievous forms which this interference takes is the attribution to him of living models for his characters. Nowadays the instinctive reply to the question "Have you read So-and-so's new novel?" is "No. Who is in it?"

I was introduced to a young woman the other day whose first words were, "Oh, I'm so excited to meet you. Now you can tell me who all the characters in your book really are! Mary says that Mrs. —— is Lady So-and-so, but I'm sure it is really Mrs. ——. I *am* right, aren't I?"

Now, reluctant as any writer must be to discourage any motive that can lead people to buy his books, it should be pointed out how unfair this is to the author and to his friends. Obviously there must be a connection of some kind between a writer's work and his life. His knowledge of the world is limited by his own experience. It is practically impossible for those who live among poor people to write about the rich; a writer who has never been seriously in love cannot make his characters seem so; upbringing, education, experience of travel, of the war, etc., all circumscribe and determine the incidents of a book.

But here the connection ends. Nothing is more insulting to a novelist than to assume that he is incapable of anything except the mere transcription of what he observes.

It is the same with one's characters. When one is describing someone's appearance it is quite likely that one will subconsciously be led to describe someone one has seen – after all, there is a very limited number of physical characters which one can enumerate. The reader, thinking she recognises the portrait, will then assume that the temperament and the adventures of the character are also taken from life.

Daily Mail, 31 May 1930, p. 10.

In the same way it sometimes happens that one's fancy is taken by a remark or a trick of speech which one overhears; everyone immediately jumps to the conclusion that the character who uses it in the book must in all points be identical with the one who used it in real life. In this way one is liable to the loss of friends and to libel actions.

Another maddening misconception is that the author must be in sympathy with all the opinions uttered by his characters. A breach of the moral law or convention in one's books is treated by many elderly and semi-literate people as a breach committed by oneself.

There is a worse trouble than any of these, however. That is the people who insist on identifying themselves. "You ought to meet So-and-so," I was told the other day. "He is just the kind of character you ought to put into one of your books." "Dear young lady," I answered. "I don't put people into my books. *They take themselves out.*"

Not long ago I published a novel in which a few pages were devoted to the description of an hotel. In order to avoid trouble I made it the most fantastic hotel I could devise. I filled it with an impossible clientèle, I invented an impossible proprietress. I gave it a fictitious address, I described its management as so eccentric and incompetent that no hotel could be run on their lines for a week without coming into the police or the bankruptcy court. Here at least, I thought, I was safely in the realm of pure imagination.*

Imagine my surprise, therefore, when I received threatening letters from two irate old ladies in London, one in Newcastle and one in New York, all identifying themselves and their establishments with my invention!

I had the same experience with the heroine of the story. She was a young lady of crazy and rather dissolute habits. No one, I should have thought, would see herself in that character without shame. But nearly all the young women of my acquaintance, and many whom I have not had the delight of meeting, claim with apparent gratitude and pride that they were the originals of that sordid character.

If only the amateurs would get it into their heads that novel writing is a highly skilled and laborious trade. One does not just sit behind a screen jotting down other people's conversation. One has for one's raw material every single thing one has ever seen or heard or felt, and one has to go over that vast, smouldering rubbish-heap of experience, half stifled by the fumes and dust, scraping and delving until one finds a few discarded valuables.

---

* Waugh's Preface to *Vile Bodies*, London, 1965, admits that the novel contains "a pretty accurate description of Mrs Rosa Lewis and her Cavendish Hotel, just on the brink of their decline but still famous." Ed.

Then one has to assemble these tarnished and dented fragments, polish them, set them in order, and try to make a coherent and significant arrangement of them. It is not merely a matter of filling up a dust-bin haphazard and emptying it out again in another place.

Was Oxford Worth While?

Last week-end I went down to Oxford for an undergraduate party. It is near the end of term, and half the guests were just out of the schools in the middle of their final examinations. They replied to polite inquiries about their progress: "Oh, I don't know. With any luck in my *viva* I may scrape a second" – which is the stock answer of everyone who hopes for a first. I said that six years ago. I got a third.

I have reached the age when most of my friends in the University are dons. They go on, term after term – hospitable, malicious, unchanged. It was an unusual experience to see so many undergraduates, most of them in the last days of their last year, in the absurd white bow ties that are supposed to convey an academic appearance. It set me wondering whether Oxford had been worth while.

When parents and schoolmasters ask themselves and each other that question they often mean only one thing: Is the money spent on university education a sound capital investment? From three to four years of a young man's life, at an age when he might be earning a certain amount of money, are occupied instead in spending it. The amount, of course, varies a great deal from one man to another, but I suppose that it costs on the average about £1,000 to take a degree.

Is there a corresponding increase in the graduate's earning capacity? Would the money have been better employed at some technical training college?

From this point of view, as far as I can judge from my own experience and that of my friends, Oxford is certainly not worth while. When I went down the only job I could get was that of teaching elementary classics to turbulent little boys at the salary of £160 a year. Of my contemporaries only one is earning "real money"; he is a film star at Hollywood; incidentally he was sent down for failing to pass his preliminary schools.

Another friend, on the other hand, took high honours in Mods and Greats and has also devoted himself to cinema work. He gets a part in the crowd at Elstree about once a month. Another scholar who took a double first and was president of the Junior Common Room has become a curate.

Another friend who had an exemplary career in all branches of University life was for a month last year actually starving until he was discovered; another, who had a brilliant reputation among his fellow-undergraduates, lives in a dingy bed-sitting room and does occasional reviews for journals of precarious financial stability.

As far as direct monetary returns are considered, our parents would have done far better to have packed us off to Monte Carlo to try our luck at the tables.

But, of course, that is a narrow and silly way to regard education. A much more pertinent question is : Do Oxford and Cambridge maintain a tradition of genuine culture?

To judge by the blank faces and blanker conversation of the young men in a London ballroom one would suspect that they did not. To judge by the decoration of my tutor's rooms, one would say with certainty that they did not. Oxford is not up to date in the latest theories of aesthetics and psychology from Berlin and Paris. Many of the colleges are far from hygienic. A great number of the undergraduates express the heartiest contempt for everything to do with Art or intellect.

But there is another side. Oxford is architecturally a city of peculiar grace and magnificence, and it is impossible for anyone, however deep his apparent preoccupation with hunting or golf or bridge, to live there for three or four years without being influenced by it.

All the misunderstanding of the value of university life seems to me to come from two extreme heresies. On the one hand are those who expect a University to be a kind of insurance company into which so much money is paid and from which so much, eventually, is extracted. They expect a B.A. degree to be a badge which will gain them instant preference over poorer competitors, and in nine cases out of ten they are disappointed.

On the other hand, there are those who expect Oxford to be like an Oxford novel. A place of easy living, subtle conversation, and illuminating friendships. They expect it to be a kind of microcosm of eighteenth-century Whig society, combined with an infinitely sophisticated modernism. They, too, are disappointed.

The truth is that Oxford is simply a very beautiful city in which it is convenient to segregate a certain number of the young of the nation while they are growing up. It is absurd to pretend that a boy of eighteen, however sound he has been as a school prefect, is a fully grown man. Those who choose or are obliged to begin regular, remunerative, responsible work at the moment they leave school, particularly if they have had a fairly carefully tended adolescence, often show signs of a kind of arrested development.

It is just because Oxford keeps them back from their careers that it is of most value.

It gives them another four years in which to grow up gradually. It puts them out of the way of their fellow-citizens while they are making fools of themselves. They can learn to get drunk or not to get drunk; they can edit their own papers and air their opinions; they can learn how to give parties; they can find out, before they are too busy, what really amuses and excites them; and they can do all this in a town by themselves.

After that they can begin on the dreary and futile jobs that wait for most of them, with a great deal more chance of keeping their sense of humour and self-respect.

This Sun-bathing Business

I have been reading with the deepest amusement the accounts of the scene at the Welsh Harp last week-end when a mixed but united party attempted to sun themselves on a stretch of private ground by the shores of the lake. If we ever tend to feel a little superior to the squabbles of our earnest fellow-subjects in India or Malta, let us remember with humility the outburst last week-end. This man boils salt water; that man takes off his shirt; all men are brothers.

Not that I have the smallest enthusiasm for sun-bathing myself. I hate the whole business. Now and then I am forced to do it.

The first effect of this extensive unclothing is a mild interest in one another's colour – sometimes envious, usually sympathetic. This, however, very quickly passes and is succeeded by a sensation of gentle intoxication and content. That, too, is of short duration. Complete stupefaction sets

Daily Mail, 5 July 1930, p. 8.

in succeeded, at a long interval, by irritation, inflammation, and other symptoms of sunburn.

Then you rub on oil, and bits of sand and waste-paper adhere to you. At the end of the process you go indoors feeling completely tired out, as if you had been doing a decent afternoon's work, half awake and morose.

If you are lucky you are now discoloured evenly all over, if you have fair hair you look ludicrous, if you are dark you are a tolerable imitation of a Spanish donkey-boy.

But if you are unlucky, like me, you turn a mottled crimson, with white flakes in places as though you were afflicted with some noisome skin-disease.

All this is supposed to be good for you. Doctors say so. Nowadays people believe anything they are told by "scientists," just as they used to believe anything they were told by clergymen.

Of one thing, however, I am suspicious. I am doubtful whether all the addle-headed young women who encumber the country were really born as stupid as they seem. Their brown limbs give away their secret, like the scars of the cocaine taker. They have just lain out too long in the sun and their wits have got hard boiled. They have their annual orgy of stultification on the Riviera, and whenever they can get it in England – mercifully rarely – they fall back on their craving for their drug, sunlight.

It is astonishing how alert and intelligent many of these poor dolts become by Christmas.

However, that is their own look out.

If I had a daughter I should take good care to shut her up indoors. Hamlet gave just this advice to Polonius. The astonishing thing about the Welsh Harp incident was that large crowds of people assembled to disturb the sun-bathing of a number of total strangers. Moreover, they were not impelled by an officious solicitude for their poor baking brains, but by indignation that they should sit there on the grass imperfectly clothed.

Now, I can quite understand that many people may be depressed by the spectacle of naked humanity. Personally I cannot see that an ugly body is any more offensive than an ugly dress.

This, however, is not the point. The people who made a fuss at the Welsh Harp simply detest the spectacle of bodies of any kind, beautiful or ugly.

But do they cherish their over-delicate sensibility and avoid places where they are liable to shock? (After all, England is still full of places where one can be pretty certain that everyone will be fully clothed.) No. These astonishing people assemble in a large crowd at the one place where they know they will see the very thing which displeases them. There are some types of mind which it is hopeless to try to understand.

But there is another equally odd conclusion which emerges from the situation; that is, the devastating self-righteousness of all parties. The sun-bathers are not merely content to enjoy themselves in a fashionable but slightly idiotic manner. They must pretend that they are full of exalted moral purpose, martyrs in the cause of hygiene and true decency.

That is one of the queer characteristics of our countrymen. They will always quote the highest motives for whatever they do. If an Italian, say, overcharges one's bill or gives one the wrong change and is detected, he grins and admits failure. An Englishman will always attempt to prove himself right, will go on grumbling until one is out of earshot and will think one "no gentleman" for pointing out his dishonesty.

So it is with the disturbers of the peace at the Welsh Harp. If only the sun-bathers will be frank and say: "We like to lie and cook in the sun, because (a) someone told us it was fashionable; (b) it is rather fun seeing what our friends look like without their clothes; (c) it is comfortable to let our brains dry up completely so that we haven't got to bother about thinking."

If only the other side would say: "It was a hot day and we felt pugnacious and thought it would be fun to push those cranks into a pond."

But no. There must be all the usual clap-trap about "Freedom," "Health," "Purity," and even, most fantastic cry of all, "Save the children!"

What a funny lot we are!

Let Us Return to the Nineties
BUT NOT TO OSCAR WILDE

There seems to be every indication that we are in for another of those revivalist movements to which European, and particularly English, taste is so fatally liable. This time it is to be the eighteen-nineties. The early Victorian tide in which, before luncheon, we paddled and splashed so gaily has washed up its wreckage and retreated, and all those glittering bits of shell and seaweed – the coloured glass paper weights, wax fruit, Rex Whistler decorations, paper lace Valentines, which we collected –

Harper's Bazaar (London), November 1930, pp. 50–51, 98.

have by late afternoon dried out very drab and disappointing and hardly discernible at all from the rest of the beach, while the enamelled buckets, silver paper and banana skins of our own age still attract attention among the sand castles. Nurse is exhorting us to tidy up our own territory round the bathing tent, and even sets the example by digging in the confectioner's box which held the buns for tea; but all eyes are fixed on the sea; the tide has turned; the waves come tumbling up again with all manner of flotsam and jetsam bobbing in the surf, and with shrill cries the children scamper down to welcome the Nineties.

These recurrent outbursts of enthusiasm for the fashions of bygone periods are due to a very simple cause; the fact that it is a very arduous business to keep up with one's own period. People talk about "being modern" as though it were simply a matter of buying a new dress, drinking some cocktails, putting on the most recent gramophone record, and letting a mysterious "spirit of the age" do the rest. That way lie all the terrors of the pseudo. It takes as much serious effort to be sincerely and completely modern as to swim the Channel – and it is just about as profitable. There is an unhappy man in Paris called M. Cocteau whose whole life is occupied in trying to be modern (and there are some people in Bloomsbury with the same idea, but – whether because they started later, or work less feverishly, I do not know – these poor Britons have never quite caught up). There are many kind, rich ladies in London who think that they are attaining this modernity, by inviting coloured people or the authors of the latest best sellers to luncheon; there are editors who imagine they are keeping up to date by hiring very young people to write for them. But it is more complicated than these people believe.

One great difficulty is that, individually, people become more modern as they grow older. Undergraduates are absorbed in Rossetti and questions of right and wrong, their own sex adventures, and ideas of liberty and justice; the artists and writers who can justly claim to be thought *avant garde* are almost always middle-aged or quite elderly people – M. Picasso or Mr. James Joyce. It is as though it took an entire lifetime to bring oneself up to the spirit of one's own age. More than this, there is the discouraging conclusion that by the time one has really become modern, there is almost nothing to be said about it. There was unlimited material for conversation in an Academy painting of eighty years ago – what a sweet face the model had, and was the view from the window done in Dorset or Wilts, and what was the doggy with the limpid eyes really thinking about?

If one had learned the jargon there was quite a lot one could say about the painting of ten years ago – "recession," "planes," "significance," etc.; but before a painting by M. Picasso in his latest manner, the most glib tongue is compelled to silence.

Now, it is the essence of fashion that it should be fluid. When it finds itself dammed in one direction, it finds a new level elsewhere. Unable to go forward, it goes back. Little rivulets find out paths for themselves and fall in sparkling cascades – Mr. Byron to Byzantium, Mr. Sitwell to Baroque, M. Maritain to Aquinum, but the broad stream flows unimpeded. It is not to be wondered at if some of the nutshell boats, spinning in the eddies, lose their bearings a little and one hears such odd judgments as I read recently that "the Nineties are the last word in modernity."

It is perfectly natural that the fashionable flow should have come to temporary stagnation at that particular decade. Any period acquires a certain glamour after twenty-five years or so. Among simple minds the clothes of even a few years back excite derisive glee in theatre or cinematograph; to the more sophisticated the aesthetic and social codes of another generation are always instructive; but whereas almost any other period requires an acquaintance with Art and History far beyond the capacity of the young women who most eagerly follow the fashion, the Nineties, or rather the fiction that has come to represent the Nineties to the present generation, requires for its appreciation and imitation no sort of endowment of intellect or culture.

For the Nineties have come to mean for us only one thing – the great, booby figure of Oscar Wilde. Even he was by no means as comic as his admirers have made him. He was overdressed, pompous, snobbish, sentimental and vain, but he had an undeniable *flair* for the possibilities of the contemporary, commercial theatre. He got himself into trouble, poor old thing, by the infringement of a very silly law, which was just as culpable and just as boring as an infringement of traffic or licensing regulations. For the rest of his life he became a professional sponge. But it is this unremarkable figure that has become the type to which the new fashion is tending. It is natural that one of the first signs of the new movement should have been the revival of his plays. No one can object to this, because they are in their own strictly limited way perfectly competent works. The sad thing for poor Wilde's reputation was that, in the grim social circles which he wished to penetrate, anything that was not Politics or Sport was Art. If he wore scent, or jewellery, or eccentric waistcoats, or collected knick-knacks of porcelain, or *chinoiserie* – it was all unusual and therefore was Art. If he lay a long time on a sofa in a silk dressing-gown – that was Art, too. Wilde went bowling all over the country to lecture about Art. He even persuaded himself that he suffered for Art.

It is no wonder that fashionable people in London look back wistfully to that happy decade. The word Art still has the same glamour. They long ardently to be artistic, but all the arts have withdrawn themselves far beyond their comprehension. How they have hungered for a time when a reputation for wit might be achieved through paradox and epigram – those monkey-tricks of the intellect. The revival of interest in the Nineties is another – possibly a last – attempt of the amateurs and dilettani to persuade themselves that they are cultured.

Well, we are in for this revival and we must put up with it as best we may; there seems to me only one way in which we can meet the rising flood. Let us, if we must, return to the Nineties, but not to Oscar Wilde. There was much in those ten splendid years to which we can still look with approval. There was, for instance, the cult of the safety bicycle – that boon to postmen and University dons. Instead of sprawling about on divans, burning cheap joss sticks (or expensive ones for that matter) and fanning themselves with peacock's feathers, I should like to see fashionable society pedalling out among the motor-cars for picnic lunches on Epping Common or Hampstead Heath.

While Beardsley and Condor were being admired in London, Cézanne, quite unknown to the æsthetes, was just entering upon the noblest phase of his art. We can thus be true to the Nineties without denying the existence of responsible painting.

The truth is that the poor decadents were, less than anyone, in touch with their own age. All the time that they imagined themselves lapsing into over-civilised and slightly drugged repose, that apostle of over-civilisation, Mr. Edison, was hard at work devising the telephone bell which was to render the whole of the next generation permanently sleepless. While they talked about the earth slowing down at the *fin de siècle,* and of "an age of inertia," the finishing touches were being put to the motor-car and plans were being made for heavier-than-air flying machines. While they vied with one another in exaggerating their moods and poses, the psychologists on the Continent were developing a system of thought in which these conscious waves of emotion became the most negligible and valueless of human faculties. Let us by all means return to this splendid, fashionable decade – the decade of W. G. Grace and General Kitchener. In the words of that great laureate of the decadence, Mr. Kipling,

> *So it's knock out your pipes an' follow me!*
> *An' it's finish up your swipes an' follow me!*
> *Oh, 'ark to the big drum callin',*
> *Follow me — follow me 'ome!*

Why Glorify Youth?

Three years ago I was asked for the first time to write an article for a London paper. The subject set me was "Give Youth a Chance." My heart sank, but I was in no position in those days to pick or choose among the chances that came my way of earning a few guineas.

I wrote the article,* stuffing it with all the clichés I could remember and doing all I could by bombast and exaggeration to qualify it for the trade label of "challenging." I got my guineas and was grateful, but all the time I reflected what a fatuous subject it was. Now, three years later, I am invited to write on "Why Glorify Youth?" – and it seems to me that this reversal of theme reveals a most salutary change of attitude, a cool wave of sanity that has swept public opinion during the intervening time, washing away the picnic litter of Youth-movement sentimentality.

Why Glorify Youth? Why, indeed? And it may be worth while pointing out at once that young people never – except in the way of business – evinced the smallest disposition to do so. The whole Glorious Youth legend was invented by the elderly and middle-aged. It took two main forms, according to the temperament of the particular worshipper. There was the Beauty of Youth Legend. This assured the success of such works as *Dusty Answer* and *Young Woodley.* Oh, lovely youths and maidens! Oh, bodies of classic grace and splendour! Rapturous calf love! Important doubts and disillusionments! Oh, grand apotheosis of pimply adolescence! The novels in their tens of thousands swirled and eddied like flood water through the circulating libraries: the curtains rose and fell to rapturous applause.

The Responsibility of Youth Legend took a soberer form. I hardly remember a single speech or sermon made to us at school which did not touch on this topic. "You are the men of to-morrow," they used to say to us. "You are succeeding to the leadership of a broken and shaken world. The cure is in your hands," etc., etc.

One or two people took this message seriously and have buried themselves in minor secretarial posts at Geneva, or forfeited their deposits

    * "Too Young at Forty." Ed.

regularly each general election, or are passing on the same clap-trap to university classes in remote parts of the globe. For the most part, however, the reply of my generation to all these glowing expectations was the period which will no doubt presently be known as the "roaring 'twenties." In the last year of that decade I wrote *Vile Bodies*, in which I attempted to summarise the chief features of those topsy-turvy years in which the younger generation succeeded in knocking the nonsense out of the attempts to sentimentalise them.

It is now abundantly clear that the "roaring 'twenties" are over. The chief figures of the time have settled down to marriage and children, and others have become submerged completely. It seems clear enough that their successors have not the inclination to carry on the same tradition. The " 'twenties" of this century will soon become a phrase like the " 'nineties" of the last. But just as the " 'nineties," odious as they now seem to us with their "greenery-yallery" artiness, did do a valuable social service in finally breaking up British insular, bourgeois materialism, so the " 'twenties" – futile, obstreperous, anarchic, vulgar, call them what you will – broke up post-war Rupert Brooke magnificently-unprepared-for-the-long-bitterness-of-life sentimentality, and made youth openly and ludicrously inglorious.

It is, on the face of it, odd that such a decade should have been needed – fraught as it was with so much distress to parents, not to mention children – to emphasise what should be a self-evident truth. Who but the muddle-headed, mist-haunted races of Northern Europe would ever commit the folly of glorifying incompleteness and immaturity? For what is youth except a man or woman before it is ready or fit to be seen?

What could be more depressing or perverse than to imagine the whole active life of man as a gradual declivity from the perfection of nineteen, as those seedy old men must feel who once broke their public school record for the hundred yards and have spent the succeeding fifty years or so of their lives re-living the event? And what a pathetic attainment to be proud of. If Youth is our most valuable possession, then we are every one of us poorer and more pitiable every moment of our lives from birth to death. Not everyone grows to be old but everyone has been younger than he now is.

No doubt much of this mistaken pessimism comes from the typically Teutonic confusion of general value with sex appeal. As a race we are constitutionally so shy about sex that we are rarely prepared to praise anyone on those terms alone; we will insert some moral justification for our physical inclinations. Thus when people wish to say that they find youthfulness a desirable and exciting quality in a lover, they feel themselves obliged to set up a hymn of praise for the wholly contemptible concomitant qualities of mind and character.

But I am even sceptical of youth's supremacy in the very narrow field of physical attraction. Disembarrass the issue of all other considerations, refuse to attach importance to charm, wit, experience, prestige, and what have you left? A pretty small residue of puppyish, rubbery limb, clear skin, bright eyes, untidy hair; nothing to fall in love with, nothing to obsess one to the exclusion of other interests. Sex appeal is made up of an infinite number of different stimuli, and in all but very few the woman of over thirty has the debutante hopelessly beaten.

Oh, how maddening after five minutes' conversation, those perky, fresh little faces, those bright blank eyes, those lips bubbling with senseless prattle. "Oh, English girl, divine, demure," how one longs to give you a marron glacé, a light kiss and put you under the chair, with the puppies and kittens who are your true associates.

The English debutante is fit only for the schoolroom, but it is our absurd custom to impose her on terms of social equality upon unfortunate young men ten years her senior. And here she is fighting on her own ground. Clumsy, gauche, ignorant and ill-dressed as she is, she is engaged in the contest in which the single weapon of Youth is of some value. In everything except sex appeal Youth is a positive disadvantage.

A great mistake is made in confusing Youth with Modernity. One of the most sickening qualities of the young is that they are nearly always grossly old-fashioned. In the ordinary arts of civilisation – eating, drinking, clothes, hospitality, furnishing – all fashions are set by people between the ages of thirty and fifty-five. The reason why Sport is civilised while Athletics are not, is that the sportsman profits almost indefinitely by experience, whereas the athlete has as a rule to retire from competition before his mind has begun to work at all. Still more with the fine Arts of Literature, Music, Painting, the real "moderns" are all men in late middle age. Undergraduates are still coquetting with the artistic fashions of 1910. It is many years before they begin to grow into their own age. The "moderns" are mature artists, such as Mr. James Joyce and M. Picasso.

There seems to me to be in the Fine Arts no question of Youth and Age, but simply one of greater or less growth. An artist is not better through being old in years, but he has had the opportunity of being better. There is an antecedent improbability against any young man being a first-rate artist, because he has not had time to grow. Yet one constantly overhears silly old women pottering round art exhibitions saying "Only twenty-two, my dear. I am all for Modernity. One wants new blood." While if they only had the eyes to see it there is more advance in some invention or discovery of an elderly painter next door than in all the groping of the young genius.

How one wishes that the Arts had the same standards of age as Politics, where the "promising" young men of the party are all forty or fifty, and the real hard work is left to those in the prime of life between sixty and seventy. Why will literary critics not realise that Mr. George Moore is every bit as "promising" as Lady Eleanor Smith.

The Youth boom has been very convenient for young men like myself who have made a living out of it, but it seems to me time that criticism adopted some more significant standard.

Tolerance

Twenty-five years ago it was the fashion for those who considered themselves enlightened and progressive to cry out against intolerance as the one damning sin of their time.

The agitation was well founded and it resulted in the elimination from our social system of many elements that are cruel and unjust. But in the general revolution of opinion which followed, has not more been lost than gained?

It is better to be narrow-minded than to have no mind, to hold limited and rigid principles than none at all.

That is the danger which faces so many people to-day – to have no considered opinions on any subject, to put up with what is wasteful and harmful with the excuse that there is "good in everything" – which in most cases means an inability to distinguish between good and bad.

There are still things which are worth fighting *against*.

General Conversation: Myself . . .

A winter morning; a sombre and secluded library; leather bound unread, unreadable books lining the walls; below the windows, subdued,

This is a contribution to "The Seven Deadly Sins of Today by Seven Famous Authors", *John Bull*, 2 April 1932, p. 7. It announces the theme of a short story by Waugh, "Too Much Tolerance", *John Bull*, 21 May 1932, pp. 22, 24.

Nash's Pall Mall Magazine, March 1937, pp. 8, 10–11.

barely perceptible, like the hum of a mowing machine in summer on distant lawns, the sound of London traffic; overhead, in blue and white plaster, an elegant Adam ceiling; a huge heap of glowing coal in the marble fireplace; a leather topped, mahogany writing-table; the pen poised indecisively above the foolscap – what more is needed to complete the picture of a leisured litterateur embarking upon his delicate labour?

Alas! too much. An elderly man has just entered, picked up a French novel and glanced at me resentfully. This is not my library. Nor, in the words of a French exercise, are these my pens, ink or paper. I am in my Club, in the room set aside for silence and heavy after-luncheon sleep. It is three days past the date on which I promised delivery of copy. Leisured litterateur my foot.

"Eats well, sleeps well, but the moment he sees a job of work he comes over queer." That is my trouble, an almost fanatical aversion from pens, ink or paper.

I keep seeing books – though not, I think, as often as I used – about young men who have literary souls and are thwarted and even made to go into the family business and become mere money-makers and breeders of children instead of great writers. My plight is the exact opposite. I was driven into writing because I found it was the only way a lazy and ill-educated man could make a decent living. I am not complaining about the wages. They always seem to me disproportionately high. What I mind so much is the work.

Of course, in my case, writing happens to be the family business; that takes away some of the glamour. My father is a literary critic and publisher. I think he can claim to have more books dedicated to him than any living man. They used to stand together on his shelves, among hundreds of inscribed copies from almost every English writer of eminence, until on one of my rather rare, recent visits to my home, I inadvertently set the house on fire, destroying the carefully garnered fruits of a lifetime of literary friendships.

I remember in childhood the Saturday morning hush over the home, when he was at work on his weekly article. I remember the numerous, patronising literary elders who frequented our table.

My brother took to the trade without a moment's reluctance. He wrote a best seller before he was eighteen and has been at it uninterruptedly ever since. You can see his fingers twitching for a pen as he talks to you.

I held out until I was twenty-four, swimming manfully against the tide; then I was sucked under. I tried everything I could think of first. After an inglorious career at the University I tried to be a painter, and went daily for some months to an Art School crowded with young women in pinafores whose highest ambition was to design trade-marks for patent medicines. We stood at easels in a large, hideously overheated studio and drew from the nude from ten until four. Heavens, how badly I drew! The trouble about my upbringing was that whereas my family knew very well how badly I wrote, they had rosy illusions about my drawing. They could turn out a fine graphic picture in paper games, but none of them had drawn from the nude from ten till four, and they were fatally encouraging about my horrible, charcoal cartoons. It took me about three months to realise that I should not ever be up to designing a trade-mark. Meanwhile the annual deficit of expenditure over allowance had reached a formidable total and I looked for some way of making money – or, at any rate, of avoiding spending it.

There are only two sorts of job always open under the English social system – domestic service and education. However abominable one's record, though one may be fresh from prison or the lunatic asylum, one can always look after the silver or teach the young. I had not the right presence for a footman, so I chose the latter. For eighteen happy months I taught the young. I taught them almost everything – classics, history, modern languages, boxing, tennis and Rugby football – games I had never before played – the elements of religion, shooting and (believe it or not) drawing. At first the boys despised me, but I bought a motor bicycle and from that moment was the idol of the school. I bribed them to behave well by letting them take down the engine. I thought the system was working well, but after the fourth term I got the sack.

My next plan was to be a carpenter, and for a winter I went regularly to classes in a government polytechnic. Those were delightful days, under the tuition of a brilliant and completely speechless little cabinet-maker who could explain nothing and demonstrate everything. To see him cutting concealed dovetails gave me the thrill which, I suppose, others get from seeing their favourite batsman at the wicket or bull fighter in the ring. It was a charming class too. There was one young woman who, during the whole time I was there, was engaged in sawing longways an immense log of teak. She worked and worked at it hour by hour and had cut about a yard when I left. I often wonder if she is still at it. There were two Egyptians who did veneering of exquisite skill and the most atrocious designs conceivable. I never got as far as veneering curved surfaces, but I made an indestructible mahogany bed-table, which I gave to my father, and which survived the fire.

It soon became apparent, however, that it would be many years before I should qualify for a wage, and then for a few shillings a week. That did not worry me, but I had an inclination to get married, so I looked for more remunerative work. Some dreary weeks followed during which, though I cannot claim to have trudged the streets without food, I certainly made a great number of fruitless and rather humiliating calls upon prospective employers.

Dickens held it against his parents that they tried to force him into a blacking factory instead of letting him write. The last firm at which I solicited a job was engaged, among other things, in the manufacture of blacking. I pleaded desperately. If I wasn't employed there I should be driven to Literature. But the manager was relentless. It was no use my thinking of blacking. That was not for the likes of me. I had better make up my mind and settle down to the humble rut which fate had ordained for me. I must write a book.

The value of writing books is that it gives one a market for articles. So here I am, pen poised indecisively over the foolscap, earning my living.

But I am not utterly enslaved. I still have dreams of shaking off the chains of creative endeavour. Rimbaud got away from it and became a gun runner. Vanbrugh gave up writing plays to build the most lovely houses in England. Disraeli and A. P. Herbert went into politics and did themselves proud. John Buchan is lording it in Quebec. Boulestin took to cooking. Perhaps there is a chance of freedom.

Fan-Fare

Frequently, unobtrusively, in the last 17 years I have had books published in the United States of America. No one noticed them. A parcel would appear on my breakfast table containing a familiar work with a strange wrapper and sometimes a strange title; an item would recur in my agent's accounts: "Unearned advance on American edition," and that was the end of the matter. Now, unseasonably, like a shy waterfowl who has hatched out a dragon's egg, I find that I have written a "best-seller." "Unseasonably," because the time has passed when the event brings any substantial reward. In a civilized age this unexpected moment of popularity would have endowed me with a competency for life. But perhaps in a civilized age I should not be so popular. As it is the politicians confiscate my earnings and I am left with the correspondence.

Life (International: Chicago), 8 April 1946, pp. 53–60.

This is something new to me, for Englishwomen do not write letters to men they do not know; indeed they seldom write letters to anyone nowadays; they are too hard-driven at home. Even before the war English readers were seldom seen or heard. It is true that there are facilities for writers whose vanity so inclines them to join literary associations, make speeches and even expose themselves to view at public luncheons, but no one expects it of them or respects them for it. Instead of the Liberty, Equality and Fraternity of the Americas, Europe offers its artists Liberty, Diversity and Privacy. Perhaps it is for this that so many of the best American writers go abroad. But, as Hitler observed, there are no islands in the modern world. I have momentarily become an object of curiosity to Americans and I find that they believe that my friendship and confidence are included in the price of my book.

My father taught me that it was flagitious to leave a letter of any kind unanswered. (Indeed his courtesy was somewhat extravagant. He would write and thank people who wrote to thank him for wedding presents and when he encountered anyone as punctilious as himself the correspondence ended only with death.) I therefore eagerly accept this chance of answering collectively all the cordial inquiries I have received. Please believe me, dear ladies, it is not sloth or "snootiness" that prevents my writing to you individually. It is simply that I cannot afford it. The royalty on your copy, by the time I have paid my taxes, literally does not leave me the price of a stamp.

You require to know what I look like? Well, I am 42 years of age, in good health, stockily built – no, I really cannot go on. Let me merely say that the tailors and hairdressers and hosiers of the small parish of St. James's, London do all they can to render a naturally commonplace appearance completely inconspicuous. Stand on the pavement and scan the aquarium-faces which pass and gape and pass again in my club window; try and spot a novelist. You will not spot me. I once had an intellectual friend who complained that my appearance was noticeable in Bloomsbury. But I seldom leave St. James's when I am in London, and I seldom go to London at all. I live in a shabby stone house in the country, where nothing is under a hundred years old except the plumbing and that does not work. I collect old books in an inexpensive, desultory way. I have a fast-emptying cellar of wine and gardens fast reverting to jungle. I am very contentedly married. I have numerous children whom I see once a day for ten, I hope, awe-inspiring minutes. In the first ten years of adult life I made a large number of friends. Now on the average I make one new one a year and lose two. It is all quite dull, you see : nothing here is worth the poke of a sightseer's sunshade.

It was not always thus with me. In youth I gadded about, and in

those years and in the preposterous years of the Second World War I
collected enough experience to last several lifetimes of novel writing. If
you hear a novelist say he needs to collect "copy," be sure he is no good.
Most of the great writers led very quiet lives; when, like Cervantes, they
were adventurous, it was not for professional reasons. When I gadded,
among savages and people of fashion and politicians and crazy generals,
it was because I enjoyed them. I have settled down now because I ceased
to enjoy them and because I have found a much more abiding interest
– the English language. My father, who was a respected literary critic of
his day, first imbued me with the desire to learn this language, of which
he had a mastery. It is the most lavish and delicate which mankind has
ever known. It is in perpetual danger of extinction and has survived so far
by the combination of a high civilized society, where it was spoken and
given its authority and sanctity, with a thin line of devotees who made
its refinement and adornment their life's work. The first of these is being
destroyed; if the thing is to be saved it will be by the second. I did not
set out to be a writer. My first ambition was to paint. I had little talent
but I enjoyed it as, I believe, many very bad writers enjoy writing. I
spent some time at an art school which was not as wantonly wasted as
it seemed then. Those hours with the plaster casts taught me to enjoy
architecture, just as the hours with the Greek paradigms, now forgotten,
taught me to enjoy reading English. I have never, until quite lately,
enjoyed writing. I am lazy and it is intensely hard work. I wanted to
be a man of the world and I took to writing as I might have taken to
archaeology or diplomacy or any other profession as a means of coming
to terms with the world. Now I see it as an end in itself. Most European
writers suffer a climacteric at the age of 40. Youthful volubility carries
them so far. After that they either become prophets or hacks or esthetes.
(American writers, I think, nearly all become hacks.) I am no prophet
and, I hope, no hack.

That, I think, answers the second question so often put to me in the
last few weeks: "When can we expect another *Brideshead Revisited*?"
Dear ladies, never. I can never hope to engage your attention again in
quite the same way. I have already shaken off one of the American
critics, Mr. Edmund Wilson, who once professed a generous interest in
me. He was outraged (quite legitimately by his standards) at finding God
introduced into my story. I believe that you can only leave God out
by making your characters pure abstractions. Countless admirable
writers, perhaps some of the best in the world, succeed in this. Henry
James was the last of them. The failure of modern novelists since and
including James Joyce is one of presumption and exorbitance. They
are not content with the artificial figures which hitherto passed so grace-
fully as men and women. They try to represent the whole human mind

and soul and yet omit its determining character – that of being God's
creature with a defined purpose.

So in my future books there will be two things to make them unpopular : a preoccupation with style and the attempt to represent man
more fully, which, to me, means only one thing, man in his relation to
God.

But before we part company there are other questions you ask which
I will try to answer. A lady in Hempstead, N.Y. asks me whether I
consider my characters "typical." No, Mrs. Schultz, I do not. It is
horrible of you to ask. A novelist has no business with types; they are
the property of economists and politicians and advertisers and the other
professional bores of our period. The artist is interested only in indivi-
duals. The statesman who damned the age with the name "the Century
of the Common Man" neglected to notice the simple, historical fact
that it is the artists, not the statesmen, who decide the character of a
period. The Common Man does not exist. He is an abstraction invented
by bores for bores. Even you, dear Mrs. Schultz, are an individual. Do
not ask yourself, when you read a story, "Is this the behaviour common
to such and such an age group, income group, psychologically conditioned group?" but, "Why did these particular people behave in this
particular way?" Otherwise you are wasting your time in reading works
of imagination at all.

There is another more intelligent question more often asked : "Are
your characters drawn from life?" In the broadest sense, of course, they
are. None except one or two negligible minor figures is a portrait; all the
major characters are the result of numberless diverse observations fusing
in the imagination into a single whole. My problem has been to distill
comedy and sometimes tragedy from the knockabout farce of people's
outward behaviour. Men and women as I see them would not be credible
if they were literally transcribed; for instance the international journalists whom I met for a few delirious weeks in Addis Ababa, some of
whose abandoned acts I tried to introduce into *Scoop*. Or there is the
character Captain Grimes in *Decline and Fall*. I knew such a man.
One of the more absurd escapades of my youth, the result of a debt-
settlement conference with my father after which I undertook to make
myself financially independent of him, was to take a job as master at a
private school. There I met a man who made what has seemed to me
the lapidary statement, "This looks like being the first end of term I've
seen, old boy, for two years." But had I written anything like a full
account of his iniquities, my publishers and I would have been in the
police court.

As for the major characters, I really have very little control over them.
I start them off with certain preconceived notions of what they will do

and say in certain circumstances but I constantly find them moving another way. For example there was the heroine of *Put Out More Flags*, a Mrs. Lyne. I had no idea until halfway through the book that she drank secretly. I could not understand why she behaved so oddly. Then when she sat down suddenly on the steps of the cinema I understood all and I had to go back and introduce a series of empty bottles into her flat. I was on board a troopship at the time. There is a young destroyer commander who sat next to me at table who can bear witness of this. He asked me one day at luncheon how my book was going. I said, "Badly. I can't understand it at all" and then quite suddenly "I know. Mrs. Lyne has been drinking."

A Handful of Dust, on the other hand, began at the end. I had written a short story about a man trapped in the jungle, ending his days reading Dickens aloud. The idea came quite naturally from the experience of visiting a lonely settler of that kind and reflecting how easily he could hold me prisoner. Then, after the short story was written and published, the idea kept working in my mind. I wanted to discover how the prisoner got there, and eventually the thing grew into a study of other sorts of savage at home and the civilized man's helpless plight among them.

People sometimes say to me, "I met someone exactly like a character out of one of your books." I meet them everywhere, not by choice but luck. I believe the world is populated by them. Before the war it was sometimes said that I must move in a very peculiar circle. Then I joined the army and served six years, mostly with regular soldiers who are reputed to be uniformly conventional. I found myself under the command and in the mess with one man of startling singularity after another. I have come to the conclusion that there is no such thing as normality. That is what makes story telling such an absorbing task, the attempt to reduce to order the anarchic raw materials of life.

That leads to another question: "Are your books meant to be satirical?" No. Satire is a matter of period. It flourishes in a stable society and presupposes homogeneous moral standards – the early Roman Empire and 18th Century Europe. It is aimed at inconsistency and hypocrisy. It exposes polite cruelty and folly by exaggerating them. It seeks to produce shame. All this has no place in the Century of the Common Man where vice no longer pays lip service to virtue. The artist's only service to the distintegrated society of today is to create little independent systems of order of his own. I foresee in the dark age opening that the scribes may play the part of the monks after the first barbarian victories. They were not satirists.

A final question: "Do you consider *Brideshead Revisited* your best book?" Yes. *A Handful of Dust*, my favourite hitherto, dealt entirely with behaviour. It was humanist and contained all I had to say about humanism. *Brideshead Revisited* is vastly more ambitious; perhaps less successful, but I am not deterred either by popular applause or critical blame from being rather proud of the attempt. In particular I am not the least worried about the charge of using clichés. I think to be over-sensitive about clichés is like being oversensitive about table manners. It comes from keeping second-rate company. Professional reviewers read so many bad books in the course of duty that they get an unhealthy craving for arresting phrases. There are many occasions in writing when one needs an unobtrusive background to action, when the landscape *must* become conventionalized if the foreground is to have the right promin-ence. I do not believe that a serious writer has ever been shy of an expression because it has been used before. It is the writer of advertise-ments who is always straining to find bizarre epithets for commonplace objects.

Nor am I worried at the charge of snobbery. Class consciousness, par-ticularly in England, has been so much inflamed nowadays that to mention a nobleman is like mentioning a prostitute 60 years ago. The new prudes say, "No doubt such people do exist but we would sooner not hear about them." I reserve the right to deal with the kind of people I know best.

One criticism does deeply discourage me : a postcard from a man (my sole male correspondent) in Alexandria, Va. He says, "Your *Brideshead Revisited* is a strange way to show that Catholicism is an answer to anything. Seems more like the kiss of Death." I can only say : I am sorry Mr. McClose, I did my best. I am not quite clear what you mean by the "kiss of Death" but I am sure it is gruesome. Is it something to do with halitosis? If so I have failed indeed and my characters have got wildly out of hand once more.

Why Hollywood is a Term of Disparagement

It may seem both presumptuous and unkind to return from six weeks' generous entertainment abroad and at once to sit down and criticize one's hosts. In the case of Hollywood it is neither.

Daily Telegraph and Morning Post, 30 April 1947, p. 4 and 1 May 1947, p. 4.

Not presumptuous : first, because a fortnight is ample time in which to appreciate the character of that remote community; there are no secrets under those unflickering floodlights; no undertones to which the stranger must attune his ear. All is loud, obvious and prosaic.

Secondly, because Hollywood has made its business the business of half the world. Morally, intellectually, aesthetically, financially, Hollywood's entries are written huge in the household books of every nation outside the U.S.S.R.; largest of all in those of America but, because of our common language, second only to them in our own.

Nor is it unkind, for one may say what one likes in perfect confidence that one is powerless to wound. No game licences are issued in the Reserve where the great pachyderms of the film trade bask and browse complacently. They have no suspicion that in most of America and in the whole of Europe the word "Hollywood" is pejorative.

Even in Southern California the film community are a people apart. They are like monks in a desert oasis, their lives revolving about a few shrines – half a dozen immense studios, two hotels, one restaurant; their sacred texts are their own publicity and the local gossip columns.

The only strangers they ever meet have come to seek their fortunes; refugees from Central Europe for whom the ease and plenty and affability of the place, seen against the background of the concentration camp, appear as supreme goods, and astute renegades from the civilizations of the East who know that flattery is the first step to preferment.

None of these will hold a mirror up to Caliban; all feel their own security threatened by a whisper of criticism. Artists and public men elsewhere live under a fusillade of detraction and derision; they accept it as a condition of their calling. Not so in Hollywood, where all is a continuous psalm of self-praise.

Place and people have the aspect of Philo's Alexandria; such, one thinks in one's first few days, must have been the life there in the great days of the Mouseion; some such withdrawal of the arts is necessary everywhere if culture is to survive the present century.

But this is a whimsy. Things are not really like that. The seclusion of these hermits is purely one-sided. They live for and by the outer world of which they know nothing at first hand and whose needs they judge by gross quantitative standards.

"No film of ours is ever a failure," an executive said to me. "Some are greater successes than others, but we reckon to get our money back on everything we produce."

There is the impasse, the insurmountable barrier of financial prosperity. Behold the endless succession of Hollywood films, the slick second-rateness of the best of them, the blank fatuity of the worst – and none of them failures ! What goes on there ?

Three groups are responsible for making a film, the technicians, the players and the writers. (Producers-directors bear the guilt of all three.)

Of these the least culpable are the technicians. It is they who make the studio the vast, enchanted toyshop which delights the visitors.

In only two respects are the technicians guilty. It is their fault that the studios are there, 3,000 miles from the world's theatrical centre in New York, 6,000 miles from the intellectual centres of London and Paris.

They came there because in the early days they needed the sun. Now almost all photography is done by artificial light. The sun serves only to enervate and stultify. But by now the thing has become too heavy to move.

And the technicians are too enterprising. Their itch for invention keeps them always a move ahead of the producers.

Twenty years ago the silent film was just beginning to develop into a fine art; then talking apparatus set it back to its infancy. Technicolor is the present retarding revolution. Soon no doubt we shall have some trick of third-dimensional projection.

Mr. Charles Chaplain, abused everywhere as a "progressive," is the one genuine conservative artistically, in Hollywood. The others allow themselves no time to get at ease with their materials.

The technicians are almost anonymous. All the devices of publicity are employed to give exclusive prominence to a few leading players. They possess the popular imagination and excite the visitor's curiosity.

What of them? Dramatic critics often ask why the cinema has produced no actors comparable with the great figures of the stage, and point to the fact that in many "documentaries" and Continental films the best performances are given by unknown and untrained players. Even in Hollywood this year the highest Academy honours have gone to a man who was chosen simply because he had been maimed in the war.

The wonder should be that so many stars are able to give as much as they do, for the conditions of their work are hostile to dramatic tradition. Certain disabilities seem to be inherent in the film; others are peculiar to Hollywood; all are exaggerated there.

There is an essential inhumanity about a film star's life. Compare it with that of a leading actress of 50 years ago. The latter worked in the capitals of the world; once her play was running smoothly her days were her own; she lived a life of leisure and fashion in an infinitely various society of her own choosing.

The company formed a corporate unit with its own intimacies, scandals and jokes; each performance was a separate artistic achievement; the play was conceived as an artistic whole which was nightly brought into existence in a sustained and cumulative emotional mood which is the essence of acting.

The players were in direct contact with their audience. Each audience was different; the manager would nightly visit the dressing-rooms with news of who was "in front."

Above all, acting was recognized as an art which it took a lifetime to learn. Almost all great plays were written for mature players; the "juvenile lead" and the "ingenue" were for youngsters learning their trade.

The Hollywood star lives in a remote suburb. She sees no one from one year's end to another except a handful of people all in the same trade as herself. She remains in purdah in the studio, inhabiting a tiny bathing-machine, surrounded by satellites who groom her and feed her until the technicians have finished with the "stand-in" and require her presence on the set.

When her work begins it consists of isolated fragments, chosen at the convenience of the technicians. It is rehearsal, hour after hour, for a few minutes of finished acting.

At last in a Trilby-like trance she achieves the expression the director requires. She is "shot," and they proceed to another, often unrelated fragment.

And finally she has produced only the raw material for the "cutter," who may nonchalantly discard the work of weeks or dovetail it into an entirely different situation.

And she must be young. Her life is as brief as a prize fighter's. By the time that she has become a finished actress she is relegated to "supporting" rôles.

The work is physically exhausting and intellectually stultifying and there are no very great material rewards. A myth survives from past years that film stars live in Petronian luxury. The salary figures seem dazzling, and, indeed, she does live in a degree of comfort very enviable by contemporary European measure.

But it is no more than that. In fact her standard of life is precisely that of a moderately successful professional Englishman of 50 years ago. That is to say, she lives in a neat little villa with half an acre of garden; she has three servants, seldom more, very often fewer. Her antique furniture, collected at vast expense, would be commonplace in an English rectory.

Her main time of entertainment is Sunday luncheon when she asks half a dozen professional friends to share her joint of beef. She has more clothes than her counterpart, but her menfolk are infinitely worse dressed.

In only one substantial particular does she differ. She has a swimming pool which can be lit up at night. That is the mark of respectability, like the aspidistra in the cottage parlour.

And unlike her counterpart it is almost impossible for her to save money. If she attempted to live in simpler style she would lose "face" and be rebuked by her studio. She cannot live more elaborately, for taxation intervenes. She can make this maximum in one film. After that for the rest of the time she is working for nothing.

Consequently it is becoming increasingly hard to persuade her to do any work. Vanity is the sole inducement. She will therefore take no part in which she, and her male colleagues, are anything less than the whole film.

She must be on the stage all the time in a continuously alluring fashion. A play which depends on a team of various characters has no interest for her. A film must be her personal romantic adventures and nothing else.

It is a short-sighted preference, for it means that when she is 50 there will be no adequate parts for her. But no one in Hollywood considers the possibility of growing up.

The infinite pains taken in Hollywood over all technical matters renders all the more remarkable their nonchalance when it is a question of ideas.

Go to the Art Research Department and they will tell you in a twinkling the kind of inkpot Dante used or the orders worn by the Duke of Wellington at Queen Victoria's Coronation.

Go on the set and hear the dozen or more experts wrangling round the "stand-in" about light and sound; wait until the star appears and see how men with combs and clothes-brushes, women with elaborate catalogues, cluster round and perfect her.

You will believe yourself present at one of the great achievements of human ingenuity and devotion. Then go to a "story conference" and you find yourself in a world that is at once haphazard and banal.

It is not that they are wrong-headed, that in the interests of entertainment they deliberately choose to disregard certain human values and to distort others.

It is not that, as is often suggested, they serve sinister interests aiming to preserve or destroy (according to choice) capitalist society and bourgeois morality, to advance American imperialism, Jewish internationalism, Catholicism, Agnosticism or what you will.

It is simply that they are empty-headed and quite without any purpose at all. Thus anyone interested in ideas is inevitably shocked by Hollywood according to his prejudices.

The novelist is shocked by their complete inability to follow a plain story. For in the cinema, he would think, is the perfect medium for presenting a straight plot. The effects at which he labours so painfully may here be achieved with ease. All descriptions are superfluous. Here you have narrative reduced to its essentials – dialogue and action.

A great, simple art should have come into existence. But nothing of the kind has in fact occurred.

Literary considerations are as despised in the film studios as in those of modern painters. The producers, generally speaking, read nothing. They employ instead a staff of highly accomplished women who recite aloud, and with dramatic effects, the stories which filter down to them from a staff of readers.

The producers sit round like children while the pseudo-nannie spins a tale, two or three in an afternoon – classical novels, Broadway comedies, the Book of the Month, popular biographies, anything.

"Bags I," says the producer, when something takes his fancy. "Daddy buy that." Agents negotiate, a price is fixed. And from that moment the story belongs to the studio to deal with as they please.

Each of the books purchased has had some individual quality, good or bad, that has made it remarkable. It is the work of a staff of "writers" to distinguish this quality, separate it and obliterate it.

We all know frightful examples of favourite books we have seen thus sterilized. Perhaps of recent years the most notorious is Mr. Somerset Maugham's "Christmas Holiday," a brilliantly original story of an English schoolboy's awakening in Paris to some of the realities of life, eminently suitable for retelling in a film, which emerged from the mill as the adventure of an American airman with an escaped gangster.

Why, one wonders, do they trouble to purchase rights? I cannot believe that any action for plagiarism would lie if they had produced that film without reference to Mr. Maugham. It is simply, I think, that they like to have something to work on, and that the large sum paid to the author is an inconsiderable part of the total cost of production.

A film costs about $2,000,000. It must please 20,000,000 people. The film industry has accepted the great fallacy of the Century of the Common Man – epitomized recently in England by Dr. Summerskill's condemnation of good cheese – that a thing can have no value for anyone which is not valued by all.

In the old days a play which ran 100 nights was a success, a book which sold 5,000 copies might influence a generation. Even now a writer who sells more than 20,000 copies, instead of being elated, begins to wonder what has gone wrong with his work. But a film must please everyone.

The economics of this desperate situation illustrate the steps by which the Common Man is consolidating his victory.

It is not the large sums paid to the stars and producers and authors (the greater part of which, incidentally, goes straight to the Common Man in taxes), but the overhead expenses of the studio which overweight the costs, and these are imposed by the trade unions and their system of redundant labour.

It would not be impossible to get together a team of first-class players and producers and writers who would work for a fraction of their present salaries if they could take genuine pride in their art and make a film which appealed only to a limited audience, but this would barely affect the cost of the film.

Situations which seem fantastic elsewhere are commonplace in Hollywood. I know a "writer" who wished to put up a map on the wall of his room and asked for a hammer and four nails. He was told that all the carpenters would strike if he did the work himself.

A trade unionist arrived with his tools and found that a small bookcase had to be moved to another wall. The writer took one side and invited the carpenter to take the other. But that was a breach of rules. Two furniture movers had to be called in.

A special "florist" has to be summoned if, in rearranging a "set," the director wishes to move a vase of flowers from one table to another.

The unions determine the numbers to be employed in any film. If a band of six instruments is required, a dozen men will arrive and half of them sit idle on full pay.

Impositions of this kind, repeated hourly in a large studio, fix the exorbitant cost of a film. The capitalist at the head of the company is concerned solely with profits; the proletariat allow profits only to those who directly work for their pleasure; in this miniature class-war the artist vanishes.

The reductio ad absurdum of the principle of universal appeal is not in the intellectual or aesthetic sphere, but in the moral.

The American censors observe no such fruitful distinction as exists in England between films suitable for children and for adults. Nor do most American parents enjoy the authority common in Europe over their children. They cannot prevent them going to the cinema; all they can hope to do is prevent the cinema showing films likely to corrupt them. In fact, no one really knows what will corrupt anyone else.

There has been intense investigation of the question lately. It must be remembered that children seldom tell the truth to investigators, and that magistrates are usually sympathetic to the plea of the juvenile delinquent: "I saw it done in the pictures."

Moreover, it is the spectacle rather than the theme which impresses a child. That is to say, a boy is excited by the use of firearms whether in the hands of a gangster or a soldier; an embrace is equally inflammatory whether between licit or illicit lovers. Americans are devoted to a conception of innocence which has little relation to life.

But when all this is said it remains broadly true that some films may be harmless to adults and harmful to children. This, within all the essential finer distinction, the Americans ignore, and the function of the Hays Office is to enforce a Code which forbids the production of any film which can be harmful to anyone, or offend any racial or religious susceptibility.

No such code is feasible in a heterogeneous society. Logically applied it would condemn, for instance, almost the whole of Shakespeare.

The unhappy compromise is evident in all Hollywood films except those of Mr. Walt Disney. Every attempt is made by innuendo to pack as much lubricious material as possible into every story, while mature dramatic works intended for a morally stable, civilized audience have their essential structure hopelessly impaired.

The vagaries of the Hays Office may be quoted at indefinite length. One example must suffice here.

A script was recently condemned as likely to undermine the conception of Christian marriage. The story was of an unhappy married man and woman who wished to divorce their respective partners and remarry one another. They institute proceedings, but in the end refrain from remarriage precisely because they come to realise that this would not constitute Christian marriage.*

At the same time the excellent film "The Best Years of Our Lives" was being acclaimed as the embodiment of healthy American domesticity. That story depends for its happy end on the hero being deserted by his Bohemian wife and thus being free to marry the banker's innocent daughter. This was passed because it was never specifically stated that a divorce would have to intervene.

I have attempted to show some of the disabilities under which Hollywood works. Are they insuperable? I sincerely believe that they are. As far as the home of a living art is concerned, Hollywood has no importance. It may be a useful laboratory for technical experiment.

The great danger is that the European climate is becoming inclement for artists; they are notoriously comfort-loving people. The allurements of the modest luxury of Hollywood are strong. Will they be seduced there to their own extinction?

* The story described here strongly suggests *Brideshead Revisited*. Early in 1947 Waugh went to Hollywood to discuss a film of this novel. On 15 March he telegraphed A. D. Peters, "Censor forbids film of *Brideshead*." On 18 March Carol Brandt, Peters's New York partner, informed Peters that the Johnston-Hays office refused to pass *Brideshead* without changes which Waugh could not accept. Ed.

Mr. Waugh Replies

Some of my earliest memories are of book-reviewing. My father wrote a weekly literary article for the *Daily Telegraph*. He was also the head of a publishing firm and it is significant of the high standards of the day that no one, so far as I know, ever thought the combination odd or suspected that he might use his position to push his own wares or discriminate against rivals. He greatly enjoyed this work, would read the book under review attentively and discuss it at table. Then on Saturday mornings a hush fell on the house while he wrote his article.

My own first regular literary employment was reviewing for the *Observer* in the late '20s. I too enjoyed it. The world seemed full of exiting new books and Miss Garvin's office a free book-shop. We used to assemble among the piles of bright wrappers and each make his choice. The pay was low and we supplemented it by selling copies at half-price. There were usually one or two expensive "Art Books" and these would be surreptitiously shifted from pile to pile in the course of the afternoon. Since then, off and on, I have done a good deal of such work, always with pleasure.

In the mid '30s it became fashionable for reviewers to complain that they were ill-used. Their minds, they said, were being bruised, their creative faculties numbed, their styles corrupted by the battery of inferior minds. It is notable that the best reviewing of this time – such as Mr. Cyril Connolly's in the *New Statesman* – was hostile and derisive.

Since the war there has been some further deterioration. Few reviewers are now able to recapitulate a plot with accuracy. But perhaps the deterioration among the books has been more noticeable. I suspect that nowadays the best criticism is never seen in print. All over the country clever and learned men and women are lecturing to university students. I do not know whether our universities, like those of America, give degrees in "Creative Writing," but it is plain from the letters I get that modern books are being seriously examined and that discourses of the

Spectator, 3 July 1953, pp. 23–24. The *Spectator* invited Waugh to review the reviews of his book, *Love Among the Ruins*.

kind which used to fill the pages of the quarterly reviews, now vanish in the Biro scribbles of students' note-books.

In no periodical have we now anyone approaching a Grand Cham. The subtlest critics, such as Mr. Raymond Mortimer and Mr. Connolly, are starved of space so that they can only throw out a few luminous hints, a few charmingly written paragraphs, as it were from *Trivia*. Many of the papers with the largest circulations do not notice the Arts at all. The most influential among book buyers and librarians are said to be: *The Times Literary Supplement*, the *New Statesman*, the *Spectator*, *Time and Tide*, *The Listener*, the *Observer*, the *Sunday Times*, and of daily papers *The Times* and the *Telegraph*. The *Daily Mail* alone of the popular papers has some literary prestige. Mr. Quennell is a widely-read, fastidious critic and a competent writer. One may be sure that, if it were not his job, he would not spend ten minutes on nine out of ten of the books he commends. He tells his readers week by week, with self-effacement and high competence, what books are likely to interest them. He writes the most useful, if not the most exhilarating, literary journalism today but I am told that even he, with his great circulation, has little influence on the market and that his laurel wreath of the "Book of the Month" is barely worth £25 to the author, unless of a first book. Reviewers can greatly encourage or cruelly wound a young writer; perhaps also a very old one, fearful of failing powers. They do not much concern the middle-aged. For this reason I can, I hope, without rancour or egotism, examine the work of the modern reviewer in the single light of my own latest book which has been pretty generally condemned.

It is a brief, very prettily produced phantasy about life in the near future with certain obvious defects. It was begun as a longer work three years ago, abandoned, and resumed with the realisation that the characters lacked substance for more than a short story. As it stands it is designed purely to amuse and is therefore subject to a snap verdict, yes or no. Either it comes off or it fails. It was an easy job for the reviewer in contrast, say, to a new work by Mr. David Jones. I may add that I myself live in seclusion. I do not attend gatherings of P.E.N. or Foyle's Lunches or literary cocktail parties (if such things really exist), so that I cannot have incurred personal enmity in my profession. Despite its reception this book is selling in numbers which seem to satisfy its publishers.

If we take the snap-decision of the periodicals listed above, we find: *Times Literary Supplement*; yes, "we laugh helplessly." *New Statesman*; yes, "wit crackles drily on every page." *Spectator*; no, "his satire has ceased to be a laughing matter. . . . Not in the same class as *The Loved One*. . . . He is left more or less speechless." *Time and Tide*; yes and no, "this isn't vintage Waugh." *The Listener*; yes, "pre-Brideshead Waugh." *Observer*; no, modified, "it would be amusing if it were by a beginner."

Sunday Times; yes, "delight and pleasure." *Times*; yes, modified, "bland satirical extravagance raises more smiles than laughter." *Telegraph*; yes, modified. *Daily Mail*; yes, modified, "the joke is a little too complicated – and possibly a little too bitter."

All this seems to amount to an audible chuckle, if not a hearty laugh. No funny man should expect more every time he attempts a joke. There is a general mild tone of regret that it disappoints expectations, though there is no unanimity as to the exact moment of my decline; some put it eight, some twenty-five years ago, some this month. It is when we come to the less influential papers that the criticism becomes uniformly adverse and oddly violent.

Where the reviewers of even the well-mannered papers seem to have deteriorated, in a way my father would have thought intolerable, is in their tendency to write about the author rather than the book and in assuming a personal intimacy with him which in fact they do not enjoy. The young lady, for instance, who says many kind things about me in the *New States-man* ventures to question my good faith in religion and imputes to me lack of compassion for the poor. No doubt she has no conception of the deadliness of her accusation. If at all true, it would be a matter for my confessor not for her. Others equally unknown to me impute a hankering for the eighteenth century. It was Mr. Clive Bell, the champion of post-impressionism, who wrote of "the adorable century," not I, whose preferences are for the thirteenth or the fourth. But it is in the Beaverbrook press that I find the most curious claims to intimacy.

Mr. George Malcolm Thomson of the *Evening Standard* seems to have studied some file of gossip paragraphs and to have transcribed all the most offensive, inaccurate and irrelevant. He reports that I do not like oysters, that I advocate slavery, that I am sensitive about my low stature. Mr. Thomson, alas, is a cypher to me (no doubt he is a fine gangling fellow), but I have some acquaintance with Lord Beaverbrook. Over the years I have heard him give tongue on a great variety of topics but it never occurred to me until now to speculate whether he suffered from humiliation at being slightly shorter than myself. How does Mr. Thomson know my height? It is not recorded in any book of reference. How can he possibly know whether I am sensitive about it? Has he seen me tripping about Shoe Lane on stilts? Has he had an eye to the keyhole of a gymnasium where I was engaged in stretching exercises? And, really, what has it got to do with my writing? Are my plots a continual retelling of the story of David and Goliath, where evil giants are overcome by heroic pigmies?

Mr. Shulman of the *Sunday Express* accuses me of snobbery. He goes further and predicts that "in future" only snobs will enjoy my books. This seems very odd since the book under review is the only novel I have ever written in which there appears no member of the upper class, either as buffoon or heroine.

The critic of the *Daily Express* merely says he yawned and yawned and yawned, without indicating the time of day or night when he attempted to read it, or even whether he is adept at reading at all.

This unanimity of the Beaverbrook press is striking. All abuse, not so much my little book, as me, in terms which, used of a coal-miner, would precipitate a General Strike. Now it so happens that quite recently my solitude has been disturbed on several occasions by appeals for help from their office. One of their gossip writers politely asked me for information I was unwilling to give. The *Sunday Express* offered me a seat in the Abbey for the Coronation. The *Evening Standard* suggested my going abroad to interview a royal person (not, I hasten to say, the ex-King of Egypt). If I am such a bad writer why do they solicit my work? For different good reasons I was obliged to refuse these flattering offers. I know these Beaverbrook men to be busy. I was brief with them. Did I seem curt? Can it be that I gave offence and that those fiery, independent spirits, the arbiters of literary taste of millions, are influenced by other than purely artistic considerations?

I See Nothing But Boredom . . . Everywhere

It is presumptuous to interpret what Mr Vincent Cronin has cleverly called "the deaf and dumb language of Providence." All I can do is predict what will be the character of the next decade, if present tendencies continue uninterrupted.

I must confess that I face the immediate future with gloomy apprehensions. I am not the least nervous about the much-advertised threats of the nuclear scientists: First, because I can see nothing objectionable in the total destruction of the earth, provided it is done, as seems most likely, inadvertently. If it is done in malice someone will have behaved culpably. But every well-instructed child knows that the world is going to end one day. The only certain information we have on the subject is that the catastrophe will be fiery and unexpected: the only certain instructions, that we must live every day as though it were to be our last.

Daily Mail, 28 December 1959, p. 4.

Secondly, because I believe scientists and publicists enjoy a sense of importance when they make our flesh creep. I well remember the nonsense that was talked in 1938 by the experts on chemical and bacteriological warfare; the wholesale massacres that were threatened from aerial bombardment. And thirdly, because I do not think the next world war will break out in the period we are discussing.

No, what I fear is not alarm but boredom. I am thinking primarily of this kingdom. In other parts of the world there will no doubt be appalling events. The foundation of empires is often an occasion of woe; their dissolution, invariably; and I believe that the peoples of Asia and Africa who have lately enjoyed British rule are in for great distress. But I believe that in this country we have settled down to a period of stagnation which will last just about ten years. I have no fears of political upheaval or of the oppression foreseen by George Orwell for 1984. We endured a full socialist regime, with all its features – one-party government, control of industry, imprisonment without trial, forced labour in the mines, and so on – from 1940 to 1945. The Socialist Government very slightly alleviated it; the Conservatives rather more. The Labour Party will continue its useful function of posing annoying questions to Ministers but I do not think the electorate will ever again vote them into authority.

At the moment it is popular to talk of universal affluence and increased comfort. It is worth noticing that this enrichment is enjoyed by only a part of the nation; the largest, but, I think, the least interesting. Almost everyone I know is much worse off. I, for example, was earning about £3,000 a year in the middle '30's. I see from the official figures lately given by the Financial Secretary to the Treasury that in order to enjoy the standard of living I had in 1938 I must now earn £20,750. I find it hard work to earn half that amount and my income has, on paper, greatly increased. Those whose incomes have remained the same are, notoriously, very much more impoverished. Numerically, as voters, this almost submerged class are of small importance; they will dwindle in the coming decade.

I do not think that the newly enriched will continue to get much richer, but they have been trained to accept universal privation. All that upsets them is to see someone else better off. Financially we are moving towards a classless society. The morbid attention that is at the moment being paid to the minor nuances of social distinction – an attention evident not only in popular newspapers but in grave weeklies – is a sign of the weakness, not of the strength, of the social order. The British, until now, have been the most elaborately stratified people in Europe. It may be a good or a bad thing to be classless; it is certainly un-British.

The most dismal tendency I see is that with our class-system we are fast losing all national character. It was thought absurd by many and detestable by some, but it was unique and it depended for its strength and humour and achievements on variety : variety between one town and another, one county and another; one man different from another in the same village in knowledge, habits, opinions. There were different vocabularies and intonations of speech; different styles of dress. Now all those things that gave the salt to English life and were the raw material of our Arts are being dissolved. When I was last in the Tate Gallery there was exposed a series of casts from a work by Matisse, showing the disappearance of a human figure. The first showed the clumsy but recognisable back of a woman; the last a mere absurdity; and between them the earnest student could study the stages of dissolution in the master's mind. Something like this is happening to the English.

They are already hard to find in London. No one lives there who is not paid to do so. You will find strange faces and strange tongues in the streets; tourists in the hotels; and there are no private houses. Do I exaggerate? Perhaps there are still a score where more than a dozen can sit down to dinner. I do not pretend to be a popular man-about-town. My knowledge comes second-hand, but I believe that London society has ceased to exist; all hospitality is now commercial or official.

The essence of society was not, as is often represented, that it provided a setting for political and financial intrigue. It was the world where people amused themselves, and at the same time exercised a gentle discipline, imposing a standard of manners on its members and those who emulated them, distinguishing between fame and notoriety in its protegés, keeping the bumptious in their places, insisting on good workmanship from its tradesmen. It was an institution as essentially English as the Monarchy. London society has distintegrated. Those who should comprise it are scattered; most have retreated to their country houses. The rest are dispersed from Central Africa to the West Indies. Those who should enliven it are stultifying and vulgarising themselves before the television. This has happened and I see no possibility of restoration.

All this makes unwelcome reading for the editor of a newspaper whose business is to make every day new and exciting. How will he fill his columns in the next decade? I see nothing ahead but drab uniformity. The motor-car has already destroyed its own usefulness. Suppose, as seems most unlikely, it once more is rendered mobile by making the whole country into a speedway and a car-park, there will be no inducement to go anywhere because all buildings will look the same, all shops sell the same produce, all people say the same things in the same voices. Foreign travel will be scarcely more attractive for the elderly and experienced. One went abroad to observe other ways of living, to eat unfamiliar foods and see strange buildings. In a few years' time the world will be divided into zones of insecurity which one can penetrate only at the risk of murder and tourist routes along which one will fly to chain hotels, hygienic, costly and second-rate.

The Arts? Here one cannot, thank heaven, speak confidently. We have in a lifetime seen painting and sculpture come to a dead stop all over the world, but the human spirit may rise in reaction. But suppose we in England do produce a genius in the next ten years, will he stay with us? The rewards will be negligible. There will be no cultured world to entertain and encourage him. I think he will leave us as so many others have done in recent years. It is a sorry civilisation that exiles instead of honouring its artists. He will decamp not, primarily, for flattery and flesh-pots, but simply because the sort of community we all see coming will afford no stimulus to his work. If he remains, it will be as an outlaw.

The underworld will always be with us. At its present rate of growth it should surpass American proportions in 1965 and Sicilian in 1980. The editors can take comfort here. Strikes and crimes of violence will still be news all through the leaden decade. One day, I suppose we shall be asked to read as the most exciting event of the century about the adventures of some American or Russian who has sat on the moon in a sealed capsule. Heavens, how boring.

But in about 1970 I expect to read of the outbreak of the next world war. Most of my countrymen will welcome it as an escape from the slavery of boredom. Poor beasts, they will have forgotten. But they will soon learn. The epoch will end in another bout of socialism more severe than the Churchill-Attlee terror of the early 40's.

Sinking, Shadowed and Sad—the Last Glory of Europe

Venice is the most beautiful city in the world. It is not very old as the great cities of Asia count time. It is about the same age as London. Moralists of the last century used to draw comparisons between the two places – mercantile, maritime, and imperial – and warn Londoners that they might decline like the Venetians if they gave way to luxury and ostentation.

London has not declined. Goodness knows there is little luxury and no ostentation there today. We avert our eyes from it in shame. And Venice

Daily Mail, 30 March 1960, p. 6.

remains the object lesson in a very different sense from that predicted by our great-grandfathers. If every museum in the New World were emptied, if every famous building in the Old World were destroyed and only Venice saved, there would be enough there to fill a full lifetime with delight. Venice, with all its complexity and variety, is in itself the greatest surviving work of art in the world.

The Venetians came to their hundred islands from the mainland as a refuge from the invaders from the north. And a place of refuge it has remained. Everyone knows that there are no wheeled vehicles in Venice, but only those who have experienced it can appreciate what that means. There are now motor launches. The gondoliers have almost priced themselves out of existence. There are now scarcely a dozen private gondolas.

Not many of the palaces are in the hands of the families who built them. Some, like the Rezonico, are museums; some, like the Labia, have been restored and occupied by foreigners; most are divided into apartments. The two chief hotels have built themselves unobtrusively ugly new wings. You will find grumblers to tell you that Venice is not what it was. Don't believe them.

On this, the latest of several visits, I came for the first time in January when it is "out of season" for foreigners and the Venetians themselves feel most at their ease. It was chilly and damp and misty and I saw the city in a new aspect; one of poetic melancholy and mystery. It is not essentially a summer city. Most of its festivals occur in winter. In the great days of the Republic the nobles used to retire from their huge frescoed halls and spend the cold weather cosily in mezzanine flats. In July and August they moved to villas along the Brenta Canal and in the hills. No one who could afford to go away spent the summer in Venice. That is an American craze which began in my lifetime. Spring is an exquisite season, but, alas, too popular. I would sooner get rather wet in the streets and find many of the pictures indoors rather obscure (only two buildings have introduced modern lighting) than live in a crowd.

Never believe anyone who tells you he "knows" Venice. You can "do" it in less than a month, studying and enjoying all that the guide books recommend. And that is at the same time both an education and an inebriation. But the Venetians themselves are the last to claim that they "know" their city. It is divided into six areas, whose boundaries are inextricably confused, and even today, I am told, there are Venetians who have never been outside their own "sestiere." Each church, each well-head, is the centre of a distinct community.

How can one give an impression of the Venetians? Perhaps they are what Romans were between 1815 and 1870. But there is something of the East in the modesty of the women and the gravity of the men. This, which 200 years ago was the city of gambling and carnival, is now, outside Spain, the acme of decorum. No public love-making, no brawling, no showy clothes; withdrawn yet still traditionally cosmopolitan.

I went to tea in one of the few palaces still fully occupied by the original family – one which has not only magistrates of the Republic but a canonised saint in its pedigree. Half a dozen of us were there in the high frescoed hall. Because I was English all spoke in my language, easily, colloquially, allusively, almost without accent. They compared T. S. Eliot and Anouilh in their treatment of Thomas à Becket; they spoke of the breeds of English cattle. No one there had spent more than a week or two in England. It was an ease with the world such as one once found and no longer finds in Paris; and this is a city with no Diplomatic Corps, a provincial city comparable, I suppose, in financial and political importance to Swansea.

Later I went into another milieu to call on a local journalist; a man, I suppose, not very well off. We met at a statue and he led me through tunnels and alleys – in Venice there is no rich or poor quarter – until we emerged at his house, drab enough from the outside; an English municipal council would no doubt condemn it to demolition; under an arch, into a yard, and we were in a 15th-century arcade, up a staircase and we were in a delicate little room of 18th-century rococo plaster work such as antiquarian societies in England will create a fruitless hullabaloo about when they are doomed to destruction. In Venice they exist everywhere, out-of-sight, uncounted.

The Venetians are the most conservative people in Europe, and by a strange paradox they are at the moment deprived of self-government for fear they should turn Communist. They have no *podesta* (mayor) but are ruled by a Prefect sent from Rome. All their Civil Servants and most of their police come from Naples and Sicily. They got bored with politics at the end of the 18th century. Since then they have been ruled by French, Austrians, Piedmontese. They are far too wise and experienced to fuss. But they guard their own city fiercely.

Two years ago there was a plot to erect a "modern" house, designed by the American, Wright, on the Grand Canal. The Neapolitan officials had given their consent. Then the Venetians and their foreign friends became aware of the danger and the thing was stopped. There is only one ugly building in Venice today – the campanile of St. Mark's. It has stood there in defiance of proportion and elegance for 500 years. In 1902 it collapsed. A heaven-sent opportunity, one would say, to clear the thing away. Not at all; the Venetians patiently built an exact replica.

The present Pope was Patriarch of Venice before his election. The Venetians are proud and pleased; pleased especially because it was rumoured that he had designs to demolish Sansovino's screen in St.

Mark's. "He had to go of course," they say, "but he was a good man, so we sent him to Rome."

And yet they dare not have an election in Venice for fear that they should turn up a Communist. The reason is ironical and significant. Mussolini and his Finance Minister went to great pains to restore the prosperity of Venezia. At Mestre and Marghera on the mainland they created new industrial suburbs which were to be the glory of the Fascist regime. They, of course, have turned solid Communist. But the Venetians still have their refuge from them in their own islands, and the horses of Lysippus look down from the porch of St. Mark's not at all surprised or alarmed by what they see.

But the city is sinking. Every year, by a few inches, it subsides into its lagoon. Not in my time nor, I pray, in my children's, but one day it will silently disappear. With it will go the last glory of Europe. I hope there will still be someone alive to remember the now hackneyed lines of Wordsworth: *"And when she took unto herself a mate, she must espouse the everlasting sea."*

Aesthete

Two years after Evelyn published "In Defence of Cubism", Arthur Waugh, worried at his sixteen year old son's "Studio" becoming a "private temple of the most modern school of art", addressed to him the dedicatory letter which prefaces *Tradition and Change* (1919): he should remember the "imperishable influence of tradition", he should "change gently" and "not despise the old". In later life the same Evelyn became notorious for scornful denunciations of Picasso and Matisse; and for collecting Victorian monstrosities. But he never remotely resembled a baffled, self-satisfied Philistine.

The passages in *Rossetti* and *Labels* describing works of art reveal a striking power of analysing painting and scuplture and defining their qualities, and of conveying visual impressions in words. "Preface to the Decorative Designs of Francis Crease", as well as relating an interesting phase of Waugh's aesthetic development, displays some of this power. Very early, Waugh became an opponent of functional theories of art. *Rossetti* controverts Clive Bell in detail. The Professor Silenus episodes in *Decline and Fall* ridicule his theories hilariously. "The Philistine Age of English Decoration" shows that Waugh rebelled against the "good taste" dictated by the functional-modernists to the extent of lauding the period most antipathetic to the moderns – the mid-Victorian.

This article is one of several Waugh wrote revealing a collector's knowledge of furniture. It is also one of several expressing admiration for Victorian art. What the moderns condemned as over-elaborateness and pomposity, he regarded as the inventiveness of a "free, fecund" society, confident of the future, which exalted Liberty above Equality. "A Call to the Orders" asserts belief in the classical virtues of order and proportion, a grammar to be learned before the imagination can freely play. The interest in architecture shown in this article, and its disgust with what Waugh elsewhere calls the "Nazi-factory" style of building, enter into all of his novels.

The review of Peter Quennell's life of Hogarth conclusively proves that Waugh's promotion of Victorian narrative painting was not a tease. He seriously believed that narrative composition was a unique national achievement of which the English should be proud. "The Death of Painting" sums up a lifetime of delight in and concern for art.

In Defence of Cubism

Art can, at the best of times, reproduce only an impression, and we have to employ such optical illusions as perspective by which to deceive the eye, and try to give a flat surface the impression of depth. Thus that hackneyed argument, "unlike life," is obviously quite fatuous. And yet, in twentieth century Europe, a Europe prepared by the impressionism of Turner and Manet, we find it cropping up again and again. "That bears no possible resemblance to a figure" is a criticism which is repeated daily in every Cubist's studio – and yet it is recognised for what it is. Why?

Let us first consider the "unlike life" argument. Should Art be like life? If we consult our greatest masters, Turner, Whistler, Manet, Constable, the answer is, No. If "like life" means the irritating detail and impoverished sentiment of Frith, is it not best to shun such an ideal? And yet the anti-cubist will ask, if not life, what should Art present? The answer is, surely the impression that objects give. Of course, we are not to suppose that the Cubist receives the impression of a maze of innumerable geometrical figures, but he must use some means of putting down his sensations. The black-and-white artist does not see life composed of black lines, but he translates his impressions into his own medium. Thus the resemblance to life does not in the least concern the merits of the picture.

The average person condemns Cubism unheard, frequently unseen. You hear the self-satisfied Philistine denouncing Cubism as pure affectation; you ask him what Cubist pictures he has seen; none, or perhaps one in a halfpenny paper reproduced by a smudged half-tone block printed on the cheapest paper by a rotary press – and quite probably a Futurist one. The would-be-funny cartoons entitled "How to draw in Cubes," or "Art (?) made easy," have given an already prejudiced public an entirely erroneous idea of the Art.

Few people seem to realise that pictures in Cubes can be bad as well as good. They seldom, if ever, see a good Cubist picture. They see articles in magazines headed "That Cubist," with reproductions of the most

Drawing and Design, November 1917, p. 9.

affected pictures, and judge the whole art by these. Such is the public for whom Art has to work!

In some few cases Cubism is a mode of expression which is dangerously rivalled by Impressionism. Most notable of these cases is the landscape, but this is only an exception. In most cases it is far superior to any medium in use. Its value as an advertising art has been shown. Will Scott has made it unequalled in the many-sided art of caricature. In fact, it is a Cubist poster (Will Scott's caricature of Sidney Drew) that has the honour of being the first artistic advertisement that is used outside the ordinary cinema. Roger Fry, and all the artists and craftsmen working co-operatively with him at the Omega workshops, has shown its value in house-decoration. Jean de Bochiére has shown, by his portrait of himself, that Cubism is an unsurpassed medium for portraiture. Nevinson has demonstrated its use in almost every branch of painting and in some, notably one of a falling aeroplane, which is now on show at the Fine Arts Gallery, shows that it can attain effects where drawing of any other sort, either linear or academic painting, would fail.

And as to the coming years. I see before Cubism a glorious future. When it has passed through the fire of prejudice and contempt, it will emerge, purged of all the affectations which now beset it as it really is. The public will accept it as it has accepted the Impressionists. The Academicians will fall and die unlamented, and Nevinson, Picasso and all the early Cubists who like "The lone antagonists of destiny, who went down scornful before many spears" fought to the last against all the contempt and deliberate misunderstanding of a prejudiced public, will take their well-deserved places among the masters who paved the way for their coming. But *"quod sit futurum cras fuge quærere"* – Let us not paint to produce fame in the future, but rather Art in the present.

Preface to the Decorative Designs of Francis Crease

Only one man could suitably have undertaken to write a preface for this collection of temperate and exalted designs; that is John Ruskin. I say this carefully, knowing very well that name and period have become so indissolubly wedded in modern criticism, that by a larger and less fasti-

The Decorative Designs of Francis Crease, London, privately printed, 1927. Held in the British Museum.

dious public than this book is intended to reach, such a statement would be regarded as pertly ironical. What I mean is not that there is the most remote connexion between Mr. Crease's art and the efflorescence of Venetian Gothic and aesthetic Socialism of the Ruskin Period, but that the qualities for its just appreciation are exactly that fineness of perception and delicate equipoise of senses that Ruskin possessed in so high a degree and for which he found no adequate stimulus in the art of his own period. Ruskin would have risen exuberantly to these designs, and he alone could, without impertinence, descant upon their eloquent excellencies. They belong to no period; they are the outcome of no particular school or training, but of an individual sensibility patiently concerned with the beauty of natural form and in intimate communion with other minds of the same temper, whether in their period they showed themselves in the profuse invention of luxurious textiles, or in the austere incision of gems. They are Northern, rather than Mediterranean, more of Chartres than of Rome, but often, and particularly in the later designs, leaving a faintly discernible fragrance of the East as of a spiced wind borne to alien hills or of the Magi at some Flemish *Nativity*. They have little about them that is capricious, nothing that is mannered or superficial, nothing assertive, nothing crude, nothing debased.

It is just for these reasons that they are noticeably unsympathetic to the present period. Looking back upon the last few months in London, I think of three typical artistic events : M. Michel Sevier's Exhibition of Paintings, the Magnasco Society's Exhibition of Baroque Drawings, and the production of *Mercury* by the Russian ballet. These, with the Charvet ties and shell buttonholes, Lord Lathom's interior decorations, the paper boys crying the news of Mrs. Bonati's murder, and the gossip in the constricted foyer of the Prince's Theatre, make up "the period." They go together, the vital with the trivial; but Mr. Crease's work is aloof from all this. It cannot become old-fashioned because it is not part of a fashion. It is intended for a small circle composed almost exclusively of his personal friends, and thus it is fitly produced in a narrowly limited edition, not aiming like most limited editions at creating an artificial rarity, but rare from its own nature, appealing to few, and steadfast in its appeal.

No doubt it seems presumptuous to insist so strongly upon the good qualities necessary for the appreciation of Mr. Crease's work, and then to put myself forward to express this appreciation. Let me explain how it is that I come to be writing this preface. I am Mr. Crease's first and, so far, his only pupil; whatever I seem to be claiming for myself is derived directly from him.

It was, oddly enough, my house tutor at Lancing who first introduced me to him, when I was sixteen years old. For some time I had observed him in Chapel on Sunday evenings, an incongruously elegant figure in the side aisle, who, drawn by the music, used to sit through most of the service in meditation, bear with the sermon, and then wrapping his cloak about him, would disappear mysteriously onto the downs.

I had some interest in heraldry at the time, and, being ecclesiastically minded, in illumination, and I won a prize of some sort for decorating a collect, an architect of eminence judging the award. I began to feel artistic, and, during harvest, wore a red poppy in my buttonhole, which was thought to be rather bad form. One afternoon I was changing after a boxing competition, in which I had been characteristically unsuccessful, when I received a summons to come to my house tutor's room, and to bring with me my prize prayer. I came sulkily. Mr. Crease was at tea with him, enthroned among canes and lists. I presented my illumination and stood about uncomfortably until told to sit down. After a close inspection he politely commended the pretty colours, and then, with a touch of vehemence in his voice, deplored the 'unworthiness' of the script. It was not script at all, said Mr. Crease, and then, with bewildering diffidence, he offered to teach me how it should be done; the illumination, he said, was beautiful, far superior to anything he could ever hope to do; it was shameful that the script should be unworthy of it; with great pains he had learned a little of the art; perhaps he could be of some use to me. It was an unusual way for a master's guest to address a gauche and recently-pummelled schoolboy. I looked at my house tutor, and, to my surprise and lasting gratitude, he consented.

At the time Mr. Crease was living at Lychpole, a secluded farm on the Sompting estate. Either there or to Sompting Abbotts I went every week for my lesson, and it is no exaggeration to say that from then until Mr. Crease left Sussex, these meetings coloured and dominated everything that I did.

On the afternoon of my first visit to him, I was overtaken by a heavy storm on the top of Steep Down, and arrived very late, very wet, and very shy. He lent me dry clothes, gave me tea in a handleless Crown-Derby cup, and taught me with the utmost patience how to cut a quill pen. Everything about his rooms was tranquil and beautiful – the old furniture, the richly coloured china and embroidery on the chimney-piece, the silver candlesticks, the monochrome reproductions of the Sistine frescoes, and epitomizing all that the place stood for, the *Winter-Cherry* design with the inscription –

> *I love all beauteous things,*
> *I seek and adore them;*
> *God hath no better praise,*
> *And man in his hasty days*
> *Is honoured for them.*

It was an intoxicating contrast to the rain outside and the discomfort and rancour of the school I had left. When he set me to write I found that the verses he had put out for me were some lines on Sherborne Abbey written by my brother.

I never became much good at script; I had not the time for practice or the patience – it is, after all, a mature accomplishment – but I learned far more. In writing, once the barest respect has been paid to the determining structure of the letter, the pen is free to flourish and elaborate as it will. In the control of these often minute variations of form, in the direction of serifs, the spacing and poising of shapes, the sense of historical propriety, there is scope for every talent required in the building of a cathedral. At the time my own predilection was for the most rigid four-teenth-century Gothic hand; Mr. Crease's script was the freest possible adaption of the Celtic scripts of the ninth and tenth centuries. In learn-ing to prefer his style, I gained for the first time some insight into the underlying motives of linear design. Ruskin started his pupils with a lichened twig or spray of ivy to teach them the alphabet; Mr. Crease started me with the alphabet and led me to the lichened twig and the singularly lovely irises that grew in the garden at Sompting Abbotts.

I had lived for the most part in London among bricks and buses, and was very insensitive to natural beauty. I think that I was even disposed to regard a love of Nature as a sign of effeminacy and weakness of intellect. One afternoon Mr. Crease set me to do a water-colour of the meadows below his window and the hill beyond, and then, leaning over my shoulder as I strained and niggled at the line of the larches, suddenly transfigured my drawing with great brushfuls of gold and crimson. He used to walk back with me sometimes as far as the turn in the Roman ditch round Steep Down where Lancing Ring suddenly comes into view, I eagerly questioning him about architecture or aesthetics or Limoges or Maiolica, he trying to turn me to the beauty of the evening and the downs.

Whatever he said was devoutly entered in my diary every evening.

'The tree which moves some to tears of joy,' he would quote, 'is in the eyes of others only a green thing which stands in the way . . . some scarce see Nature at all. But to the eyes of the man of imagination, Nature is Imagination itself.'

It is this transfusion of everything with the pure joy of Beauty, in which nothing is dissected or set aside, but everything is seen as part of one moment of worship, that is so characteristic of Mr. Crease's work.

A letter of his written in March, 1920, seems to me to express his attitude to Nature as I cannot hope to do in this preface, and to explain his designs.

My dear Evelyn Waugh, he wrote,

This evening whilst you were in Chapel was one of extraordinary splendour, and I wished you also might have been touched by it. For myself, the shadows of the prison house have fallen long ago, but now and again some shape of beauty lifts the shadow for a time. It is so much easier to feel one could write 'Resentment Poems' than 'Songs of Exuberance'; I hope it may never be so with you.

What I have in mind is the hope that you, like so many others of intelligence, may not run after definitions of Art and Beauty and the the like, feeling the definition and failing to feel the Beauty itself as it approaches on an evening like this evening. I can think of an Oxford friend at this moment who feels nature described in a sonnet and sitting in his arm-chair, but seems to fail in the open air. And again I remember a Don at Oxford learned in Greek Gems, telling me how all the other Dons would be interested in curious knowledge and facts about any gem, but its beauty always, or nearly always, escaped them. I often think of that fifteenth-century writer who said, 'I would rather feel compunction than know its definition.' Happily we are not thinking of compunction at this moment, but you see what I mean. No Flemish painter of the seventeenth century or English school of the nineteenth could hope to convey more than the suggestion of the visionary splendour of this evening – Wordsworth and Gray came nearest to such an atmosphere, so I believe.

One thing in my youth I had, and it was a verse or two of Gray repeated to me – I must be more thankful.

I wish you could have seen the flight of gulls in the fields on the left of the Ring, against the softer greys and greens, blue and rose colours; hundreds of them suddenly took their way home to the sea in one long stream following each other, and changing colour in the sunlight, and making sad music as a prelude to the coming symphony of colour. I always feel that those passing through Lancing have had all that I have never had – but it does seem sad that somehow or other it so often leads to the Hotel Metropole at Brighton as an Ideal, and not to the Truth which makes you free. Don't give this to Gordon to print! [my house tutor, who owned a small hand-press].

But I have no wish to write a history of my own aesthetic awakening or to detail a development that has been lamentably incomplete and impure; my only hope is to justify myself for this pressing forward first with my homage.

It is a particularly happy moment, it seems to me, for the collection of Mr. Crease's work, for the decisive processes of stitching and pressing.

In a distinguished essay on the *Art of Francis Crease* in the August number of the *Beacon*, 1922, Mr. Osbert Burdett wrote :

> *For the return to nature that his instinct first led him to follow has been, as we already see, the first step on the road that runs beyond nature to the province of pure design, where the forms of the artist are filled entirely by imaginative life, though themselves organically derived from the motives he has left behind him.*

This tendency, so acutely discerned five years ago, has become abundantly and gloriously evident in Mr. Crease's latest designs. Compare for example No. 15 (folio 14) at the beginning of the book with Nos. 28 and 31 (folios 26 and 29) at the end, and you will see, fully achieved, the emancipation of the essential structure of design from its accidental resemblances – as fully as in the abstractions of the *Mercury* ballet. The procession climbs in decorous progress from the meadow-sweetness of the *Bats and Borage* (folio 4) to the superb luxuriance of the *Pride of the Peacock* (folio 9) and the *Wild-Carrot* (folio 10), to the almost mathematic *Cyclamen* (folio 22), and then, at another turn in the path, begins to emerge into austere and unpeopled heights, into a rarer atmosphere and more brilliant sunlight, while far below the groves of Lychpole have become a green place in the spreading horizon.

And surely another sheet is already stretched upon the drawing board?

A Call to the Orders

How profusely they are strewn over England, the monuments of our Augustan age of architecture ! They stand on all sides of us, rebuking, in their measured Johnsonian diction, their degenerate posterity. Even in London, that noble deer bayed and brought down and torn in pieces; the city of lamentations, ruled by Lilliputians and exploited by Yahoos, whose splendid streets, once one of the splendours of Europe, are now fit

Supplement to *Country Life*, 26 February 1938, pp. xii, xiv. After *Harper's Bazaar* refused this article, Waugh wrote to A. D. Peters on 30 November 1937 : "I think it is much the best thing I have writen for Nash Harpers and ought to appear somewhere." Ed.

only to serve as the promenades of pet dogs or as vast ashtrays for the stubs of a million typists – even in London, in by-ways and neglected places, a few buildings precariously survive in grace and decency.

Outside the stricken area one meets them at every turn of the road. They are in the towns, grouped as a rule round the market place or the church; solid and spacious houses of the *bourgeoisie*, with their regular rows of well placed windows, their low stone steps spread out to the pavement, fanlight and pediment above the panelled doors, and behind them half an acre of walled garden, an old mulberry tree staining the grass, sometimes a statue; the coaching inn, re-built in Georgian times on a mediæval plan, curving sympathetically to the line of the street, the porch, supported by pillars, surmounted by the sculptured sign of the house, the ample, three-centred arch of the stable entrance, and along the side of the courtyard the ballroom, built and decorated in the fashion of 1770, its walls encrusted with plaster sphinxes, garlands, goats, Muses and urns.

They are in the villages : the rectory, too large for the restricted progeny of the new incumbent, let, as often as not, to the local adjutant or to a business man who keeps horses there for week-end hunting, but still eloquent of the gossip of Jane Austen's heroines and the rotund, prosaic sermons of happier clerics; and half a mile away the gentleman's house, "standing," as the house-agents say, "in twenty acres of park-like grounds; three acres well matured gardens; entrance lodge, carriage drive, stabling for twelve and other outbuildings; may be had with or without additional 1,000 acre farmland at present let to long-established tenants; four recep., ten bed, usual offices, water by gravitation. Electric light available in near future. A feature of the property is the wealth of period decoration." A lovely house where an aged colonel plays wireless music to an obese retriever.

And beyond these, dominating and completing the landscape, the great palaces of the Whig oligarchs, with their lakes and bridges and Grand Avenues, orangeries and follies, their immense façades and towering porticos, their colonnades and pavilions and terraces; those most commodious of all palaces, planned to provide a sequestered family life; concealing beyond the saloons and galleries and state-apartments an intimate system of little breakfast rooms and sun-lit studies; very homely palaces, even now when the cold light of electricity has cast its chill over rooms once warmed by a Christmas-tree blaze of tapers.

They are all over England, these models of civilised buildings, and of late years we have been turning to them again in our convalescence from the post-War Corbusier plague that has passed over us, leaving the face of England scarred and pitted, but still recognisable. For ten or fifteen years we all had the pest-mark scrawled across our doors and the watchman cried nightly: "Bring out your dead!" From Tromso to Angora the horrible little architects crept about – curly-headed, horn-spectacled, volubly explaining their "machines for living." Villas like sewage farms, mansions like half-submerged Channel steamers, offices like vast bee-hives and cucumber frames sprang up round their feet, furnished with electric fires that blistered the ankles, windows that blinded the eyes, patent "sound-proof" partitions which resounded with the rattle of a hundred typewriters and the buzzing of a hundred telephones. In England we have an artistic constitution which can still put up a good fight; our own manifold diseases render us impervious to many microbes which work havoc upon the sounder but slighter races. We suffered less from the concrete-and-glass functional architecture than any country in Europe. In a few months our climate began to expose the imposture. The white flat walls that had looked as cheerful as a surgical sterilising plant became mottled with damp; our east winds howled through the steel frames of the windows. The triumphs of the New Architecture began to assume the melancholy air of a deserted exhibition, almost before the tubular furniture within had become bent and tarnished. It has now become *par excellence* the style of the arterial highroads, the cinema studios, the face-cream factories, the Tube stations of the farthest suburbs, the radio-ridden villas of the Sussex coast. We have had a fright – a period of high fever and delirium, a long depression, and now we are well on the way to recovery. We are again thinking of stone and brick and timber that will mellow and richen with age, and we have instinctively turned to the school in which our fathers excelled. The baroque has never had a place in England; its brief fashion was of short duration; it has been relegated to the holidays – a memory of the happy days in sun-glasses, washing away the dust of the Southern roads with heady Southern wines – and the fashion has returned for more austere models – that superb succession of masterpieces from Vanbrugh to Soane which are grouped, far too vaguely, under the absurdly insular title of "Georgian."

Now the trouble is all the other way; enthusiasm has outrun knowledge, and we are in danger of doing to the styles of the eighteenth century what our fathers and grandfathers did to Tudor and Jacobean. It is a serious danger, because imitation, if extensive enough, really does debauch one's taste for the genuine. It is almost impossible now to take any real delight in Elizabethan half-timber – logical and honourable as it is – because we are so sickened with the miles of shoddy imitation with which we are surrounded. We are now threatened with a new disorder, the first symptom of which is, usually, a formidable outcrop of urns; they are bristling up everywhere – on filling stations and cafés and cottage chimneypieces. Now, there is nothing specifically beautiful about an urn as such – its value depends on its precise shape and where it is put. The builders of the eighteenth century used them liberally, but with clear purpose. Nowadays, we not only scatter them indiscriminately, but we seem to have lost the art of designing them – witness the ghastly jars that have been stuck up in Oxford along the St. Aldates wall of the new gardens at Christ Church. And even where recent decorators have been to the trouble to buy up – only too easily, from the yards of the contractors who are demolishing London – genuine pieces of eighteenth-century work, they have often re-erected them with scant regard for architectural propriety. There is the Devil of Crazy Pavement constantly tugging at most English women. Crazy pavement itself, with Welsh dressers, warming-pans, fowling-pieces, and harness brasses, have disappeared from civilised life and can only be seen in the cottages of actresses and columnists; but the yearning for *bric-à-brac* persists. Eighteenth-century ornament is singularly ill adapted for use as *bric-à-brac*; every piece of it has been designed for a specific purpose in accordance with a system of artistic law. I know of a house whose owner lately bought at an auction sale a pair of very fine columns; they are of fluted mahogany surmounted by graceful composite capitals, torn presumably from some dismantled library and sold apart from their surrounding panels and shelves. The happy purchaser has embedded them in the wall on either side of his fireplace; there they stand, supporting nothing. Of course, there is nothing remotely improper in using columns, like key-stones, in a purely decorative way – it has, in fact, been one of the main decorative devices of every great architect; but if you are having a sham column you must also have a sham architrave : the eye, with an instinctive understanding of the laws of physics, demands it.

There is a further trap into which the amateurs have sometimes fallen – the illusion that a design which looks pretty as a drawing will look equally pretty in stone. It is one of the arts of decorative draughtsmanship to exaggerate and accentuate; nothing looks more elegant, literally on paper, than the attenuated lines and fantasies of unimaginative buildings. People will sometimes think that they are saving themselves money by going to the local builder with a modish book-plate or programme-cover and asking him to copy it as a pavilion for their swimming pool or a porch to their garden. The result is almost always a gruesome failure. Gothic was made to be played with, and its misuse, like that of Oriental styles, has often had the most enchanting effect; but classical architecture must be taken seriously if it is taken at all; in the great age, the classicists were full of jokes – Gothic, Indian, Chinese – but never classical jokes. They remained true to the Vitruvian canons, and it is to those canons that we must return. One of the difficulties is that during the last twenty years the architecture schools have been getting into the hands of a generation who do not understand the Orders; they can most of them do you a presentable reproduction of a Cotswold farm (for exactly ten times the cost of buying a genuine one), or they can advise you, with a flourish of scientfic data, about the wearing qualities of different patent compositions for the kitchen floor; but very few of them have had that grinding, back-breaking apprenticeship with the "Orders" about which the great architects of the past complained so bitterly and from which they profited so much. Very few Englishmen have read Vitruvius. It is rather discouraging to try. He is anything but the lucid grammarian of taste which those who have not attempted him imagine. In fact, when we say "Vitruvius" we are really using a snob name for Palladio. While in England our forefathers were still building with gables and beams and mullioned windows, in Italy Palladio was evolving the style which was to come to us a hundred and fifty years later, which we, with typical arrogance, were to re-name after our line of kings. It was a style based on that of Imperial Rome and adapted to the changed habits of Renaissance noblemen. It was a style based on exact measurement and proportion; the relation of height to thickness in a column, the degree of its taper, the relation of capital to architrave, the particular ranges of ornament that were grouped together by convention. The whole thing was worked out, and the system was learnt by everyone who had any pretension to artistic interests – not only by the architect and his patron, but by the cabinet-maker. It is a highly significant thing that the first pages of the three great furniture albums of the eighteenth century all set out "the Orders" – Tuscan, Doric, Ionic, Corinthian, and Composite – in delicate introductory plates. It was by being drilled in these until the mind was conditioned to move automatically in the golden proportions, that the designers were able to indulge the most exuberant fancies. By studying "the Orders" you can produce Chippendale Chinese; by studying Chippendale Chinese you will produce nothing but magazine covers.

The Philistine Age of English Decoration

When William Morris married and set up house at the beginning of the '60s he found there was nothing for sale in the shops which he wanted to put in his home. He was almost unique in his dislike of the furniture of his decade. An aesthete as fastidious as Ruskin was perfectly content with

Harper's Bazaar (London), March 1938, pp. 79, 96, 98.

his mother's drawing-room; he and the connoisseurs of the time took their pleasures in natural scenery and the fine arts; they no more expected Art in the drawing-room chairs than we do to-day in our morning newspaper. When they had occasion to furnish a house they bought what they could afford from what was on show, new, varnished, straight from the workshop. Antique dealers did not exist except in mean streets and behind hawkers' barrows; scraps of fine furniture and china could be picked up cheaply as junk, but it was as unlikely that a mid-Victorian, who could afford anything new, would furnish at second-hand, as that a modern woman would dress herself at the cast-off-clothes-man's. It was typical of the sanguine spirit of his age that instead of becoming a collector, Morris became a designer; he designed every conceivable thing from printing type to commonwealths and changed the whole visible aspect of the English home; but it was ten years before his influence was felt outside his own circle, and the period between the Great Exhibition and the fall of the Second Empire remains a monument of what the plain Briton can do to his home when he is not badgered by his daughters into buying what he does not like.

Architecture, good or bad, cannot be said to have played much part in the formation of the Victorian home. It is, mostly, prosaic, nondescript, and as slavishly functional as any 1920 theorist could demand. The mid-Victorian householder liked a large family well out of sight and sound; he liked numerous indoor servants who lived underground by day, high overhead by night, were crammed with food like poultry being fattened for the market and were seldom seen except before breakfast, in the dining-room, at family prayers; he did not want to entertain on any spectacular scale; he had no use for the communicating suites of state apartments beloved of his grandfather; he preferred a series of substantially constructed retreats. The hip-bath before the bedroom fire provided a luxurious predecessor of the chromium and decalite cubicals of his degenerate grandchildren. These requirements determined the plan of the house. For elevation he cared very little. He was not disposed to spend much on what was, after all, primarily for the enjoyment of strangers outside. Such ornament as he indulged was economical in material and, in form, bewilderingly eclectic. The nations of the world were coming to the City of London to borrow, and its citizens adorned their homes with motives arranged as capriciously as the unredeemed pledges in a pawnbroker's window – here a Venetian window, there a Gothic; over the door a terra-cotta plaque faintly reminiscent of the French Renaissance, round the porch columns which showed a perfunctory regard for the classics; a Swiss gable, a Moorish chimney. It is the only period of English architecture that cannot be said to have any style of any kind at all.

His garden was more expressive, if not more lavish; it can only be seen now in its reduced, shabby-genteel form, but, to judge by the water-colour drawings which were produced so plentifully by mid-Victorian debutantes, it was much the same in its prime. Its essential was privacy. The eighteenth-century gentleman liked to overlook the most extensive possible landscape, much of which he owned, most of which he ruled, and of all of which he regarded himself and his house as the principal orna-ments. He liked to see and be seen.

The Victorian home was the retreat of the business man; he wanted something snug and private; he valued land, as most of us value it to-day, as a protection from being overlooked; hence his coniferous plantations and his shrubbery – especially the shrubbery; he was agoraphobic; he had no inclination to drive down enormous avenues lined with curtsying tenantry, but preferred to saunter unobserved, completely enclosed, in winding green tunnels of variegated laurel. When faced with a lawn he filled it with Monkey Puzzles and Wellingtonias.

It is to the interior, the exclusive and domestic circle, that one must penetrate to appreciate the fine flower of the period. In those great days there was no doubt about an interior being an interior; none of the blaze of light and blast of fog-laden air that vex the modern flat dweller. There was little need of open windows in rooms where no one smoked and a large coal fire maintained the continuous circulation of warm air; when a certain closeness of atmosphere was regarded as salubrious. The mid-Victorian home was a place of rest and retirement, indissolubly associ-ated with Sunday afternoons, to be enjoyed to its full in the coma that comes of heavy eating. And yet, such was the national hardiness of body and conscience that our grandparents went to no extreme in search of physical ease. Eighteenth-century chairs were always accommodating; it takes a very righteous man to be comfortable in a chair of 1860. Now-adays we have to be coaxed into repose with every ingenuity of spring and padding; our grandparents lay stupefied on the most uncompromising horsehair and on structures which outraged every principle of human anatomy. But in one matter of comfort they had the advantage of us. Their rooms were wonderfully dark. Great trees stood within a few yards of the plate-glass windows and touching them, dank and acrid ivy softened still further the gross daylight. Inside, double curtains of happily contrasted lace and plush induced a perpetual twilight. They were silent too. Oak boards and maybe pavings were close covered with dense, machine-milled carpets. In the library-smoking-room – inviolable mas-culine sanctuary where the *pot de chambre* stood screened in the corner – morocco leather prevailed, but everywhere else materials were thick and woolly and deadening to sound.

It must not, however, be thought that the plain man had – or to this day has – any natural taste for plainness. Poor fellow, it has been drummed into him by a hundred experts, writing on what are ironically termed "home pages", that ornament is vulgar, and to-day he endures blank slabs of concrete and bakelite, prisonlike bars of steel and aluminium; his only protest is to spend longer hours among the aspidistras of the bar parlour. Left to himself, in that golden age of philistinism, he ransacked the whole animal and vegetable kingdom and the realms of geometry for decorative notions. How few survive to-day of the rich suites that were turned out in their thousand! They are scattered and broken and maimed and burnt. But we need not despair. There was precious little Chippendale mahogany about until forty years ago when fashion set the forgers to work. The inevitable cycle of taste will restore all and more than all that was lost. Now is the time to form the collections of genuine pieces. One need not at present be on one's guard against counterfeit. What looks mid-Victorian to-day *is* mid-Victorian. The collector's art is to select what was most extravagantly representative of the period.

In this quest which has been zealously followed by a few for several years there is no better guide than Blackie's *Cabinet Makers' Assistant*, which is to the amateur of the '60s what Chippendale's and Sheraton's books are to the preceding century; whereas these cost £10 to £30 according to the address of the bookseller, Blackie can be got for five or ten shillings. These engravings, like their more famous predecessors, are idealised; they bear the same relation to the completed piece of furniture as do the illustrations in the seedman's catalogue to the growing plant; probably in the prosaic light of the workshop much of the detail was omitted or blunted; it is not by any means certain that all these designs were ever actually executed; doubtless they will be in future years – by the forger. Meanwhile where can they be sought? In the collections of the future a set of "National Emblem Chairs" will be a magnificent possession. Where are those chairs to-day? There must be specimens of them loyally dusted by lonely spinsters in a dozen shady and secluded parlours. But where are the State Bedsteads? It seems only too probable that they have ceased to exist. They are too large for the homes which are now the chief guardians of the art of their age, unless perhaps a few still survive in the villas which adorn the grimy countryside round the industrial cities, habitations of widows of the commercial magnates of the past, mayors and provincial knights and pioneers of mechanisation; proud, still affluent old ladies who never sought to cut a splash in the capital – they may still guard some treasures of their bridal days. These elaborate pieces of furniture can scarcely have been broken up for the manufacture of others; they are so veneered and chiselled that there is hardly a square foot of honest wood in them. The dining-room tables are going fast – those groaning boards of Dickensian hospitality; their legs have been sawn off, replaced by claw and ball cabrioles, and their massive mahogany tops shipped across the Atlantic as Chippendale. The wardrobes, too, are suffering daily, but the Canterbury Fire Screens must survive and the piano stools.

All these, however, are interesting only as showing the Victorian treatment of traditional types; the specialist will concentrate on collecting those peculiar articles of furniture which were devised by the Victorians for their own special uses, and died with them. What the Gout Stool is to the late Georgians, the What-not, the Umbrella-stand, and the Chiffonier are to the mid-Victorians.

The What-not rose to popularity with the Photograph and is unique among mid-Victorian creations in its flimsiness. Blackie defines it rather loosely as "a piece of furniture which serves occasional or incidental use and belongs indifferently to the dining-room, drawing-room, or parlour." It is a common error to regard the What-not as, essentially, a piece to put in the corner; examples exist which stand square to the wall and, even, isolated in the centre of the room. Its determining character is a series of trays set one above the other, usually of graduated sizes; the ornament is usually in fretwork and correspondingly fragile; perfect specimens are therefore exceedingly rare.

The mid-Victorian Hat and Umbrella Stand may still be found in use in provincial hotels; its chief defect is an unusual combination of weight and instability; if use is made of nearly all the pegs it offers, it tends to fall forwards upon the user. Its chief attraction is the almost infinite invention to which it gave scope. Elizabethan design was at this period considered most appropriate for the hall as being both sombre and aristocratic, and the best hat stands are ornamented with lozenges and frets boldly borrowed from Tudor stonework. A graceful but rather brittle kind has the form of a growing tree; there is an immense variety, but the collector will certainly seek the wheel pattern where the pegs are set in a single hoop which is crowned with geometrical scroll-work and supported on turned spirals.

The Chiffonier is perhaps the most enigmatic of all articles of furniture. It has nearly all the marks of the sideboard and is, in fact, often debased to this use in the lodging houses of Oxford and Cambridge. In its own day, however, it graced the drawing-room. Its essential feature is the pleated drapery in the panels behind latticework of metal or wood. It has been suggested that it was used for keeping novels in households where that type of reading was not publicly indulged.

The paintings of the period survive too plentifully to require description. In the age between the first Academicians and the pre-Raphaelites picture-buying became the hobby of a class who were somewhat exacting in the matter of subject; classical subjects tended to the obscene, scriptural subjects to the popish; animals, therefore, living or dead, provided the most popular models. These in their sumptuous contemporary frames will form an important part of the collection.

The Forerunner

It is notorious that Great Britain, as compared with Italy, France, Spain and the Netherlands, has made a meagre contribution to the visual arts. We had a brief period of fine landscape, some sound portraits, but in what elsewhere were the highest achievements, in religious devotion and in secular magnificence, our painters and sculptors are negligible. In only one branch of painting, and that not the most honoured even in our own country, did we produce a unique, idiosyncratic national school. That is the school of narrative composition founded by Hogarth and perfected a hundred years later. It would be absurd to claim a place for him beside Titian and Velasquez, even beside Goya. He was in no sense a great painter, but he is a national figure comparable to Dr. Johnson or Trollope, of whom we may well be proud. He was an excellent craftsman, trained in the discipline of the silversmith's shop. He painted better every year of his life. He was frivolously versatile, always hankering, like poor Benjamin Haydon, for the heroic and the sublime. Haydon is honoured today only for *Waiting for the Times*. Hogarth's Bristol altar-piece is disregarded, his *Marriage à la Mode* has given continuous pleasure for two hundred years and has inspired generations of worthy disciples.

The school which Hogarth founded may be defined as the detailed representation of contemporary groups, posed to tell a story and inculcate a moral precept. The figures are not merely caught and preserved in certain attitudes; previous and subsequent events are implicit in the scene portrayed. Hogarth's moral lessons are commonplace, commonsensical: that extravagance leads to destitution, debauchery to madness, crime to the gallows, loveless marriage to infidelity and so on. It remained for the more delicate sentiment of the Victorians to refine on these maxims. Holman Hunt's *Awakened Conscience* deals with a deeper experience than a dose

Review of *Hogarth's Progress*, by Peter Quennell, *Time and Tide*, 9 July 1955, p. 906. The second half of this review, comprising material unrelated to narrative painting, has been omitted. Ed.

of venereal disease. Augustus Egg's *Past and Present* gives a more poignant revelation of deserted childhood than the Countess's crippled orphan. There is more pathos in Orchardson's bridegroom than in the Earl. Frith's *Derby Day* is better composed and better painted than *The March to Finchley*. But Hogarth was the rude originator of these refined works and shares our gratitude.

He was pure Cockney, intolerant of everything foreign. English painting, so far as it has excelled at all, has done so in inverse relation to the influence of Italy and France. I do not know of any foreign painter except Svoboda who rivalled the English School in their own *métier*. Comparable Parisians of the nineteenth century tended towards the lubricious or the allegorical. There is one corner of the artistic field that will remain for ever England.

In writing Hogarth's life, Mr. Quennell has had a task which few will envy. Hard-working craftsmen give little scope for the biographer. All that can be told of Hogarth's affairs is contained in Austen Dobson's admirable article in the *Dictionary of National Biography*. His full-length study, which until now has held the field, is largely padding. So, indeed, inevitably, is Mr. Quennell's. The difference is that whereas Dobson's padding makes rather dull reading, Mr. Quennell's is entirely enjoyable. He knows eighteenth century London, particularly its underworld, very well indeed. Any account of Hogarth's day to day existence must be largely conjectural. Mr. Quennell has taken the occasion to give a rich, detailed conspectus of the streets and taverns, theatres and political controversies, in which Hogarth worked and from which he drew his illustrations. Often there are pages on end with no direct reference to the hero of the story, but they are vivid, elegant pages and they help us to an understanding of his art.

The Death of Painting

'From today painting is dead,' cried Paul Delaroche in 1839, when first shown a daguerreotype. He spoke too soon. For two generations there was

The Saturday Book: No. 16, ed. John Hadfield, London, 1956, pp. 49–53. This article draws heavily on Robert Goldwater and Marco Treves, *Artists on Art: from the XIV to the XX Century*, New York, 1945. Ed.

life – vigour, sometimes – in the stricken body. Even today in odd corners painters may still be found plying their ancient craft for the pleasure of a few impoverished private patrons. But for the professional critics, the public committees, the directors of galleries, the art is indeed dead, picked white; not a smell survives. It is noteworthy that a Frenchman first saw the significance of this French invention. France was the scene of the death agony. Delaroche's prognosis was sound enough. But it was based on a false diagnosis.

Nearly twenty years later an Englishman wrote: 'Photography is an enormous stride forward in the region of art. The old world was well nigh exhausted with its wearisome mothers and children called Madonnas . . . its wearisome nudities called Nymphs and Venuses . . . Then a new world slowly widens to our sight, a very heaven compared to the old earth . . . There will be photograph Raphaels, photograph Titians. . . .'

That was the prospect Delaroche feared. Here were a box, a lens, a bath of salts and with them the common man could effortlessly accomplish all that the great geniuses of the past had attempted. For until the present century the whole history of European painting was determined by man's striving to reproduce and arrange visual appearances. The critics of the last fifty years have been busy in imputing quite different motives to the Masters and in identifying quite different achievements. There is no evidence of these preoccupations in the rather sparse documents. Most of the letters and recorded precepts of the Masters deal with prices, models, and technical devices. When they speak of their aims they are unanimous. Leonardo da Vinci wrote: 'That painting is most praiseworthy which is most like the thing represented' and: 'When you wish to see whether your picture corresponds with that of the object presented by nature, take a mirror and set it so that it reflects the actual thing, and then compare the reflection with your picture.' Nicholas Hilliard wrote: 'Now knowe that all painting imitateth nature or the life in everything.' Piero della Francesca: 'Painting is nothing but a representation of surfaces and solids foreshortened or enlarged.' Poussin: 'Painting is nothing but an imitation of human actions . . . one may also imitate not only the actions of beasts but anything natural.' In the court of Louis XV it was disputed whether two perfect painters, observing the same scene, would not produce identical pictures, painters by inference differing only in their faults. There were certainly at different periods some differences of opinion about the rights of selection of the artist, about the modifications he might make in his model in the interest of ideal beauty, what details he might eliminate in the interest of grandeur. Painters represented things they had never seen, such as cherubim on the wing. Some, such as Bosch, portrayed pure fantasy but all the objects were imagined as concrete, visible and tangible and painted as such. It was never questioned that the painter's prime task was to represent. Actual illusion was never achieved except in amusing toys – dog-eared papers apparently pinned to the wall so that the fingers itch to remove them – but there is no reason to doubt that had a full-scale *trompe l'oeil* ever been effected, it would have been applauded without reserve.

Today high honours and high prices are given to the practitioners of 'non-representative art.' Patronage is in the hands of people who no longer seek joy in possession; the directors of public galleries conceive it as their duty to instruct by exemplifying 'movements,' however repugnant they may find the task. In the early days of the Post-Impressionists there were ingenious journalists who tried to demonstrate that the new painters were logically developing the discoveries of the Masters; that true aesthetic emotion had always existed in some unexplored subconscious area and was only at that moment (*circa* 1911) becoming articulate; that all original artists had begun by shocking the Philistine. As the scrupulously accurate drawing of Holman Hunt and the early Millais looked 'deformed' to Dickens, so a few years were needed before the common man could see Léger with new eyes. That particular bit of humbug has not worn well. In the last fifty years we have seen the drawings of savages, infants and idiots enjoying fashionable favour. The revolutionaries have grown old and died. No new eyes have grown in new heads. The division between the painting and sculpture of this century and its predecessors has become more pronounced, as more observers in other spheres recognize the evils of the time. There have been no sensational recantations of the kind prevalent among political writers, but the critics on the whole now admit that while Giotto and Tintoretto and Rembrandt and Degas were all in their enormously different ways practising the same art, the activities – call them what you will – of Léger belong to an entirely different order. Can this revolution be attributed to photography?

That invention certainly failed in the claims originally made for it. It has been a humble assistant to the Arts. There are mosaics and frescoes so placed that they can be seen imperfectly and then only with great fatigue. Photography has disclosed new beauties in these. The camera can reveal certain things that are invisible to the naked eye, such as the hitherto unrecognizable stains on the Holy Shroud at Turin. As in the classic hypothesis of the apes typing eternally until they write the sonnets of Shakespeare, the millions of plates exposed have inevitably, but quite fortuitously, now and then produced an attractive composition. But in its direct relations with painting, photography has never been a rival. The allegorical groups and costume-pieces produced in the '50s and '60s – such as Rejlander's celebrated *The Two Ways of Life* and Mrs. Cameron's illustrations to *The Idylls of the King* – are what Delaroche feared, and they proved to be wholly ludicrous. The mortal injury done to painters was something quite other; it was both technical and moral.

In technique it was the instantaneous snapshot, not the studio exposure, which proved revolutionary. Movements which before had eluded the eye were arrested and analysed. The simplest example is that of the galloping horse. Draughtsmen had achieved their own 'truth' about the disposal of its legs. The camera revealed a new truth that was not only far less graceful but also far less in accordance with human experience. Similarly with the human figure. In posing a model a painter was at great pains to place her. His sense of composition, her sense of comfort, the feasibility of maintaining and resuming the pose, were important. It was a frequent complaint of young artists that their elders were content with the repetition of art-school clichés. They struggled to build up from sketches entirely novel attitudes. Then came the camera shutter to make permanent the most ungainly postures. The 'slice of life' became the principle of many compositions at the end of the nineteenth century. At the same time 'gum prints' were invented by the photographers, a process by which the surface of painting was imitated. For a decade or more painting and photography were very close. There are 'gum prints' by the Parisians Demachy and Bucquet made at the turn of the century which at first glance may be mistaken for photographs of Impressionist canvases. How far the founders of Impressionism worked from snapshots is conjectural. Their followers were quite open in the matter. Sickert used to translate photographs into paint in just the same way as Victorian ladies translated paint into needlework – and in both cases with very pretty results.

Many early photographers, among them the herald of the 'photograph Titians' quoted above, were unsuccessful painters. There was a fair livelihood to be made out of the new device, especially by a man with the air of an artist; nothing comparable, certainly, to the splendid earnings of the popular painters, but the photographer did not have to work for it, as they did. Perhaps no painters in history worked so hard as the eminent Victorians. They knew little of the easy student days of *Trilby* or of the versatile apprenticeship of the renaissance. Painting had become a profession, respectable, rewarded, specialized. They trained as hard as for the law or for medicine, and they kept in training through the long years of rich commissions and hereditary honours. The physical exertion of covering their great canvases was immense. They used 'assistants,' but very furtively. Not for them the teeming studios of Rembrandt or the factory of Alan Ramsay. The English patron who was paying two or three thousand pounds for a picture demanded that it should be all the artist's own work.

Photography provided the ideological justification for sloth. The camera was capable of verisimilitude; it was not capable of art; therefore art, the only concern of the artist, was not verisimilitude. Verisimilitude was what took the time and trouble. Art was a unique property of the spirit, possessed only by the artist. You could be awfully artistic between luncheon and tea. So the argument ran.

In 1877 Ruskin denounced Whistler's pretentious *Nocturne in Black and Gold* with the felicitous expression : 'a coxcomb flinging a pot of paint in the public's face.' The prospect of enlarging this opinion in court was 'nuts and nectar' to him. 'The whole thing,' he wrote to Burne-Jones, 'will enable me to assert some principles of art economy which I've tried to get into the public's head, by writing, but may get sent over all the world vividly in a newspaper report or two.' Alas, that great projected trial came to nothing. Ruskin was too ill to appear. Whistler was given contemptuous damages without costs; Ruskin's costs were paid by public subscription. But it was not the hoped-for triumph of high principle. The pert American scored some verbal points and gentle Burne-Jones reluctantly gave evidence that Whistler's work lacked 'finish.' This clearly was not the point at issue with the early and life-long adulator of Turner. What a tremendous occasion had Ruskin at the height of his authority and eloquence stood up to warn the world of the danger he acutely foresaw! Something as salutary as Sir Winston Churchill's utterance at Fulton, U.S.A., and perhaps more efficacious. By a curious aberration of popular history the trial was for more than a generation represented as a triumph of Whistler against the Philistines. Today, it is reported, there is an honoured American painter who literally does 'fling' pots of paint at his canvas. What would Whistler have to say about that? Ruskin, we may be sure, would be serenely confident in his early judgment.

The German demagogues of the '30s attempted an exposure of 'decadent' art, so ill-informed and ill-natured and allied to so much evil that honourable protests were unheard or unspoken. The art dealers were able to appeal to a new loyalty; if one hinted that Klee was the acme of futility one proclaimed oneself a Nazi. That phase is ended. Today we need a new Ruskin to assert 'some principles of art economy.' First, that the painter must represent visual objects. Anatomy and perspective must be laboriously learned and conscientiously practised. That is the elementary grammar of his communication. Secondly, that by composition, the choice and arrangement of his visual objects, he must charm, amuse, instruct, edify, awe his fellow men, according as his idosyncrasy directs. Verisimilitude is not enough, but it is the prerequisite. That is the lesson of the photographer's and of the abstractionist's failure.

3

Man of Letters

Reactionary in most matters, Waugh was not conservative about literature. Though always ready to allow himself "the pleasure of a few sharp
expressions" about fashionable authors he thought overpraised (witness the
savage review of Stephen Spender's *World Within World*), he normally
recognized literary merit in a work regardless of the writer's opinions:
he wholeheartedly praised the novels of Christopher Isherwood and Arthur
Calder Marshall, both Marxist.

Later in life Waugh pronounced absurd condemnations on Joyce and
Lawrence, but he had himself reacted against the Georgian standards of his
own youth and embarked on an innovative, if not revolutionary, career as
a novelist – although it was Harold Acton and the Sitwells, not Bloomsbury,
who inspired him. The essay on Ronald Firbank acknowledges an influence
which, much modified, became the basis of a new approach to novel writing.
The conclusion of "People Who Want to Sue Me" (in Chapter One), which
emphasizes the importance of selectivity, is one of many passages describing
Waugh's own technique. He admired experiment if it was successful, witness
the review of Henry Green's *Living*, "A Neglected Masterpiece."

As a general reviewer, Waugh dealt with a wide range of books, judging
according to the standards of the book under consideration and the likely
taste of the reader. "Dropmore Press Makes Good" is one fruit of a life-long
interest in book-making and printing. The review of Belloc's verse, "Here's
Richness", reveals a consistent interest in poetry.

If Waugh had a genuine idiosyncrasy as a literary critic it was attempting
to treat divinity as a normal part of humane culture: hence appreciations of
Ronald Knox's sermons and theological books in terms proper to literature
rather than piety. (None is printed here since their substance can be found in
the Knox biography.) He said less than might be expected about the
"Catholic novel" as such, but did review religious novels in explicitly theological terms (e.g. Graham Greene's *The Heart of the Matter*; see "Felix
Culpa?", Chapter Five), and often introduced a religious dimension into
criticism of secular novelists, like Angus Wilson. However, for the most part
his criticism is to be seen as the comment of a well-read, perceptive practi-
tioner. The standards implicit in it are respect for craftsmanship and insist-
ence on structure, as in the review of Cyril Connolly's *Enemies of Promise*

(in Chapter Four); then lucidity, elegance and individuality, and in the absence of elegance, vitality. Fact always attracted him more than fiction. Most of the essays reprinted here deal with authors by whom he was influenced, like P. G. Wodehouse, or those with whom he had some affinity, like the young Aldous Huxley, "Saki", and Max Beerbohm. He expected the Galsworthy Introduction to be included in a volume of his own work. Presumably because he was thoroughly equipped to deal with literature, and therefore confident when writing about it, these essays are the most objective and temperate of his works and show him at his best.

Ronald Firbank

It is no longer necessary to be even mildly defiant in one's appreciation of Ronald Firbank. There is, it is true, small probability of his ever achieving very wide recognition, and even among critics of culture and intelligence there will, no doubt, always be many to whom his work will remain essentially repugnant, but already in the short time which has elapsed since his death, his fame has become appreciably stabilized so that condemnation of him implies not merely a lack of interest in what may or may not have been the amiable eccentricities of a rich young man, but also the distaste for a wide and vigorous tendency in modern fiction.

Those who delight in literary genealogy will find his ancestry somewhat obscure. He owes something to *Under the Hill* and Baron Corvo, but the more attentively he is studied, the more superficial does the debt appear. His progeny is unmistakably apparent. In quite diverse ways Mr. Osbert Sitwell, Mr. Carl Van Vechten, Mr. Harold Acton, Mr. William Gerhardi, and Mr. Ernest Hemingway are developing the technical discoveries upon which Ronald Firbank so negligently stumbled.

These technical peculiarities are late in appearance in Firbank's work and are the result of an almost incommunicable sense of humour attempting to achieve means of expression. His early books are open to the charge, so indefatigably launched against them, of obscurity and silliness. When he had in *The Flower Beneath the Foot, Prancing Nigger,* and *Cardinal Pirelli* fully developed his technical method the obscurity gives way to radiant lucidity and most of the silliness is discovered to be, when properly expressed, exquisitely significant. Some silliness, a certain ineradicable fatuity, seems to have been inherent in him. His introduction of his own name in *The Flower Beneath the Foot* and *Prancing Nigger* is intolerable *vieux jeu*; perhaps Firbank's sense of humour had reached a degree of sophistication when it could turn on itself and find the best fun of all in the doubly banal; if so it was a development where few will be able to follow him. His coy naughtiness about birches and pretty boys will bore most people with its repetition. He exhibits at times a certain intemperance in portraiture, indulging too gluttonously an appetite other novelists,

Life and Letters, March 1929, pp. 191–96.

even his most zealous admirers, struggle to repress. These defects, and perhaps some others, may be granted to his detractors, but when everything has been said which can intelligently be brought against him there remains a figure of essential artistic integrity and importance.

It is the peculiar temper of Firbank's humour which divides him from the 'nineties. His raw material, allowing for the inevitable changes of fashion, is almost identical with Oscar Wilde's – the lives of rich, slightly decadent people seen against a background of traditional culture, grand opera, the picture galleries, and the Court; but Wilde was at heart radically sentimental. His wit is ornamental; Firbank's is structural. Wilde is rococo; Firbank is baroque. It is very rarely that Firbank 'makes a joke'. In *The Princess Zoubaroff* there is the much-quoted introduction :

NADINE : My husband.
BLANCHE [*genially*] : I think we've slept together once ?
ADRIAN : I don't remember.
BLANCHE : At the opera. During *Bérénice.*

Even here the real wit is not in the pun, but in Adrian's 'I don't remember'; one of those suddenly illuminated fragments of the commonplace of which Firbank's novels are full and which, Mr. Gerhardi has shown, are not inimitable. Any writer with a more or less dexterous literary sense can evolve 'jokes' without the least exercise of his sense of humour. In his later work the only verbal jokes are the proper names, Mrs. Mouth, Lady Something, Mr. Limpness, etc. The humour is no longer a mosaic of extricable little cubes of wit. It cannot be repeated from mouth to mouth prefaced by any 'Have-you-heard-this-one?'

> Floor of copper, floor of gold. . . . Beyond the custom-house door, ajar, the street at sunrise seemed aflame.
> 'Have you nothing, young man, to declare ?'
> '. . . Butterflies !'
> 'Exempt of duty. Pass.'
> Floor of silver, floor of pearl. . .
> Trailing a muslin net, and laughing for happiness, Charlie Mouth marched into the town.
> Oh, Cuna-Cuna ! Little city of Lies and Peril ! How many careless young nigger boys have gone thus to seal their doom !

But by its nature Firbank's humour defies quotation. Perhaps it is a shade nearer to the abiding and inscrutable wit of the Chinese. It is there to be enjoyed by those who have a taste for it, but it is too individual and intangible to become a literary influence. The importance of Firbank which justifies the writing of a critical essay about him, lies in his literary method. He is the first quite modern writer to solve for himself, quite unobtrusively and probably more or less unconsciously, the aesthetic problem of representation in fiction; to achieve, that is to say, a new, balanced interrelation of subject and form. Nineteenth-century novelists achieved a balance only by complete submission to the idea of the succession of events in an arbitrarily limited period of time. Just as in painting until the last generation the aesthetically significant activity of the artist had always to be occasioned by anecdote and representation, so the novelist was fettered by the chain of cause and effect. Almost all the important novels of this century have been experiments in making an art form out of this raw material of narration. It is a problem capable of many solutions, of which Firbank discovered one that was peculiarly appropriate and delicate.

His later novels are almost wholly devoid of any attributions of cause to effect; there is the barest minimum of direct description; his compositions are built up, intricately and with a balanced alternation of the wildest extravagance and the most austere economy, with conversational *nuances*. They may be compared to cinema films in which the relation of caption and photograph is directly reversed; occasionally a brief, visual image flashes out to illumine and explain the flickering succession of spoken words.

One sunny May Day morning, full of unrest, Lady Parvula de Pantzoust left the Hotel for a turn on the promenade. It was a morning of pure delight. Great clouds, breaking into dream, swept slowly across the sky, rolling down from the uplands behind Hare Hatch House, above whose crumbling pleasances one single sable streak, in the guise of a coal black negress, prognosticated rain.

"Life would be perfect," she mused. . . .

And the dialogue begins anew.

But nothing could be farther from Firbank's achievement than the 'novel of conversation'. In his dialogue there is no exchange of opinion. His art is purely selective. From the fashionable chatter of his period, vapid and interminable, he has plucked, like tiny brilliant feathers from the breast of a bird, the particles of his design.

'I would give all my soul to him, Rara . . . my chances of heaven !'
'Your chances, Olga——', Mademoiselle de Nazianzi murmured, avoiding some bird-droppings with her skirt.
'How I envy *the men*, Rara, in his platoon !'
'Take away his uniform, Olga, and what does he become ?'
'Ah *what*——'

The talk goes on, delicate, chic, exquisitely humorous, and seemingly without point or plan. Then, quite gradually, the reader is aware that a casual reference on one page links up with some particular inflexion of phrase on another until there emerges a plot; usually a plot so outrageous that he distrusts his own inferences. The case of the Ritz Hotel *v.* Lady Something in *The Flower Beneath the Foot* is typical of the Firbank method. The King at a dinner-party employs the expression:

'I could not be more astonished if you told me there where fleas at the Ritz', a part of which assertion Lady Something, who was blandly listening, imperfectly chanced to hear.

'Who would credit it. . . ! It's almost *too* appalling. . . . Fleas have been found at the Ritz.'

Nothing more is said for forty pages, and then:

'Had I known, Lady Something, I was going to be ill, I would have gone to the Ritz!' the Hon. 'Eddy' gasped.

'And you'd have been bitten all over,' Lady Something replied.

Twenty pages pass and then an 'eloquent and moderately victorious young barrister' is mentioned as 'engaged in the approaching suit with the Ritz'. A few pages farther on it is casually observed that the Ritz is empty save for one guest.

In the same way in *Cardinal Pirelli* the scandal of the Cardinal's un-orthodox baptism of the Duchesse's pet dog is gradually built up. The actual baptism described; then it is approached circumspectly from another angle, touched and left alone. There is a long scene in the Vatican, apparently without relation to the rest of the story; at the end the Cardinal's name is mentioned; another touch and then retreat. There is a social climber who wants *her* dog to be baptized. Suddenly the Cardinal is in disgrace.

In this way Firbank achieved a new art form primarily as a vehicle for bringing coherence to his own elusive humour. But in doing this he solved the problem which most vexes the novelist of the present time. Other solutions are offered of the same problem, but in them the author has been forced into a subjective attitude to his material; Firbank remained objective and emphasized the fact which his contemporaries were neglecting that the novel should be directed for entertainment. This is the debt which the present generation owes to him.

A Neglected Masterpiece

A few days ago I came upon an illuminating paragraph in a Sunday newspaper. It was in the column where a lady of fashion dispenses advice to those who consult her about their private concerns. A correspondent wrote ". . . I am not outstandingly brilliant at anything. I can't leave home as my mother is delicate, but I want to do something to earn not less than £3 a week. I've tried chicken farming and it doesn't pay." The answer was, "You might get a job as a reader to a publisher . . . that or book reviewing."

That explains everything about our literary critics; they are young ladies, not outstandingly brilliant at anything, who have failed to make a success with poultry. It explains, too, the tepid and negligent reception accorded to Mr. Henry Green's *Living*.

This novel has been out for nearly a year but I make no apology for writing about it. It is a work of genius. I am as sure about this as I am about any question of taste. And no one outside a very narrow circle has read it.

There are several reasons for its neglect. One is the author's name. From motives inscrutable to his friends, the author of *Living* chooses to publish his work under a pseudonym of peculiar drabness. Moreover, the book lacks many of the qualities that attract attention – it is neither abnormally long nor abnormally short, it is not about the war, it is not about unnatural vice or religious doubt, it is not translated from any foreign language, it does not "contain easily recognisable portraits of people prominent in Society." Above all it cannot be "skipped." It has to be read with great care and humility – if possible three or four times.

It deals with an iron foundry in Birmingham and it may be as well to explain here that "Mr. Green" knows this subject intimately. After a normal education at Eton and Magdalen, Oxford, he went for two years to work in a factory, living in a workman's dwelling and following a workman's daily routine. There are two sets of characters; there are the Duprets who own the factory and their friends in London. Young Mr. Dupret is, in an indefinable way, the hero of the story, which begins with his visit to the Birmingham works.

Review of *Living*, by Henry Green, *Graphic*, 14 June 1930, p. 588.

In the course of the book old Mr. Dupret dies and his son succeeds him as head of the business. Young Mr. Dupret falls in love with a girl in London society but fails to make any impression on her; she in her turn falls in love with a genial bounder called Tyler and fails to make any lasting impression on him. All this part of the book is conceived with exquisite irony. Old Mr. Dupret's illness and the attempts to stir him from his lethargy, the house party with Tom Tyler being "the life and soul" of it, are satirical passages only equalled in modern literature by Miss Compton Burnett's *Brothers and Sisters* (another book that is not half as well known as it should be). In the second half of *Living* the rich characters fade away, having done their part, and the field is left to the factory workers in Birmingham.

These are treated in a manner which, as far as I know, is unique. "Mr. Green" has no political or sociological axe to grind; he is not distracted by any Tolstoyan illusions about the dignity of manual labour. He sees the working class with a humorous sympathy; we are accustomed to seeing them treated by *bourgeois* writers either as brutes or noble savages. For Mr. Green they are like a pack of unruly schoolboys, full of intense enmities and jealousies and odd superstitions (particularly a fear of the bourgeois professions of medicine and law). He shows them as tortured by continuous social embarrassments in their intercourse with each other, and by all kinds of ill-digested moral precepts.

At first the book is so much about the *whole* factory that it is impossible to distinguish the characters from their background.

Soon, however, if one reads carefully, five or six clearly articulated characters begin to assert their importance; those who live in the household of old Mr. Craigan "the best moulder in Birmingham." Joe Gates lives in the same house and Lily Gates, his daughter. Craigan wants her to marry a melancholy young man who works under him in the factory; he has saved money, owns the house, and is a powerful man. She wants to marry a still more melancholy young man called Jones.

Her abortive elopement with Jones, which forms the crisis of the narrative, is a superb piece of writing. Next door live the Eames family, who symbolise fecundity and nature as opposed to the mechanised lives of the other characters.

Technically, *Living* is without exception the most interesting book I have read. Those who are troubled with school-ma'am minds will be continually shocked by the diction and construction. In a great number of instances, Mr. Green omits the definite article where we expect to find it; he does worse violence to our feelings by such sentences as "this was only but nervousness because her he was taking in was so pretty," and "he still had some of his Friday's money which he had not been able to drink away all of it."

These are the very opposite of slovenly writing. The effects which Mr. Green wishes to make and the information he wishes to give are so accurately and subtly conceived that it becomes necessary to take language one step further than its grammatical limits allow. The more I read it the more I appreciate the structural necessity of all the features which at first disconcerted me.

There are no unrelated bits such as one finds in most books. A danger in novel writing is to make one's immediate effect and then discard the means one employed. Modern novelists taught by Mr. James Joyce are at last realising the importance of re-echoing and remodifying the same themes. Note, for instance, the repeated metaphor of "pigeons" in *Living*. (Dickens vaguely saw the importance of this, but he used it purely rhetorically – for instance, in the recurring image of Steerforth lying with his head on his arm as he had done at school.)

Let me add one other comparison, for one can in some way circumscribe and localise a book by stating its bearing in relation to other works. I see in *Living* very much the same technical apparatus at work as in many of Mr. T. S. Eliot's poems – particularly in the narrative passages of the *Waste Land* and the two *Fragments of an Agon*. Space does not allow me to say more; let me conclude by urging everyone who has the energy to tackle a book which is modern in the real sense of the word, and which is not predigested for weak literary stomachs, to read and *study Living.*

An Angelic Doctor

THE WORK OF MR. P. G. WODEHOUSE

Oxford men – or, to employ the periphrasis which Doctor Buchman and the Board of Trade have now imposed on us, men who are or were members of the University – have in recent years suffered many strains on their loyalty. News of Oxford in the papers has been disquieting; personal experience has often been worse. Undergraduates drink milk and eat sweets in the day and, in the evening, to the strains of the ocarina, pass resolutions to exempt themselves from military service; the dons think and write like provincial school-mistresses; philosophy has become a parlour game of logical quibbles; the history school a conditioning pro-

Review of *Week End Wodehouse, Tablet,* 17 June 1939, pp. 786–87.

cess in tepid Marxism; the new Bodleian outrages one of the finest streets
in Europe . . . all this may be true, but the University in conferring an
honorary degree on Mr. P. G. Wodehouse has suddenly exerted its failing
strength in an action worthy of its tradition. It is speaking, as is one of
its most splendid functions to speak, for the educated class of the country,
in recognizing Mr. Wodehouse's place in literature, not perhaps, as Mr.
Agate claims, as "a little below Shakespeare's and any distance you like
above anybody else's," but certainly as the equal among his contemporaries, as Sir Max Beerbohm and Mgr. Knox, and high in the historic
succession of the master-craftsmen of his trade.

At the same time there has appeared, with Mr. Belloc's introduction,
a somewhat daring volume under the title *Week End Wodehouse*. The
anonymous editor deserves both our thanks and our commiseration, for to
make one's own selection from a writer as popular and as fertile as Mr.
Wodehouse, is to invite the envy and recriminations of half the English-
speaking world. We all have in our own hearts our own "Week End
Wodehouse" and, inevitably, it differs widely from anyone else's. I cannot refrain from certain regrets about the present volume. First, its appearance. I do not like the type or the paper or the decorations. Secondly, its
arrangement, which is far from scholarly; it will outrage the serious
collector who treasures his *Gold Bat* of 1904 and the advertisement pages
of "Blacks' Boys and Girls Library" with which the master's earlier
works appeared; it will, also, prove a difficulty to the younger student
who is given no references for a great number of the quotations; the
bibliography at the end is flagrantly inadequate, omitting as it does even
some of the works (e.g. *The Man with Two Left Feet*) referred to in the
text. Moreover, delicious as the passage is, I can see no reason why on
page 366 there should be an extract which has already appeared earlier
in the same volume in its proper context. Thirdly – but here we are in
dispute about a matter of personal taste – I do not think the collection
is fairly representative of Mr. Wodehouse's versatility. The English public
school, the English Church and Hollywood are important themes throughout Mr. Wodehouse's work which are scarcely, if at all, represented here.
No anthology, however small, should omit the scene from *Mike* when Mr.
Outwood enlists Psmith's help in tracing the painted boot. *Mike*, indeed,
is one of the most important of Mr. Wodehouse's books; it is there, halfway through, that the author of the *Tales of St. Austin's* suddenly reveals
the genius of his later work. *The Bishop's Move* might well have taken
the place of one or other of the two Ukridge stories which are included.
Hollywood Interlude should have been reinforced with the superb tale
of the young man who went to retrieve his hat from a cinema magnate
and found himself contracted to write dialogue. Moreover, for a tale of
discomfort in a country house – though I agree in esteeming Sir Mortimer

Prenbery very highly as an individual creation – I think *Goodbye to All Cats* falls short of *Strychnine in the Soup*.

Against these criticisms must be put admiration for an idea which might have escaped most of us – the inclusion of the prefaces and dedications; these provide a superb example of how to grow famous with perfect good manners. On the whole it is as good a selection as one has the right to expect.

Mr. Belloc's introduction is a model of correct and graceful approach. He does not expatiate on how funny Mr. Wodehouse is, or adopt that patronizing bravado with which some critics express their praise. He treats him as he deserves, soberly and seriously, as a prose stylist and as the expression of a culture for the safety of which Mr. Belloc feels anxiety. He emphasizes the important fact that Mr. Wodehouse cannot be imitated; that every phrase is simple, exact and original. (To those he singles out for particular attention I would add one from the *Fiery Wooing of Mordred* – "the acrid smell of burnt poetry.") No one is better qualified than Mr. Belloc to recognize distinction of writing. It would be an impertinence to add to his judicious and deliberate technical analysis. The final passage of the introduction, however, seems to me unduly pessimistic. He is dealing with Mr. Wodehouse's prospect of lasting renown. There are reasons for uncertainty about this in the case of any humorous writer. Humour is the most ephemeral artistic quality. I never found anything really laughable in Aristophanes or Shakespeare; the kind of laugh which an audience gives to the classics is something quite different from the spontaneous, irresistible impulse that comes from even quite feeble contemporary jokes; moreover much of Mr. Wodehouse's humour is allusive in a peculiarly subtle way; it depends on the differences between contemporary spoken English and his own version of it. A later generation may take Mr. Wodehouse literally and suppose that his was merely the language of his day. For these reasons I think it possible that he will never give quite the same intoxicating delight to any generation after our own. But Mr. Belloc's apprehensions are based on the belief that the upper class, and in particular its butlers, are a dying race. Although few have inveighed more pungently than he against the corruption and arrogance of the rich and their servants, Mr. Belloc finds something regrettable in the change. But is the change inevitable? Or even probable? Supposing, as is still reasonable to suppose, that disparities of wealth are likely to continue, butling seems a trade certain to survive. Modern labour-saving devices have almost eliminated the housemaid, but the work of butler and cook remains essentially a handy-craft. It is true that much of the majesty of the butler rose from the fact that, although a servant in half of the house, he exercised despotic rights over a teeming population in the other half; that authority is likely to be reduced, but there is the compensating consideration that in the average modern household it is only the butler who understands the various switches and taps, the water softener, the fuse boxes, the ventilators and burglar traps which have taken the place of a large part of the domestic staff. Moreover Jeeves is no butler but a valet, and the more people live in hotels and temporary flats, the more valuable does a valet become as mediator and stabiliser between the individual and a mechanical universe.

I am confident that Mr. Wodehouse's characters will live. It is the half-real characters of the ordinary popular novelist who disappear. Literary characters may survive either through being so real and round that they are true of any age and race, or through being so stylized that they carry their own world with them. Of the first group is the Pooter family, whose physical circumstances now correspond to those of no existing class; of the second are Mr. Wodehouse's characters. They live in their own universe like the characters of a fairy story. "Jeeves knows his place," says Mr. Wodehouse, in the introduction to the *Jeeves Omnibus*, "and it is between the covers of a book." That is his secret. Just as, say, the sculptured figures on the west front at Wells are patently sculptured figures, exciting a purely aesthetic interest – not a lot of real old ladies and gentlemen whose precarious position would move us to thoughts of calling out the fire escape and getting them down – so Mr. Wodehouse's characters are purely and essentially *literary* characters. We do not concern ourselves with the economic implications of their position; we are not sceptical about their quite astonishing celibacy. We do not except them to grow any older, like the Three Musketeers or the Forsytes. We are not interested in how they would "react to changing social conditions" as publishers' blurbs invite us to be interested in other sagas. They are untroubled by wars; (Jeeves first appeared, it should be noted, in 1917, and Bertie Wooster, then unquestionably of military age, was "in the dreamless" at 11.30 a.m.) The "Drones," with its piano, swimming baths, sugar throwing, and borrowing and lending of fivers, has no conceivable resemblance to any London club; its Beans and Crumpets even wear a distinguishing, archaic costume of spats (like the Renaissance livery of the papal guard); their language has never been heard on human lips. Their desperate, transitory, romantic passions are unconnected with the hope or fear of procreation; age in their world is usually cantankerous, extreme youth, obnoxious; they all live, year after year, in their robust middle twenties; their only sickness is an occasional hangover. It is a world that cannot become dated because it has never existed. It may well be that in future generations Mr. Wodehouse's public may shrink; the vast and grateful masses who now devour him and Mr. Dornford Yates with equal relish will turn to other more topical entertainment, and Mr. Wodehouse, the Honorary Doctor of Oxford University, will survive solely as an epicures' delight, the equivalent perhaps of Miss Compton Burnett today. In a hundred years' time "the kind of man who reads P. G. Wodehouse for pleasure" may become synonymous with an extravagantly fastidious taste. And that is indeed as it should be. What can be more enviable than to enjoy the rewards of limitless contemporary popularity with the confidence, in the distant years, when copyrights have lapsed and royalties lost their importance, of a serene ascent into a rarer atmosphere, a little above the clouds, away from the crush where only the keen and the noble can follow? It is pleasant to picture the shade of Mr. Wodehouse in Olympian converse with his peers; the conversation turns upon the privations through which the immortals on earth attained their immortality; they tell their stories of garret and gutter; Mr. Wodehouse remains silent and then, lightly improvising an anecdote from the life of Ukridge, leaves them all silent and abashed until he courteously puts them once more at their ease by turning the talk to the subject of academic honours.

Introduction to The Unbearable Bassington

'Saki' Munro was not a young man when the First World War ended his career as a writer and, at length, his life. His talent was mature. He left a large number of short stories, some horrific, the greater part humorous, and one novel, *The Unbearable Bassington*. It is for his short stories that he is most widely known and loved. He produced them year by year with apparently effortless invention and elegance. His one difficulty seems to have been length; perhaps he conformed too complacently to the requirements of the editors of his time; perhaps there was a defect in his exemplary literary tact. Whatever the reason, these stories too often have the air of being fancies and passing jests unduly expanded, or of dramatic themes unduly cramped. Occasionally, seven or eight times perhaps, the theme, by chance, it seems, exactly fits the prescribed dimensions and the result is a masterpiece. To have written seven or eight masterpieces is a notable achievement.

As a work of art *The Unbearable Bassington* is inferior to the best of the short stories; faults in construction, which are the more disconcerting by contrast with the high skill of the writing, betray the first novel. For

H. H. Munro (Saki), *The Unbearable Bassington*, London, 1947, pp. v–viii.

example, the opening seems to presage a series of episodes, an *enfant terrible* repeatedly, in various ways, upsetting the plans of his mother; it is not until the fourth chapter that the story truly starts. There is an inexplicable interlude in chapter eight which only serves to arouse unfulfilled expectations in chapter fifteen. (Surely the mysterious Keriway will reappear in Vienna? But no.) The life of the book is lived within conventions more of the stage than of letters and already antiquated in 1912 – the complete exclusion of sex, for instance – which strain the apparatus of illusion. It is, however, with all its manifest defects a curiously interesting book.

Here, for the only time, 'Saki' offers, instead of the cut gardenia, the tree flowering in its pot, still the product of the hothouse, artifically nurtured, but a complete growth, leaf, stem, root, mould and all, and the rare object is found when in full view to be a sentimental tragedy; not, as a cursory reading might suggest, the tragedy of youth, but of the London drawing-room of a middle-aged lady.

The room, we are explicitly informed at the outset so that there shall be no mistaking it, is the lady's soul. It is also her life. It is one of countless similar drawing-rooms in the London of 1912, with its Bokhara rugs, buhl cabinets, and Dresden figures; it is more precisely dated by the Frémiet bronze on the chimney-piece. It is dominated by an urbane battle-piece supposedly by Van der Meulen. In this room, by a tenure which is one of the frequent insupportable improbabilities of the story, surrounded by treasures and trophies, lives Francesca Bassington, once a beauty, still 'svelte', and at forty, one might suppose, still ripe for love. But her pleasures are limited to bridge, the theatre and a succession of small luncheon and dinner parties. This life in and of her drawing-room is Francesca's entire life. It has no obvious attraction, for she has surrounded herself with what must, surely, be the dreariest people in London. With the single exception of Lady Caroline Benaresq, who is a Meredithian abstraction, a mere vehicle for the tart comments normally left unspoken, Francesca knows no one but bores. She has no particular liking for them and is often fretful in their company, but they are her world. With their talk of 'the dear archdeacon' and of bandicoots, they are caricatures from Cheltenham and Torquay. What are they doing at fashionable first nights? Why are they asked anywhere? 'Saki' endows them with titles and houses in Mayfair, but they remain obviously and hopelessly provincial. Among them Francesca has so atrophied that she is incapable of imagining any other life than they embody.

Of this life, threatened by penury, her son Comus may be either the saviour or the destroyer. He, the eponymous hero, exists for the reader only as he exists for his mother. We really know nothing of him. We are told he has friends, but he is not seen with them; at his last 'first night' he is alone; when he goes to his club we part company with him on the steps. We know about his extravagant tailor's bills and his modest losses at cards (two pounds down on the week). He exists only as a problem: how to use him in the service of the drawing-room. In real life, with the qualities ascribed to him, his future would be plain enough. A contemporary of Francesca's would take him in hand and educate him, but within the peculiar conventions in which the book is conceived, Comus must at once marry an heiress or perish. He perishes, of course. Heiresses are not captured by good-looking, self-centred boys fresh from school, but by men, of any age and appearance, who have learned from women the art of pleasing. So without more ado he is despatched to West Africa, where he dies, and the drawing-room is left in sole possession of Francesca. Then comes the catastrophe. The Van der Meulen, genuine or spurious, is not enough. This book, which is prefaced with the callow statement that it 'has no moral', discloses the ancient precept of the vanity of worldly goods, though 'Saki' chooses to translate it into his own less accurate idiom: 'What shall it profit a man if he save his soul and slay his heart in torment?'

The defects of the book have been remarked; its virtues are abundant and delectable. 'Saki' stands in succession between Wilde and Firbank in the extinct line of literary dandies. The wit is continuous and almost unfailing; there are phrases on every page which are as fresh and brilliant after thirty-four years (most cruel of all periods) as on the day they were written. 'Saki' has attempted and achieved a *tour de force* in limiting himself to the most commonplace material in its most commonplace aspect, in eschewing all the eccentrics which come so easily to English humorists, and the strong passions which are foundations of satire, and producing a work that is wholly brilliant.

It is impossible in reading *The Unbearable Bassington* at this date to avoid a prophetic and allegorical interpretation which cannot have been consciously present to the author. It was 1912. Comus had only to wait two years to find full employment for all his talents. He was cannon-fodder in a time of peace. And it is impossible, now, not to see Francesca as a type of the English civilization which sends its sons to death for a home whose chief ornament turns out, too late, to be spurious.

World Within World

It is a commonplace that while in the last ten years of the last century England was full of vigorous and original writers, the phrase "the Nineties" means, and always will mean, Ernest Dowson and the decadence. In the same way "the thirties" of this century mean a particular group which by no means comprised the best of the period. Messrs. Graham Greene, John Betjeman, Henry Green, Anthony Powell, among others, were then all in the first phase of their careers; a dozen or more of their elders were in full fruit; but each worked alone in quiet self-sufficiency. Certain young men ganged up and captured the decade. These were by no means untalented. Among many interesting writers there was one of bright accomplishment, Mr. Christopher Isherwood. There was also the enigmatic Mr. Auden. It seems one had to know Mr. Auden to appreciate him. Nothing in his written work explains the dominating position he held. There was something, apparently, in the tone of his voice reading his and his friend's work, which greatly excited his hearers. (After all, it was the age of Hitler). To this group Mr. Stephen Spender early attached himself with ardent hero-worship.

The obvious common characteristic of the group was their Marxist philosophy, and they profited hugely by it, having at their disposal all the publicity-machine of the Left Book Club; hitting the jackpot of popular enthusiasm for the losing causes in Spain and also of the equally prevalent mean panic at the prospect of bombs and gas. But their politics were not their most interesting characteristic. What made them unlike any writers in English history except the early pre-Raphaelites was their chumminess. They clung together. They collaborated. It seemed always to take at least two of them to generate any literary work however modest. They praised one another tirelessly and an unfavourable review anywhere raised a babble of protest from the authors' young friends. Mr. Spender describes how he was moved to fury by a criticism of Mr. Isherwood's first novel before he had read the book or even met the author. And these young cards convinced half the reading public not only that

Review of *World Within World*, by Stephen Spender, *Tablet*, 5 May 1951, pp. 356–57. Originally titled "Two Unquiet Lives", this review was followed by another of John Miller's *Saints and Parachutes*. Ed.

they were very clever fellows, but that they represented all that was noble and beautiful and unworldly, that they alone inherited the glories of the past, that the future was theirs alone and that anyone who differed from them was either a blackguard or a freak.

At the time it all seemed a bit too sharp; but the nuisance is past. At the first squeak of an air-raid warning the gang dispersed. One can look back now with simple curiosity. How was the trick worked? Mr. Spender offers himself as a guide to the ruins and one opens his book with pleasant anticipation. Here, perhaps, is the William Rossetti or the Theodore Watts-Dunton of the movement. But, alas, something is lacking. At his christening the fairy godparents showered on Mr. Spender all the fashionable neuroses but they quite forgot the gift of literary skill.

At one stage of his life Mr. Spender took to painting and, he naïvely tells us, then learned the great lesson that "it is possible entirely to lack talent in an art where one believes oneself to have creative feeling." It is odd that this never occurred to him while he was writing, for to see him fumbling with our rich and delicate language is to experience all the horror of seeing a Sévres vase in the hands of a chimpanzee. "When I write prose," he blandly admits, "I am impatient with that side of writing which consists in balancing a sentence, choosing the exact word, writing grammatically even." It would, therefore, be idle to risk Mr. Spender's impatience by exposing in detail his numerous, manifest failures in "that side" of his work. Only when he imputes his own illiteracy to others must the critic protest. He really should not represent Dr. Edith Sitwell as saying: "The ghost brings extreme misfortune to whomever sees it."

One is reminded of the Anglican Bishop who remarked that "the spiritual side of the job" did not greatly appeal to him. Why, one asks, does Mr. Spender write at all? The answer seems to be that he early fell in love with The Literary Life. When he met Mr. T. S. Eliot he confessed the desire "to be a poet."

"I can understand your wanting to write poems," replied the Master. "But I don't know what you mean by 'being a poet'."

Mr. Spender knew very well. He meant going to literary luncheons, addressing Youth Rallies, and Summer Schools, saluting the great and "discovering" the young, adding his name to letters to *The Times*, flitting about the world to Cultural Congresses. All the penalties of eminence which real writers shirk Mr. Spender pays with enthusiasm and they may very well be grateful to him. In middle age he forms a valuable dummy who draws off the bores while they get on with their work.

Nevertheless, it is a great pity that he did not hire one of them as a "ghost" to put his reminiscences into shape for he has a number of interesting things to tell. He has led a various and even adventurous life. Even he, with all his natural disadvantages, is far from tedious when describing Mr. Auden at Oxford recruiting his gang or the homosexuals of pre-Hitler Hamburg, or the quest for a deserter in communist Spain.

Was there no one among all the illustrious acquaintances whom Mr. Spender names in the preface as his advisers, who would say to him : "Climb down. Don't call your book *The Autobiography of Stephen Spender*. Write instead : '*An Autobiography by* . . .' Don't hold up your parents to contempt. After all, you are their son and it is just possible that you may take after them. Don't give your opinions about Art and the Purpose of Life. They are of little interest and, anyway, you can't express them. Don't analyse yourself. Give the relevant facts and let your readers make their own judgments. Stick to your story. It is not the most important subject in history but it is one about which you are uniquely qualified to speak. Here and there you show a gift for pertinent anecdote. Exploit that and you may produce a permanently interesting little book." ?

A Clean Sweep

The reviewer who comes late to his task, is at great advantage for he joins the debate after the question has been defined. All interested in novels may now be presumed to have read *Hemlock and After* or to have read enough about it to have decided that the book is not for them. The temptation of the late critic is to deal only with his predecessors, the least intelligent of whom were those of the B.B.C. These savants, who discuss books and things on Sunday morning, sought a way out of their puzzlement by saying that the book could be treated "on two levels," as though it comprised two complementary cellophane tracings, ignoring the fact that any book worth discussing at length exists in three dimensions, a solid thing which can be viewed from any angle and cut in any section. Most good novels vary in mood and method – satire, comedy, drama, allegory, analysis, description, comment and criticism, all have their part.

Hemlock and After is a singularly rich, compact and intricate artifact, and the first thing any critic should make clear is that whatever its defects, it is a thing to rejoice over. In England, in any branch of literature from detective stories to theology, we are reading precisely the same writers as

Review of *Hemlock and After,* by Angus Wilson, *Month,* October 1952, pp. 238–40.

we were reading eighteen years ago. Here at last is someone new. Mr. Wilson has already shown himself to be incomparably the cleverest and most skilful story-teller since the brief passage across our skies of Mr. Christopher Isherwood. Now he has produced a novel which in less precise hands might have run to three times its length. Indeed almost the only just complaint that can be made of his craftsmanship is that it puts a considerable strain on the reader. Let the mind slacken for the length of a line and you will miss something important.

Thus the plot defies adequate summary. The "Hemlock" of the title is, of course, an allusion to the death of Socrates. The central theme is the tragedy of an elderly man of letters, a liberal-humanist. He desires to crown his life's work by the establishment of a Home for young poets. The test of his prestige is his success or failure in enlisting the support of all the political and scholarly bodies who can make his conception practicable. He triumphs. For the Inauguration Mr. Wilson provides all the traditional comic effects of an English function – the drunk servants, the gate-crashers, the bores and snobs and frauds, the incompetent and insolent workmen. But there is a deep personal tragedy in the personal life of the hero of the day, which causes him to deliver a message of despair instead of one of hope. His wife is out of her mind and he, Mr. Sands, the great man, has in advanced years developed and indulged homosexual tendencies, which have attached him successively to two contrasted youths, a pert young cad and the feeble, retarded victim of a "graciously living" American mother. More than this, there has established herself at his gates (he lives in Metroland) a formidable woman named Mrs. Curry, a procuress, who carries on her trade in a rose-embowered cottage. Almost unanimously the critics have condemned this character as preposterous. The present writer was able, at a pinch, to accept her, but he found her methods of trading quite incredible. It would not be surprising to learn that she had in fact been drawn quite accurately from life. That is often the case with the least plausible characters in fiction and when it happens it marks an artistic failure on the part of the writer. Mrs. Curry's horrible *ménage* forms a caricature of the secret life of Mr. Sands. When she plans a particularly nasty service for one of her neighbours, Mr. Sands is disgusted and determines to intervene. But he has nothing except his disgust. His liberal-humanism has been invoked to justify his own vices. He has silenced his conscience by professing that his interest in his catamites is benevolent. By what standard are he and his set the superiors of Mrs. Curry and hers? He acts, but dies in an agony of mind. It is left to Mrs. Sands, who comes to her senses in the crisis, to complete the work of purgation.

First and last it is the story of "a bad conscience," though the scene is so densely thronged with minor but essential characters, that it needs hard reading to follow it. The characters are "unpleasant" and this is a fact which the reviewers have firmly grasped. The broadcasting critics found the characters so odious as to forfeit all interest. But the case is odder than that. There is a superfluity of the outrageously wicked certainly, but there is almost an equal number of people who under other eyes than Mr. Wilson's might be quite likeable. Mr. Wilson is unique in his detestation of all of his creatures; their most innocent hobbies are as reprehensible as their vices. The facts that they wear certain clothes or decorate their rooms in certain ways or speak with certain mannerisms are noted as damning evidence – of what?

There seem two prepossessions of Mr. Wilson's which greatly detract from his power as an artist. Perhaps they are Marxist in origin. One is his hypersensitiveness to class. Nowhere, except perhaps in parts of Asia, is the class structure as subtle and elaborate as in England. Everyone in England has a precise and particular place in the social scale and constantly manifests the fact in habit and word. Many writers have found a rich source in this national idiosyncrasy. Few writers have a sharper nose for class than Mr. Wilson. But when he defines he seems to condemn. It is as though he found something obscene in the mere fact of class membership. Can he be troubled by remote dreams of The Classless Society?

The other characteristic may spring from the same indoctrination. He appears to believe that revolution is just around the corner. This apocalyptic sense puts all his creation in a dubious light. If his characters are really the products of economic forces and if those forces are about to cease; if his whole story is simply a flickering shadow on a screen which, any moment, will rise on Real Life; if there are no abiding consequences to anything they do; if there is no heaven or hell for them – then indeed the broadcasters are right in saying that they are devoid of interest or meaning.

But Mr. Wilson is too true an artist to be a victim for long of these fatuous views – if indeed he holds them at all. When he is really wholeheartedly engaged with his characters, however obscure, he *knows* they matter, and the reader knows too.

And there is another aspect from which the book can be read. A writer's relation with his symbols is on the whole a private concern. A reader is entitled to find his own allegory. For this reader, at any rate, there was great significance in the return to sanity of Mrs. Sands. It was as though she had been the Conscience of the book, atrophied at first, then stirring and coming to action, and triumphantly and serenely making a great clean sweep. All that is lacking in a work elsewhere so full of fine definition, is the name of the new life-giving power.

Urbane Enjoyment Personified: Sir Osbert Sitwell

The physical profile is familiar. The bland, patrician features have been cast in brass by Frank Dobson and exquisitely limned by Sir Max Beerbohm; they have been photographed by Mr. Beaton and snapped by a host of camera men. The tall, well-dressed figure, the courteous manner (Mr. Turveydrop ameliorates the stern carriage of Sir Leicester Dedlock in this baronet) might, at first glance, belong to any well-to-do, cultivated English bachelor of a passing generation. Closer scrutiny reveals a hint of alertness and menace, as though a rattlesnake may be expected round the next corner and the nice conduct of the clouded cane might any minute require a good whack. There is little to indicate the transition that has occurred in the last fifteen years between the *enfant terrible* and the Grand Old Man of English Letters.

For that, beyond dispute, is Sir Osbert's present position. He is not our only one. We are fairly free with the title; less so than the French; more, I think, than Americans. It comes in the end to all genuine talent which has not been prematurely extinguished. It comes sometimes to men who have ceased writing for twenty years or more. The interest of Sir Osbert's fame is that it rests on a lifetime of uninterrupted development and enrichment. His natural growth has continued into late middle age so that his latest book has always been his best. He acquired his reputation first, then seriously settled down to earn it.

In my youth, when Sir Osbert's literary achievement was still very small, the English scene was full of august figures – Hardy, Yeats, Bridges – but there was little doubt in any of our minds as to whom we aspired to know. Already it was the Sitwells, for they radiated an aura of high spirit, elegance, impudence, unpredictability; above all of sheer enjoyment. Most writers are best known in their work. They are dull dogs to meet and only come alive at their desks pen in hand. Sir Osbert is a full, rich, singular personality first, and a shelf of books second. His achievement is to have mastered the art of recording and communicating his personality. There has never, I think, been a writer who has had at the same time so great an influence and so few imitators. Mr. Hemingway pre-eminently, to a less degree D. H. Lawrence, Virginia Woolf and Mr. Eliot, are all overcast and tainted by the crop of disciples they have sowed.

There is no identifiable school of Sitwell. Three of them was enough.

No one sought to ape their escapades. They spread no infectious literary rash. We simply basked in the warmth they generated and went back to our several tasks exhilarated. But their influence permeates all that remains of civilized English life.

It is best defined I think as pure enjoyment – of people and places, art and absurdity, the latest thing and the oldest; an equal zest for battle and for placid contemplation.

Sir Osbert was a regular soldier before the first World War. He belongs to a generation most of whom were killed or fatally embittered. He emerged from the war with some bitterness too, but this he extruded in his satirical writing. It never appeared in his life, which was unfailingly gay even in his rages. A great waste of time had been forced on him in stables and trenches. He was determined to make up for it. Where others sought mere distraction, he and his brother found real enjoyment.

They declared war on dullness. The British bourgeoisie were no longer fair game. Their self-complacency had gone with their power during the war. The Sitwells attacked from within that still-depressing section of the upper class that devoted itself solely to sport and politics. By 1939 English society had been revolutionized, lightened and brightened, very largely through the Sitwell influence. They taught the grandees to enjoy their possessions while they still had them. They made the bore recognized and abhorred as the prime social sinner.

They attacked from without the professional worlds of art and literature, where a new and insidious philistinism was being preached. Mud from the fields, where "conscientious objectors" had played at farming, bespattered everything. There was a shrinking from the rare and lovely and elaborate, and a welcome for the commonplace. Scrawls from the Infant School were as "significant" as the finest draftsmanship. Vocabularies were purged of all but their drabbest epithets. A decade later all this bilge was canalized by the Marxists. Then it had half London and Paris awash. The Sitwells careered like Indians round these covered wagons, loosing their flaming arrows into the Bible readings.

Sir Osbert and his brother Sacheverell had a well-bred disdain for the conventions of good taste. They revelled in publicity. Most English writers genuinely shrink from it. Others have a guilty vanity that makes them woo it in secret. The Sitwells left their press cuttings in bowls on the drawing-room table. Popular newspapers with all their absurd vulgarity were just a part of the exciting contemporary world in which the Sitwells romped. They were weapons in the total warfare against dullness.

The Sitwells were frankly and recklessly resolved to be conspicuous.

Others produced slim volumes of verse and waited timidly for the reviews. Miss Edith Sitwell's poems were recited through a megaphone from behind a screen. I vividly remember the first night of "Façade." My memory differs slightly from Sir Osbert's. He was aware of hostile demonstrators among an audience which seemed to me uniformly enthusiastic. No one could mistake the subsequent swish and smack of the tomahawks when a critical head showed itself.

The world is united now in their deference toward Sir Osbert. In those days he saw it – perhaps with exaggeration – as divided into opposed camps of his friends and enemies. Toward his enemies he was implacable and deadly. No one was too trivial or too august to escape savage retaliation for an insult. Most writers, in the course of their careers, become thick-skinned and learn to accept vituperation, which in any other profession would be unimaginably offensive, as a healthy counterpoise to unintelligent praise. Not so the Sitwells. If those bowlfuls of press cuttings survive – and I suspect that they do, somewhere among the archives of Renishaw – they will make a rich store of material for future biographers; controversies on every conceivable subject, appalling snubs, sledge-hammer blows on thick skulls and frail insects alike. At one time indeed, these ferocious campaigns threatened to undo their own work of publicity, for editors and critics alike became timid of mentioning Sir Osbert at all for fear of the consequences.

And meanwhile Sir Osbert continued to enjoy things. He has three enchanting houses but no one has got more than he out of travel. Like all good travellers, he rejected accustomed amenities and sought in every place what is idiosyncratic of it. In America, for instance, where the friendliest visitors tend to wilt in the central heating, Sir Osbert finds the fierce temperature highly stimulating, just as in China he rejoiced at the whistling pigeons. Books will no doubt multiply about Sir Osbert's social and artistic adventures.

One quality, perhaps because it lends itself least to the raconteur, is seldom emphasized; that is Sir Osbert's continuous kindness to other artists. Many of his battles have been fought in defence of others. And he has been recklessly liberal in the role of patron. There can be few painters or writers or musicians of his period who are not bound to him with gratitude. Two instances come to my mind, for they involve acquaintances. A penniless undergraduate, thought at the time a promising poet, was sent down from Oxford. He was immediately invited to make Renishaw his home until he had found his feet. Another young man, now a fine novelist, then unknown, worked in the publishing office which produced Sir Osbert's earlier books. He seemed lonely and dispirited. Sir Osbert invited him to give a dinner party for his friends at his London house.

Throughout his life, too, Sir Osbert has shown the far rarer generosity of encouraging the successful.

And all the time that Sir Osbert was enjoying himself, "going everywhere" as they used to say, "and knowing everyone," he was hard at work mastering his difficult art. His life and his writing are indivisible. It is fitting that his masterpiece should be the five lucid, opulent volumes of his autobiography.

These calm, leisurely pages were written during the stresses of the second World War. Sir Osbert refused to be hurried; refused to modify his idiosyncratic attitude to life in deference to the debased standards of the time. He knew he had a valuable message to deliver – one of urbane enjoyment. He knew he had an artistic creation to perfect – his portrait of his own father. He knew he had a uniquely rich experience to develop – a lifetime lived in and for the arts. Those five volumes have given him a secure place in English literature.

Here's Richness

Hilaire Belloc's death last summer came at the end of nearly fifteen years during which he had written nothing and made no public appearance. Most of his books were out of print. The weekly paper to which he had devoted himself so prodigally had ceased publication. And yet at his Requiem Mass the great nave of Westminster Cathedral was thronged and by a congregation the greater part of whom, it seemed to one observer, were drawn by Belloc's fame rather than by personal acquaintance. It was not a literary occasion. Belloc was strictly, perhaps even ruthlessly, professional as a writer, but he made his life among men of action and women of society. Younger writers were often disconcerted when they discerned behind his massive courtesy an absolute ignorance of who they were and what they had written. There were friends in plenty in the Cathedral that August morning, men and women whose wide variety gave witness of the fulness of the man they were commemorating. (Belloc has been spoken of as a bigot and it is worth noting that of his close friends not more than half shared his religious faith and very few, if any, his political opinions.) But mingling with them and outnumbering

Review of *The Verses of Hilaire Belloc*, ed. W. N. Roughead, *Spectator*, 21 May 1954, pp. 498, 501.

them were people of all kinds and ages who may never have set eyes on Belloc but loved him in his work.

Those are Belloc's prime characters as a man and as a writer, his breadth of scope and the love he inspires. His poetry is quintessential of him. He himself recognised this fact most clearly. His prose works are copious, always lucid, often rising to fine passages of rhetoric, often memorable in their sharp definition of word, but they are for the most part the work of a craftsman, often a craftsman hired for an imposed task. His poetry is his art, something he kept quite distinct from literary commerce, to which he gave his full concentrated attention, into which he distilled all the noble essences which made him unique as a man, in which he confided as his warranty of lasting fame. Most of it was written before 1914, none after 1939. But in his years of leisure and rumination he never undertook the task of collection and collation. That, he was confident, would come later and here, very punctually, we have it; a most welcome and worthy book. Mr. Roughead is an editor of Scottish prudence and precision. Sir Francis Meynell, a publisher of unwearied charm. The arrangement, the rare notes, the apparatus of reference are admirably convenient. The verses are set in the fine, clear italic of the Romulus fount and printed on paper which it is a pleasure to handle. One thousand six hundred and fifty copies have so far been printed. It is to be hoped that an unlimited popular edition will follow.

In only one particular can fault be found with this admirable pair, editor and publisher. Mr. Roughead states: "This book contains what I believe to be the whole of Hilaire Belloc's poetry, except for a few manuscript verses and printed fragments too slight to be worth including and some oral-tradition verses vague as to text and over-sharp in intention." It is not quite clear how many categories of exception Mr. Roughead here intends. Are all the manuscript verses not included held to be too slight? Are the 'over-sharp' verses all also vague in text? What is certain is that, for fear of offence some of Belloc's wittiest and most characteristic verses have been omitted. The second Lord Devonport has set an example of truly noble magnanimity in giving his approval to the publication of 'The grocer Hudson Kearley.' Lords Swaythling, Wimborne and Rothschild and Mr. Edward James seem, with some reason, to have been less accommodating. Could not a few blank leaves have been included at the end of the volume on which owners might transcribe their favourite *expurgata*?

There are more than 370 items in the collection, ranging in size and dignity from:

> I said to Heart, "How goes it?" Heart replied:
> "Right as a Ribstone Pippin!" But it lied.

to the sonorous ode on wine. The children's rhymes, almost every syllable of them a familiar quotation, are here reprinted without the illustrations which seemed an inalienable part of them. It is remarkable how well they stand alone. The order of the original books of verses has been broken and the various poems felicitously regrouped under their forms as sonnets, songs, epigrams, ballades and so on. There are eleven items never before printed, thirteen that were privately printed, and forty-six that have not appeared in any previous collection. Now that all is gathered in, it can be seen how small a part of Belloc's work was 'Bellocian' in the vulgar usage.

> May all good fellows that here agree
> Drink Audit Ale in heaven with me,
> And may all my enemies go to hell!
> Noël! Noël! Noël! Noël!

Early lines, interpolations in a prose fantasy, far from typical, but meat for the parodist; the ebullience of a brief mood. Belloc's verse is by turn humorous, comic, tender, witty, angry, melancholy, formal; very seldom jolly. It is in large the complete expression of a man's soul – and a great soul. His themes are the stuff of common life as he knew it in a warmer age; strenuous male companionship, romantic love of woman, the sea, the seasons, the transience of earthly beauty, the unremitting benevolent watchfulness of Our Lady and the angels, the innocence of childhood, the absurdity of pedantry and ambition, the wickedness and stark danger of power. His diction and prosody are the fruit of classical schooling. He was a Christian Shropshire Lad and, by that enrichment, immeasurably Housman's superior. He needs no critical interpretation. He is here to be enjoyed. For that reason there were few articles about him in the literary reviews and many mourners at his obsequies.

He had an idiosyncratic conspectus, formed early, which seemed not to vary from 1912 until the day of his death. In his opinions, he was a traditionalist and a revolutionary. It will be the gracious task of Mr. Robert Speaight, his biographer, to count the components of his intellectual structure and trace the origins of those seemingly discordant convictions which coexisted harmoniously in him. The reviewer of his *Verses* has an easier task, to express wonder at their variety and richness.

For satire:

> Distinguish carefully between these two,
> This thing is yours, that other thing is mine.
> You have a shirt, a brimless hat, a shoe
> And half a coat. I am the Lord benign

Of fifty hundred acres . . .
. . . I do not envy you your hat, your shoe,
Why should you envy me my small estate ?

And the 'Verses to a Lord who, in the House of Lords, said that those
who opposed the South African adventure confused soldiers with money-
grubbers.'

For humour :

Sir ! you have disappointed us !
We had intended you to be
The next Prime Minister but three :
The stocks were sold : the Press was squared;
The Middle Class was quite prepared.
But as it is ! My language fails !
Go out and govern New South Wales.

For sustained classic dignity, the 'Heroic Poem on Wine.'
For pure lyric beauty the lyric beginning :

O my companion, O my sister Sleep,
The valley is all before us . . . .

But it is tedious to call attention to such established landmarks. Lines
of Belloc's sing a multitude of memories. The wonder is, in finding them
all collected, how profuse and how pure a genius is here displayed.

Dropmore Press Makes Good

The Dropmore Press and the closely allied Queen Anne Press have in
recent years produced a number of enterprising, experimental little books
and one massive monument of frivolity in the reproduction of postage
stamps. Now at last they have done what their well-wishers have always
hoped for them and have created a work of art. *The Holkham Bible*

Review of *The Holkham Bible Picture Book,* ed. W. O. Hassall, *Spectator,* 16
July 1954, pp. 93–94.

Picture Book is in this reviewer's experience the most beautiful piece of book-making to appear anywhere since the war and one of the finest of the century. It comes at the right time when the decay of craftsmanship is being everywhere deplored. Future historians will have to qualify their generalisations. 1954 cannot be such a bleak year as is generally supposed.

'Bible Picture Book' is a convenient but not very accurate name for the manuscript here reproduced. It is a series of drawings, made probably in London in about 1325, under Dominican patronage. The 42 parchment leaves were taken out of the country, presumably at the Reformation, purchased abroad for £30 in 1816 on behalf of Thomas William Coke of Holkham – the celebrated 'Coke of Norfolk' who was later created Earl of Leicester – and remained in the possession of the family until the famous library was denuded by death duties in 1952. They are now in the British Museum. This is not an illuminated manuscript. The drawings are not intended as an embellishment of the text; the text, in Anglo-Norman, is explanatory of the drawings and fitted into the page where the artist allows. The pictures are not merely illustrative of the bible narrative. More than a quarter of them portray subjects which lack scriptural authority and all are enriched with details, legendary, traditional, symbolic and, it seems, occasionally purely imaginative. This is a theological tract in pictorial form dealing with man's creation, fall, redemption and final judgement. It is also plainly intended as an aid to meditation. It is addressed, the editor argues, to city burgesses rather than to the court or the convent.

The drawings are in pen and ink. The colouring is by another, less accomplished hand. Indeed there must have been a great temptation to the publishers to disregard the painting entirely and with the searching technique of modern photography to reproduce the original line alone. A beautiful series of plates would have resulted for the drawing is brilliant, elegant, vigorous and versatile. The drowned woman in the Deluge is of arresting beauty. It has been plausibly suggested that these were cartoons for mural decorations.

For the mediævalist this is clearly a source of prime importance. The present reviewer is not qualified to give any opinion on this specialised topic beyond remarking that to the layman Mr. W. O. Hassall's introduction and notes seem to provide all that the scholar will demand. It is a matter for sorrow that even in this vineyard of four years' loving labour the snake of imperfect proof-reading rears his ugly head; on page 12, line 19, '15v' should read '15.'

The volume is very moderately priced at £12 12s. and will doubtless appreciate in value. The Roxburghe *Sherborne Missal* of 1920 for example, a less sumptuous work, usually sells today for about £35. The *Grimani Breviary*, about twelve times its size, sells for £275. Perhaps it is ungracious for the reviewer who has received this splendid work as a gift, to suggest that a few shillings added to the price and a gilt top-edge might have been an advantage. The binding is excellent. The back and fore edges of the covers are of niger morocco, the sides of parchment with a fine blind stamp of Regency Gothic design on the top-side and a dove of more modern aspect on the back-side. Paper and typography are entirely admirable. The 84 plates are in collotype, eight in colour, the remainder in monochrome. The character of the original is particularly apt for 'facsimile.' There is no gilding, always the snag in reproduction. The paint, though more opaque than one could wish, has not the solidity of most mediæval manuscripts. This solidity, so brilliantly and arduously counterfeited early in the last century by the hand-colouring of Henry Shaw and the lithography of Owen Jones, was quite lost in the photographic, three colour process at the beginning of this century. The collotypes here displayed, the work of the Oxford University Press, are models of fidelity. One can distinguish the hairside from the inside in the grain of the parchment. Only the wide margins destroy the illusion of identity.

The planners of this noble volume are all too modest. Only the editor's name is given. One would have welcomed a list of 'credits' in the manner of the cinema. Credit is indeed due to everyone from the magnate who financed the undertaking to the journeyman in the workshop; more than credit; joyous gratitude that an object of such rare beauty should have taken shape among us.

Youth at the Helm and Pleasure at the Prow

Not everyone in 1923, not I for one, knew without recourse to the dictionary that a 'hey' or 'hay' was a country jig. As we sped from Blackwell's with our eagerly awaited copies of Mr. Aldous Huxley's second novel, its title suggested a neglected stable and, strange to recall, as we read it in that fragrant age, the tale did smack a little sour. To be quite accurate in reminiscence I got my own copy second-hand from the present literary critic of the *Daily Mail* – a young man already plainly destined for high position – and he passed it to me (for a financial con-

Part of a critical symposium on Aldous Huxley, *London Magazine*, August 1955, pp. 51–53.

sideration) saying I should find it 'dreary'. *Dreary*! Re-read now after all that has happened, after all that has been written, after all Mr. Huxley has written, the book has the lilt of Old Vienna.

It is placed in London in springtime. The weather, page after page, is warm and airy and brilliant. Did we ever enjoy quite such a delightful climate? We certainly do not find it in modern fiction. And London is still in 1923 eminently habitable, a city of private houses and private lives, leisurely, not too full even in the season, all leafy squares and stucco façades and Piranesan mewses. The pavements of Bond Street are 'perfumed', the shops are full of desirable goods. All one needs is a little money – not much; £300 a year is a competence, £5,000 is wealth – and that little is easily acquired by some whimsical invention such as a pair of pneumatic trousers. Regent Street is doomed but Verrey's is still open, open after luncheon until it is time to go out to tea. A few miles out in Surrey and Sussex an arcadian countryside is opening to the never-failing sun. Although all the inhabitants of this delicious city have been everywhere and speak every language they are thoroughly English, at home in their own capital. No character in *Antic Hay* ever uses the telephone. They write letters, they telegraph, they call, and there are always suitable servants to say 'not at home' to bores. It is Henry James's London possessed by carnival. A chain of brilliant young people linked and interlaced winds past the burnished front-doors in pursuit of happiness. Happiness is growing wild for anyone to pick, only the perverse miss it. There has been the single unpredictable, inexplicable, unrepeatable calamity of 'the Great War'. It has left broken hearts – Mrs. Viveash's among them – but the other characters are newly liberated from their comfortable refuges of Conscientious Objection, to run wild through the streets.

The central theme of the book is the study of two falterers 'more or less in' their 'great task of happiness', Mrs. Viveash and Theodore Gumbril. Everyone else, if young, has a good time. Two clowns, Lypiatt and Shearwater, get knocked about, but that is the clown's *métier*. Rosie is happy in her pink underclothes and her daze of romantic fantasy, picked up, rolled over, passed on, giving and gaining pleasure and all the time astutely learning the *nuances* of cultural advancement. Coleman is happy, uproariously blaspheming. Men rather like him turn up later in Mr. Huxley's works, miserable men, haunted and damned. Coleman is boisterously happy, a sort of diabolic Belloc. And Mercaptan is happy, unambitious, sensual, accomplished, radiantly second-rate. He is a period piece, still in his twenties with the tastes and pretentions of ripe middle-age. They do not come like that today. Today one knows quite certainly that a young bachelor with a *penchant* for white satin sofas and *bibelots* would not be running after girls and, moreover, that though he might drop into idiomatic French, he would be quite incapable of writing grammatical English.

Mrs. Viveash and Gumbril are the falterers in the Great Task and their situation is not quite desperate. She has her classic, dignified bereavement. Promiscuous sexual relations bore her. But she has, we are told, almost limitless power, power which, I must confess, has never much impressed me. She was 25 when I was 20. She seemed then appallingly mature. The girls I knew did not whisper in 'expiring' voices and 'smile agonizingly' from their 'death beds'. They grinned from ear to ear and yelled one's head off. And now thirty years on, when women of 25 seem to me moody children, I still cannot weep for Mrs. Viveash's tragic emptiness.

Gumbril rejects the chance of a *Happy Hypocrite* idyll, of love, literally, in a cottage. But it would never have done. He is a clever, zestful cad. He would have been hideously bored in a week. He is off abroad to a wide, smiling continent full of wine and pictures and loose young women. He will be all right.

The story is told richly and elegantly with few of the interruptions which, despite their intrinsic interest, mar so much of Mr. Huxley's storytelling. The disquisition on Wren's London should be in a book of essays but the parody of the night-club play is so funny that one welcomes its intrusion. The 'novel of ideas' raises its ugly head twice only, in the scenes with the tailor and the financier, crashing bores both of them but mere spectators at the dance. They do not hold up the fun for long.

And there is another delicious quality. The city is not always James's London. Sometimes it becomes Mediterranean, central to the live tradition. The dance winds through piazzas and alleys, under arches, round fountains and everywhere are the embellishments of the old religion. An ancient pagan feast, long christianized in name, is being celebrated in a christian city. The story begins in a school chapel, Domenichino's *Jerome* hangs by Rosie's bed, Coleman quotes the Fathers. There is an insistent undertone, audible through the carnival music, saying all the time, not in Mrs. Viveash's 'expiring' voice, that happiness is a reality.

Since 1923 Mr. Huxley has travelled far. He has done more than change climate and diet. I miss that undertone in his later work. It was because he was then so near the essentials of the human condition that he could write a book that is frivolous and sentimental and perennially delightful.

Literary Style in England and America

From the middle of the eighteenth century until the middle of the nineteenth there was published in England a series of architectural designs for the use of provincial builders and private patrons. The plates display buildings of varying sizes, from gate-lodges to mansions, decorated in various "styles," Palladian, Greek, Gothic, even Chinese. The ground plans are identical, the "style" consists of surface enrichment. At the end of this period it was even possible for very important works such as the Houses of Parliament in London to be the work of two hands, Barry designing the structure, Pugin overlaying it with medieval ornament. And the result is not to be despised. In the present half century we have seen architects abandon all attempt at "style" and our eyes are everywhere sickened with boredom at the blank, unlovely, unlovable facades which have arisen from Constantinople to Los Angeles. But this use of style is literally superficial. Properly understood style is not a seductive decoration added to a functional structure; it is of the essence of a work of art.

This is unconsciously recognized by popular usage. When anyone speaks of "Literary style" the probability is that he is thinking of prose. A poem is dimly recognized as existing in its form. There are no poetic ideas; only poetic utterances and, as Wordsworth pointed out, the true antithesis is not between prose and poetry, but between prose and metre. Now that poets have largely abandoned metre, the distinction has become so vague as to be hardly recognizable. Instead of two separate bodies of writing, we must see a series of innumerable gradations from the melodious and mystical to the scientific.

Literature is the right use of language irrespective of the subject or reason of the utterance. A political speech may be, and sometimes is, literature; a sonnet to the moon may be, and often is, trash. Style is what distinguishes literature from trash. Nevertheless in certain quarters the appellation "stylist" bears a pejorative sense. Logan Pearsall Smith, that splendid American, is dismissed fretfully while D. H. Lawrence, who wrote squalidly, is accepted as an artist because his themes were of wider and deeper interest. This is a paradox which academic critics, to whom one would look to correct popular misconceptions, do little to resolve. Many indeed aggravate it, for there is a lurking puritanism at Cambridge (England) and in many parts of the New World, which is ever ready to condemn pleasure even in its purest form. If this seems doubtful consider the case of James Joyce. There was a writer possessed by style. His later work lost almost all faculty of communication, so intimate, allusive and idiosyncratic did it become, so obsessed by euphony and nuance. But because he was obscure and can only be read with intense intellectual effort – and therefore without easy pleasure – he is admitted into the academic canon. But it is just in this task of communication that Joyce's style fails, for the necessary elements of style are lucidity, elegance, individuality; these three qualities combine to form a preservative which ensures the nearest approximation to permanence in the fugitive art of letters.

Lucidity does not imply universal intelligibility. Henry James is the most lucid of writers, but not the simplest. The simplest statements in law or philosophy are usually those which, in application, require the greatest weight of commentary and provoke the longest debate. A great deal of what is most worth saying must always remain unintelligible to most readers. The test of lucidity is whether the statement can be read as meaning anything other than what it intends. Military orders should be, and often are, models of lucidity. The correspondence of businessmen abounds in ambiguities.

Elegance is the quality in a work of art which imparts direct pleasure; again not universal pleasure. There is a huge, envious world to whom elegance is positively offensive. English is incomparably the richest of languages, dead or living. One can devote one's life to learning it and die without achieving mastery. No two words are identical in meaning, sound and connotation. The majority of English speakers muddle through with a minute vocabulary. To them any words not in vulgar use, are "fancy" and it is, perhaps, in ignoble deference to their susceptibilities that there has been a notable flight from magnificence in English writing. Sixty years ago, when 'jewelled prose" was all the rage, there were some pretentious efforts at fine writing which excited great ridicule. There was an inevitable reaction, but surveying the bleak prospect today, one can recognize that those absurdities are a small price to pay for the magnificence of the preceding masters. When I hear the word "tawdry," I suspect the puritan. The man who can enjoy the flimsy and fantastic decorations of Naples is much more likely to appreciate the grandeur of Roman baroque, than the prig who demands Michelangelo or nothing. It is a matter for thankfulness that the modern school of critics are unable or unwilling to compose a pleasurable sentence. It greatly limits the harm they do.

Individuality needs little explanation. It is the hand-writing, the tone of voice, that makes a work recognizable as being by a particular artist (or in rare decades of highly homogeneous culture, by one of a particular set).

Permanence is the result of the foregoing. Style is what makes a work memorable and unmistakable. We remember the false judgments of Voltaire and Gibbon and Lytton Strachey long after they have been corrected, because of their sharp, polished form and because of the sensual pleasure of dwelling on them. They come to one, not merely as printed words, but as a lively experience, with the full force of another human being personally encountered – that is to say because they are lucid, elegant and individual.

Among living writers of English prose there are few who attempt magnificence. Sir Osbert Sitwell's great five volume autobiography and Sir Winston Churchill's historical studies stand almost alone and the latter, though highly creditable for a man with so much else to occupy him, do not really survive close attention. He can seldom offer the keen, unmistakable aesthetic pleasure of the genuine artist. Elegance in the present century tends to be modest. We have no organ voice to rival Sir Thomas Browne's, but we have a volume of exquisite and haunting music. Sir Max Beerbohm and Msgr. Ronald Knox; each stands at the summit of his own art. They differ in scope. Where they attempt the same tasks, in parody, they are equal and supreme over all competitors. Sir Max has confined himself to the arts; Msgr. Knox goes higher, to the loftiest regions of the human spirit. His *Enthusiasm* should be recognized as the greatest work of literary art of the century. Below these two masters there is an honourable company of very fine craftsmen, none it must be admitted, in their first youth. Mr. E. M. Forster, particularly in the first half of *Pharos and Pharillon*, set a model of lucidity and individuality in which the elegance is so unobtrusive as to pass some readers unnoticed. Curiously enough it is not in the Universities that one finds fine writing; Sir Maurice Bowra is learned and lucid, but dull; Lord David Cecil has grace but no grammar; Mr. Isiah Berlin is diffuse and voluble; Mr. Trevor-Roper vulgar. Among critics in the press the standard is higher. Mr. Raymond Mortimer never fails. Mr. Cyril Connolly has fitfully achieved some lovely effects. Among novelists Mr. Anthony Powell, Mr. Graham Greene, Miss Compton-Burnett, Mr. Henry Green all have intensely personal and beautiful styles. One could never mistake a page of their writing for anyone else's.

It will be noticed that all these examples are drawn from England. Logan Pearsall Smith wrote :

And America, the land of my birth, America! . . . Youth has its dreams, its longings for distinction; among all the eager young men and women of that vast country . . . in not one of those resounding cities or multitudinous universities, does the thought never come to anyone, I ask myself, that the instrument of speech which they make use of all day long has resonances within it of unimaginable beauty? . . . The golden sceptre of style gilds everything it touches, and can make immortal those who grasp it : to not one of those aspiring youths does the thought ever suggest itself that it might be an adventure among adventures to try to wield that wand? . . . From the point of view of Style that whole Continent could sink beneath the sea and never leave a ripple.

That was written in 1934. Can we today qualify the severe judgment? There is Mr. Hemingway. He is lucid and individual and euphonious. He has imposed limits on his powers which only a master can survive. He has won mastery, but at the cost of a sad brood of imitators. Mr. Faulkner has individuality but nothing else. Perhaps the languages of the two continents have grown so separate that it is impossible for an Englishman to catch the nuances of American diction. From this great distance it seems that there are editorial styles only, – a rather good, dry style in *The New Yorker*, a very poor style in *Time* – and one sometimes suspects that austerity has been imposed on the contributors so that they shall not distract attention from the more luxurious wording of the advertisements. American critics, I believe, are impatient of the airs and graces of English writers. It is one of the great gulfs between our two civilizations that each finds the other effeminate. To the American, English writers are like prim spinsters fidgeting with the china, punctilious about good taste, and inwardly full of thwarted, tepid and perverse passions. We see the Americans as gushing adolescents, repetitive and slangy, rather nasty sometimes in their zest for violence and bad language. The difference, I think, is this. All English boys, of the kind who are now writers, learned Latin from the age of nine. Very few girls did. The boys did not become ripe scholars, but they acquired a basic sense of the structure of language which never left them, they learned to scan quite elaborate metres; they learned to compose Latin verses of a kind themselves. Little girls learned French and were praised for idiomatic volubility. When they grew up they wrote as though they were babbling down the telephone – often very prettily, like Miss Nancy Mitford. We regard this sort of writing as womanly and that is the quality we find in American male writers, who, I believe, learn Latin late and thoroughly in a few cases but often not at all. But in the Protestant schools in England, Latin is no longer universally taught. It may be that in the next generation only the boys from

Jesuit and Benedictine schools will carry on the tradition of English prose. That is by the way.

One thing I hold as certain, that a writer, if he is to develop, must concern himself more and more with Style. He cannot hope to interest the majority of his readers in his progress. It is his own interest that is at stake. Style alone can keep him from being bored with his own work. In youth high spirits carry one over a book or two. The world is full of discoveries that demand expression. Later a writer must face the choice of becoming an artist or a prophet. He can shut himself up at his desk and selfishly seek pleasure in the perfecting of his own skill or he can pace about, dictating dooms and exhortations on the topics of the day. The recluse at the desk has a bare chance of giving abiding pleasure to others; the publicist has none at all.

Alfred Duggan

The death of Alfred Duggan in April of this year brought an abrupt end to a literary career which was in many respects unique.

In recent years we have become so familiar with the spectacle of personal frustration and disaster in the artistic life that we have come almost to regard it as normal. Scott Fitzgerald and Dylan Thomas are typical of many less famous and less gifted writers who began with early brilliance and popular recognition only to find in early middle age that their powers were exhausted and that nothing remained for them except self-pity and drunkenness. Alfred Duggan, on the contrary, spent his youth and early manhood as a rake. Of all my contemporaries he seemed one of the least likely to succeed. Lest I should seem to be betraying the memory of the dead, let me say that a few months ago I wrote to him to ask whether, in some memoirs I was writing, I might describe his early escapades, and was given ungrudging permission to go ahead. Had we been told forty years ago, when we first became friends, that I should now be pronouncing a panegyric on him, we should both have been totally incredulous. He was forty-seven when he published his first novel, *Knight with Armour*, and in the fourteen succeeding years he produced the *opus* of a full life-

Spectator, 10 July 1964, pp. 38–39. This is the script of a talk delivered over the BBC on 2 July 1964.

time. He emerged from his years of dissipation with his mind acute, his remarkable memory unimpaired and a prose style already perfectly fitted for his use.

Most writers begin clumsily with experiments they live to regret. Alfred came into action fully equipped and, it seemed, fully exercised in arms. He wrote fifteen historical novels, one of which, *Count Bohemond*, will appear posthumously, three biographies, and seven historical studies for young readers. His repute grew steadily in the most diverse quarters. Reviewers became increasingly respectful. It seems to me that a talent so independent of fashion is certain to attract more and more admirers in the future and to establish him safely in a high place among the writers of his period.

In his lifetime he scrupulously avoided publicity and eschewed all the literary gatherings which provide less industrious craftsmen with the opportunity of self-advertisement. Some biographical information is therefore not out of place now.

His father was a rich Argentine of Irish descent who died during Alfred's childhood. His mother was the beautiful daughter of an American diplomatist. She brought him, his younger brother and his sister to England for their education and in 1917 married Lord Curzon, almost the last of the grandee English statesmen, then a member of the Inner War Cabinet, and, it seemed, a future Prime Minister. Alfred thus grew up in the heart of high political society, living in his stepfather's four great houses and himself enjoying a large fortune left him by his father. As I have suggested above, he made no attempt to use these advantages – then very considerable – to advance himself to positions of influence and power. Neither at Eton nor at Balliol did he show application for work. He lived rather flamboyantly for pleasure, alternating between the hunting field and the night club. Lord Curzon was more perspicuous than his tutors and friends and discerned the great talents which seemed to be running to seed. Alfred also travelled widely, particularly in the Levant where he early began to study the remains of the Crusaders, visiting many castles which were then quite unknown except to a handful of adventurous experts. His fortune dwindled and finally disappeared. Alfred accepted his changed circumstances with dignity and without repining. Instead of his former extravagant pleasures he read – with any ambition to professional scholarship, but from interest in his subject – mediæval military history. To the observer it seemed he was merely listlessly passing his time during his long sessions in the library at Hackwood, but all he read became sharply recorded in his memory, so that when at last his pent-up creative powers found expression he could draw on a great store of detailed knowledge.

At the age of twenty he professed Marxism and atheism, but after a few years he returned to the Church of his childhood and for the last thirty-five years of his life was a devout, if, at first, a wayward, Conservative Catholic.

With his abandonment of Marxism Alfred become a fervent patriot of the kingdom of his adoption. In 1939, though older than the normal age of recruitment, he enlisted as a private soldier and contrived to get himself posted to Norway in a company of volunteers for hazardous service. He endured the great hardships of the retreat in 1940, an experience which impaired his hitherto strong physical constitution and, no doubt, hastened his death. Invalided out of the army, he chose to serve his country at the bench of an aeroplane factory. In 1953 he married and for the eleven remaining years led a life of complete domestic happiness and unremitting industry in the seclusion of Herefordshire. He entirely overcame his inherited weakness, partly by the aid of a physician, partly by his power of will, partly by his new-found love as a husband, but essentially, I believe, from supernatural grace. It is, as I said before, the antithesis of the popular pattern, but it should be remarked that even in the time of his dissipation there was always a *gravitas* in him, a dignity and courtesy which transcended his weakness.

Such in brief was his life, known to only a few friends. His work stands as his memorial. He spoke of it with a detached modesty which sometimes gave the impression of cynicism. When asked why he habitually treated of obscure persons and periods instead of with subjects more likely to excite popular interest, he would answer, with less than candour, that the scantiness of sources in the dark ages relieved him of the labours of research. In fact, he was a dedicated artist who was at ease in remote times.

This century has been prolific in historical novels, many garish, some scholarly. I know of none which give the same sense of intimacy as Alfred's – as though he were describing personal experiences and observations. There is never anything in his work that is romantic, picturesque or sensational. It is accurate and infused throughout with a dry irony that is peculiarly his own. His religious faith is implicit in all he wrote. He was never an apologist or propagandist, but he recognised the Church as being the only proper milieu for mankind. He also recognised mankind as being constitutionally unworthy of the divine promises and he maintained a genial tolerance of the defects of human nature. I think that one of the formative influences in his life was his stepfather's purchase and restoration of Bodiam Castle in Sussex. He followed that process with intense interest and from that went on to his long study of other mediæval fortifications and to the details of arms and tactics. His first book begins at Bodiam with a knight riding East under the cross. His last ends with the triumph of Christian arms in Jerusalem. He intended to write a further book about Tancred. The Crusades were always in his mind, though he strayed into pre-Christian history very successfully. *Leopards and Lilies*, the story of the Angevins, written in 1954, was the latest historical period with which he dealt. The Renaissance and the Reformation and the Counter-Reformation were all strange to him. Romans and Normans, the worlds of empire and chivalry, were the natural founts of his imagination. Modern history he regarded with calm despair.

It would be tedious to give a list and précis of all Alfred's books. They are there to be studied by all whose taste is not debauched by modern excesses; lucid, plausible stories, humorous, wry and exact. A particular palate is required for their savour. To those who seek bawdy and sentimental tales, they will not appeal. Every reader will find his own favourite among them. For me, *Conscience of the King*, published in 1951, is outstandingly characteristic of the author. It deals with the age of King Arthur, far removed from the romances of Malory and Tennyson, the very dark age in Britain after the Romans left when the heathen barbarians were everywhere flooding in; an age which, I think, Alfred identified with our own. The hero is Cerdic, a very base man, the founder of the royal house of Wessex, through whom, by Matilda, our present Royal Family are descended. Cerdic was a Roman, an apostate Christian, who came to terms with the invading savages. Their manners revolt him, but he survives. At the end he is left reflecting that he has done the best possible for himself. He has no inkling of the days when his posterity will rule half the world. He wishes Romans were still here, but he has survived them. 'I would like to talk to a well-educated and intelligent man before I die,' he considers, 'but I know that is quite impossible.' And then comes the Duggan glint of irony. 'There is one thing that worries me, especially when I lie awake at night. Suppose all that nonsense [Christianity] that my brother Paul used to preach is really true after all?'

That seems to me the quintessence of Alfred, first in his imaginative entry into an entirely strange world, in his recognition of that world as being the progenitor of our own and in his view of both Cerdic's world and ours in the only light that makes them intelligible – the light of eternity.

The Max Behind the Mask

Because of its successful dramatization and frequent reissue in different forms, *The Happy Hypocrite* is, I suppose, the most widely known of Beerbohm's works, though it is neither his most brilliant nor most characteristic. That fairy story, it will be remembered, is the exact counterpart to *The Picture of Dorian Gray*. Wilde imagined a young man portrayed in early beauty. His life is increasingly vicious, but only the painting reveals the horrible deterioration of his character. Until death the hero retains the spurious glow of innocence. Lord George Hell in *The Happy Hypocrite* is an aging rake who prosecutes an idyllic love affair with a young girl under the disguise of a youthful mask. When it is finally torn from his face the ravages of age and debauchery are found to have totally disappeared. He has become what his innocent love has made him.

In his eagerly awaited biography, *Max*, Lord David Cecil makes a point of Beerbohm's early assumption of a mask, demure, elegant, passionless, which he wore all his life so that it became an essential part of his character. Lord David does little to unmask him. Indeed there is no reason to suppose that the mask hid anything. It was a part of his exquisite wardrobe. There were no dark secrets any more than there were deformities under his beautifully cut frock coats.

The writing of the biography was a difficult task. Beerbohm's life was happy and uneventful. For the most part Lord David has been content to tell it in tactfully chosen, familiar extracts from his subject's own writing. The connecting passages present a problem. Beerbohm's own literary grace was so complete that the juxtaposition of another hand must inevitably make a crude contrast. Any attempt to emulate the master's own style would have been disastrous. But Lord David has an easy, Whiggish negligence of grammar which gives the happy illusion that he is reading aloud in the drawing room and occasionally pausing to comment colloquially on the entertainment. A disagreeable reviewer might hold up to reprobation numerous sentences of Lord David's which offend against even colloquial syntax; but to do so would be to miss the

Reviews of *Max*, by Lord David Cecil, and *Letters to Reggie Turner by Max Beerbohm*, ed. Rupert Hart-Davis, *Atlas*, January 1965, pp. 47–49.

point of his achievement just as much as to complain of the narrow scope of Beerbohm's own genius.

For Beerbohm was a genius of the purest kind. Some English writers, he said, were weight lifters; others jugglers with golden balls. There were, he believed, rather too many weight lifters – and today he would have to add contortionists, freaks and buffoons to the literary circus.

I am told that the young, and especially the young who have fallen under the dire influence of the Cambridge School of English Literature, dismiss Beerbohm with contempt. How much high pleasure they miss! It is reasonable to impute an element of envy. The word "satire" has now been usurped by guttersnipes. Our popular caricaturists are content with types. Few of them, one must suppose, have any personal acquaintance, as Beerbohm had, with their subjects. Every phrase and line of his is a rebuke to them. After his very early days, when he gambolled with an ornate and consciously absurd vocabulary, he wrote supremely well. His essay on Venice, originally an article in the *Daily Mail*, is a model not only of imaginative observation but of variety of structure. It is, I believe, the best travel sketch ever written. In narration he was less happy except in "Maltby and Braxton". I confess to qualms about "The Dreadful Dragon of Hay Hill" and "William and Mary". As Lord David points out, Beerbohm had his own, exquisite, sharply circumscribed universe within which he was "incomparable" and from which he very rarely strayed. But Lord David writes primarily as a biographer rather than as a critic, and he has assembled all the available facts in a way to leave us grateful.

Beerbohm's was an odd environment as the youngest of a large, diverse family. His father, a German-Balt by origin, without, as has been supposed, Jewish blood, married his deceased wife's sister, so that the elder members were closer than half-brothers and half-sisters. They ranged in character from the famous, flamboyant, improvident actor-manager Sir Herbert Beerbohm Tree to the sister who became an Anglican nun (in an order which allowed a considerable freedom). There was a ne'er-do-well, dandified brother who drifted round the casinos of Europe losing money; another brother who disappeared in Australia and was said to have married a Negress; a methodical housekeeping sister; the mother who lived to great old age and could not be restrained from perpetual hospitality. There were others, less notable, and at the tail came Max, a type of the child of late love, selfish, self-sufficing, affectionate, cool, surprisingly tough, saturated in the wish and ability to please.

Until his marriage at the age of thirty-eight he lived at home, cosseted by all. They started in easy circumstances but grew poorer. Max was at times near penury. Had he been well-off his case would have been a normal one – a more versatile Logan Pearsall Smith, a more gifted Gerald Berners – but he was, I think, unique in guarding his tiny, brilliant genius against all corruption at the price of frugality which at times approached privation. He relished luxury when it was offered him by Philip Sassoon, Northcliffe or Lady Desborough, but he never aspired to riches. Indeed, it is constantly surprising to learn how little he was paid. At his first exhibition of caricatures after the First World War we find him exhilarated at making £1,000 for the fruit of eight years' work. Most of his most brilliant drawings fetched less than £50 each. "I have a public of 1,500," he said at the height of his fame.

Lord David provides more information than has hitherto been available about Beerbohm's love affairs, but they still remain (and are likely to do so forever) in deep obscurity. Is it prurient to wish we knew more? At Oxford and in his first years in London his male friends, with the exception of Rothenstein, were almost all homosexual. He did not share their pleasures, but he was fully aware of them and used the slang of the clique, referring to "renters" (male prostitutes) and "mulierasts" (heterosexual). He was captivated by Wilde but had begun to see through him long before his fall. His objection was not moral, merely aesthetic; Wilde was growing gross and arrogant. His only fear was that closer friends, such as Ross and Reggie Turner, might get into trouble with the police.

There came his "crush" on Cissy Loftus; then his strange, prolonged "engagement" to an unsuccessful American actress, Grace Conover. Then his brief "engagement" at Dieppe to the passionate Constance Collier. Did they go to bed? Did they experiment and fail? Finally there was his long, devoted marriage to the elusive, fastidious Florence Kahn. A *marriage blanc*? Lord David does not tell us, because he does not know. Nor can anyone ever know. Beerbohm remarked of Ruskin that it was surprising he should marry without knowing he was impotent. But the question is of little importance in an artist of Beerbohm's quality.

Lord David has not been well served by his publishers, Constable. The illustrations are undated; the index is contemptible. Mr. Hart-Davis' edition of Beerbohm's letters to Reggie Turner is a model of editorship. It is his misfortune that the collection should appear simultaneously with the biography. Lord David has been through it first and skimmed some of its riches, but he has chosen to eschew all references and most dates, so that it is a great pleasure to turn to the scrupulous text of Mr. Hart-Davis.

Reggie Turner had a peculiar position in relation to Beerbohm. Slightly older, better off, accounted by all the better talker, he failed completely as a writer and lived in a cosmopolitan half-world while Beerbohm was basking in fashionable favour. He never repined. His devotion to Beerbohm remained untainted by envy and graced by constant small acts of munificence. Beerbohm wrote to him with complete intimacy and Turner preserved that side of the correspondence. It is to be regretted that his letters to Beerbohm are lost. As it stands, the present volume is a valuable text, an essential complement to Lord David's biography. Every library should have both. Taken together they provide as clear a picture of Beerbohm as we are likely to get.

Introduction to The Man of Property

John Galsworthy died in 1933 with more official decorations and greater universal respect than have ever been accorded to any English novelist. His surviving contemporaries cherished his friendship. In modesty, generosity, devotion to his art, scrupulous regard for his honour in public and in private affairs, munificence, and stoic self-restraint he was a faultless representative of his nation and was recognized as such from Budapest to Stockholm and in many parts of the United States of America. He was eagerly read by foreigners as providing textbooks by which English habits could be learned and English character judged, but he was not read in England by the younger generation of writers. Ironically he had come to be identified with the very class and character whose deficiencies he had set himself to expose. His books have always found readers but not, in the last forty years, among those interested in the art of the novel. Perhaps a younger generation will atone for the neglect of his immediate successors.

The Man of Property is the foundation of his *œuvre*. It was begun in 1902 when he was in the seventh year of his nine years' passionate but furtive liaison with the wife of a cousin. The circumstance is vital to the book. Those who knew him best described this affair, which eventually became a serenely happy marriage, as the experience which made him an artist. He was a man of conventional upbringing and conventional tastes, educated in classics and the law, an athlete and a sportsman, and surrounded by a numerous, long-lived, prosperous, and conventional family. His illicit love, occurring in the heart of this circle, alienated him from them – not from his father, who was kept in ignorance of it, nor from his sisters, who were sympathetic, but from the cousins and their allies, whom he came to regard as constituting a solid, powerful, imperme-

John Galsworthy, *The Man of Property*, New York: Heritage Press, 1964, pp. v-viii.

able barrier against the free happiness of the human spirit. 'The Forsytes' were not, for him, a single family. They were a class whose values were all material and quantitative, who were actuated solely by the obsession of property. Adultery is in the plot of *The Man of Property* but its theme is the representation of a class. In other books and in his plays he successfully portrayed other classes, but 'the Forsytes' and all they stood for were his special creation.

Gilbert Murray wrote to him in 1922, when the Forsyte books appeared in a single volume : 'It is a wonderful achievement of yours to have created this Saga. The rum thing to me is that, after reading it all and admiring it and loving it, I don't feel that I know in the least what a Forstye is like, and am not conscious of having seen one. I believe you have a queer poetical method which simulates realism in order to attain beauty.'

This is a profound criticism. *The Man of Property* opens in the year 1886, when Galsworthy was nineteen years old. Most of the characters are old or middle-aged. They are seen through the eyes of youth and they are described sixteen years later when they have become the embodiment of the frustration of his love. To the social historian they pose the question : did they ever exist? Their obsession with urban commercial matters is not an English characteristic. None of them goes into the Navy, the Army, politics, the Church, the colonial service, which were in Victorian times the normal means by which families of rising wealth entered the gentry. Until 1918 it was the normal aspiration of every Englishman to become a gentleman. (Galsworthy himself was eminently one.) Commercial origins were obscured. Those of the commercial families who could afford it tended to buy or build themselves houses on agricultural properties far from the source of their incomes and to assume the privileges and obligations of the squirearchy. Soames Forsyte's move from London is the activating event of the story. He is dubbed by his relations 'the man of property'; they ridicule him for setting up as a gentleman. But in fact he is merely building an expensive villa in the purlieus of London on a modest plot of ground which he does not even own freehold. It does not ring true. Or rather, in Gilbert Murray's words, it is a queer poetical method simulating realism.

The English commercial class has been variously treated by the great novelists. Dickens's Podsnaps and Veneerings are prototypes of the Forsytes. But there is one great difference between them : their stability. In Victorian novels the disagreeable plutocrat almost invariably goes bankrupt. In the Edwardian age in which Galsworthy began his great work, wealth seemed indestructible. In the post-war era in which he finished it, it was revealed once more as precarious. One lifetime spanned the whole of British plutocracy. But *The Man of Property* was written in the heyday of security; it is tragedy in the Greek fashion where Nemesis is inescapable, and Nemesis is property itself. This explains the conclusion against which Galsworthy's sage adviser, Edward Garnett, vainly protested.

When Galsworthy wrote the book he intended a single complete tragedy. He notes August 1918 as the time when he decided to make it the opening of a series. He had destroyed the manuscript in 1913, thinking it to be something of no greater importance than his other multifarious writings. The extension of the work has won it millions of readers but it has impaired the classical finality of the original conception. He was in later life to identify many features of the narrative with his own family life. These revelations tend to impair the reader's appreciation of the imaginative vigour of his creation.

The plot is finely constructed. We are presented with a family, shown them in full detail in all their ramifications. There has been one domestic scandal – young Jolyon's – sedulously ignored. There is one rather shaky member – Dartie. Otherwise they are all prosperous and self-satisfied. There is a beautiful stranger, Mrs. Soames, who is appreciated as an ornament. It is recognized that she is not entirely happy in her marriage; the depth of her detestation of her husband is not known, nor are its causes ever made evident. Into this circle comes 'the Buccaneer,' artistic, improvident, passionate – all that the Forsytes are not. He becomes the lover of Irene Soames. He is an invention, someone to take the place which in real life Galsworthy occupied.

The drama of Galsworthy's own love affair was heightened by the fact that he was himself a Forsyte, no buccaneer, one of the circle he was disrupting. Galsworthy conscientiously attaches to Bosinney all the attributes, even unconventional dress, which a Forsyte would expect in an artist. He is arrogant towards the Philistine. He is also, alas, quite humourless. In the action at law which is the crisis of the story, the reader may well sympathize with Soames. Bosinney may have had talents – it is hard to visualize the villa with its glazed court, columns, and purple leather curtains – but costing is an essential part of an architect's equipment. To mislead a client in the matter (while seducing his wife) argues grave professional impropriety. Galsworthy's celebrated fairness of mind is seen in the judge's summing up. Bosinney is not designed to attract unqualified admiration. Does he carry conviction?

Edward Garnett, in a series of penetrating letters quoted in H. V. Marrott's compilation, urged Galsworthy against the final episode. To a man of Galsworthy's upbringing and nature the catastrophe – professional discredit, bankruptcy, and above all the shock of the forcible possession of a mistress by her husband – might well produce despair. A man such as Bosinney has been represented would take it all much more lightly. He and Irene would have crossed the Channel with her jewels and muddled along somehow. But two factors prevented this plausible solution. First, the artist's 'queer poetical method simulating realism.' Galsworthy had set out to write a tragedy, not a comedy of manners. The victims had to be duly sacrificed. And they were to be sacrificed to the ineluctable god of Galsworthy's creation – Forsytism. The lovers had defied powers too strong for them. The intruder must be destroyed, the captive returned to her odious prison. That was the law of life as Galsworthy saw it in the harrowing uncertainties of his nine years' ordeal.

4

Conservative

"I loathe politics. Please change the subject." This answer to an interviewer dramatizes what is arguably the most permanently valuable tenet of Waugh's conservative creed, his scepticism about party loyalties. Even during his own most political period in the late thirties his major theme (powerfully expressed in *Robbery Under Law*) was that incessant political agitation was stultifying for the individual and the nation. Ideology signifies next to nothing : a country prospers in so far as its citizens are intelligent, hardworking, thrifty, and enterprising. The concluding lines of "Aspirations of a Mugwump", warning against political involvement, though written in a teasing manner, represent one of Waugh's most settled convictions.

In spite of this conviction, Waugh was concerned about most of the important issues of his time. "Present Discontents" sums up his views on Fascism and anti-Fascism quite accurately. He neither wished nor expected Fascism to gain power in England; he was afraid that virulent anti-Fascism would provoke the middle classes into reaction. (An important component of anti-Fascism was belief that the English upper-classes were in sympathy with the Dictators and would be impelled by economic factors to seize power.) If the lowest common denominator of the various kinds of Fascism is belief in authoritarian rule to solve a country's ills, Waugh was no Fascist; he maintained that England's "traditional life", muddled as it was, contained the strength to surmount the crises of the thirties (*Spectator*, 8 July 1938, p. 55). "Spanish Civil War" states Waugh's position with exactness and candour : Fascism was the lesser of two evils in Spain, therefore he supported Franco. How little Franco's regime appealed to him can be read in *Scott-King's Modern Europe*.

The 1939–1945 conflict agitated Waugh in two important ways. As "Anything Wrong with Priestley?" shows, he retained a vivid sense of injury from the Left's having attempted, as he put it, to convert a war of national survival into a class conflict, while branding the upper class as potential traitors. The second source of despair, as explained by "Our Guest of Dishonour", was the transformation of large territories of Christendom into atheist police states. Both concerns are given moving expression in *Sword of Honour*.

What made Waugh very unusual was his defence of the class system. "Commentary for *The Private Man*" argues that an accepted system of

classes is the most valuable possession of any nation; "I See Nothing But
Boredom . . . Everywhere" (see Chapter One) that the result of classlessness
will be drab uniformity. What then are we to make of "Awake My
Soul! It is a Lord"? Was all this scorn of recent creations the sort of
snobbery that Jane Austen so much despised? Or was it Waugh publicizing
his belief in a class system by affecting an ironic and provocative stance?
I see Waugh's preoccupation with class as having at least the negative value
of not being about windy political generalities – like, in his own phrase,
"the idiotic dichotomy of Left and Right". For him, cultural and social
criticism must be specific. His prevailing concern was with "qualitative
standards", thus politics, as they are generally understood, seemed a diver-
sion, "the cocaine of the people" – an unhealthy stimulant producing no
tangible benefit.

Spanish Civil War

At the time of the Spanish War Louis Aragon and others sent a question-
naire to writers in the British Isles and published their answers in a
pamphlet.

The question ran:

Are you for, or against, the legal Government and the People of Republican Spain? Are you for, or against, Franco and Fascism? For it
is impossible any longer to take no side.

Waugh wrote in reply:

I know Spain only as a tourist and a reader of the newspapers. I am
no more impressed by the "legality" of the Valencia Government than
are English Communists by the legality of the Crown, Lords and
Commons. I believe it was a bad Government, rapidly deteriorating.
If I were a Spaniard I should be fighting for General Franco. As an
Englishman I am not in the predicament of choosing between two
evils. I am not a Fascist nor shall I become one unless it were the
only alternative to Marxism. It is mischievous to suggest that such a
choice is imminent.

Present Discontents

Generally speaking, the best literary criticism today is written either by
amateurs – museum officials, clergymen, diplomats and so on – or by

Authors Take Sides on the Spanish War (pamphlet), ed. Louis Aragon, London,
Left Review, 1937.

Review of *Enemies of Promise*, by Cyril Connolly, *Tablet*, 3 December 1938,
pp. 743–44. Three misprints which Waugh pointed out in a letter to the *Tablet*,
10 December 1938, p. 805, have been corrected. Ed.

blacklegs – people who normally engage in other kinds of writing and are too lazy to read, without inducement, the work of their contemporaries, who are moved to strong, personal feelings by what they read and like to give them expression; the worst is by the underworld of professional reviewers whose miseries and inevitable degradation Mr. Connolly sympathetically expounds. But above this there is the rare Art of Criticism, with its own valuable and distinct literature, its own aspirations and achievements. The only man under forty who shows any sign of reaching, or indeed, of seeking, this altitude is Mr. Cyril Connolly. It is therefore worth while enquiring, as he has enquired into the adverse conditions which beset a creative writer today, into those which seem to be holding him back from durable work.

"Creative" is an invidious term too often used at the expense of the critic. A better word, except that it would always involve explanation, would be "architectural." I believe that what makes a writer, as distinct from a clever and cultured man who can write, is an added energy and breadth of vision which enables him to conceive and complete a structure. Critics, so far as they are critics only, lack this; Mr. Connolly very evidently, for his book, full as it is of phrase after phrase of lapidary form, of delicious exercises in parody, of good narrative, of luminous metaphors, and once at any rate – in the passages describing the nightmare of the man of promise – of haunting originality, is structurally jerry-built. It consists of the secondary stages of three separate books, an autobiography, an essay on the main division of modern literature between the esoteric (which he happily names the Mandarin School) and the popular, and a kind of Rogues Handbook of practical advice to an aspiring author. He comes very near to dishonesty in the way in which he fakes the transitions between these elements and attempts to pass them off as the expansion of a single theme.

Nor does he seem to be fully aware of this defect either in his own work or in those he examines; on page nine he recommends the habit of examining isolated passages, as a wine taster judges a vintage by rinsing a spoonful round his mouth; thus, says Mr. Connolly, the style may be separated from the impure considerations of subject matter. But the style is the whole. Wine is a homogeneous substance : a spoonful and a Jeraboam have identical properties; writing is an art which exists in a time sequence; each sentence and each page is dependent on its predecessors and successors; a sentence which he admires may owe its significance to another fifty pages distant. I beg Mr. Connolly to believe that even quite popular writers take great trouble sometimes in this matter.

Not only in general plan, but in detail, Mr. Connolly shirks the extra effort which would have helped him to attain his avowed object of writing a durable book. There are numerous lapses into illiteracy –

"nobody has so squandered *their* gifts," "Davy Jones' " for "David Jones's" (Mr. Connolly's form is allowed by Fowler only in "reverential contexts'), "Nonsuch" for "Nonesuch," "Experiment and adventure *is* indicated" and so on. There are, as I have said, countless lapidary phrases but they lie jumbled up with the flattest clichés. Cliché hunting is a cruel and mischievous hobby – the badger digging of the literary blood sports – but it is one for which Mr. Connolly himself shows a particular zest; he indulges it ruthlessly upon poor Mr. Huxley and then proceeds to talk of "the war-weary and disillusioned generation" and of the time when "domestic happiness begins to cloy."

Mr. Connolly attempts to cover the whole field of the artist's relation to society; in particular his financial position in relation to his direct or indirect paymasters, and here, I think, he falls into an error in the character of the reading public. "Most readers," he says, "live in London, they are run-down, querulous, constipated, soot-ridden, stained with asphalt and nicotine, and, as a result of sitting all day in a box and eating too fast, slightly mad and sufferers from indigestion." A good description : newspaper editors have rightly taken this type as their public. But these are not the readers of novels. The London office-man reads, at the most, a book a month. The people who keep the literary market lively are the unemployed women, particularly in the provinces, and they particularly relish "robust health" in their authors. But Mr. Connolly is convinced that a writer cannot honourably earn a decent living; so much convinced that he falsifies an analysis of Mr. Hemingway's *The Sun Also Rises*; Jake, he says (page fifty-four) suffers from "economic inability to get enough to drink"; but Jake is a well paid foreign correspondent, with a balance of $2,432 (page twenty-seven, Albatross edition), he is not only able to drink lashings himself, but lends freely to fellow dipsomaniacs.

But these are trivial complaints; they are, in fact, universal to his generation and his juniors'; they give that much-sought label of being "contemporary." *Enemies of Promise* is disappointing on wider grounds. Mr. Connolly's belief in the value of art is unquestionable, and his defects like his virtues arise from the kind of art to which he inclines; he has fairly broad tastes, but in all he admires and all that strikes him as significant, whether for praise or blame, there is a single common quality – the lack of masculinity. Petronius, Gide, Firbank, Wilde . . . the names succeed one another of living and dead writers, all, or almost all, simpering and sidling across the stage with the gait of the great new British music hall joke. He loyally says all that he conscientiously can for the Left wing school of writers, but he omits from his catalogue the name of Mr. Calder Marshall, whose faults are those of boisterousness and whose virtues virility and, unique among his fellows, enough self-sufficiency to be able to do his own work alone, without collaboration. It is from Mr. Connolly's preference for the epicene – I use the word metaphorically, of their work only; I know nothing of their private characters – that his discontents spring, for the artists in whom he is interested have nearly all come to feel themselves outcasts and to transpose the antagonism, real or imagined, of society from themselves to their art. Now female authors like to live in jolly intimacy with their fellows; they rejoice in literary luncheons, publishers' teas and "getting up" books together as if they were charades; male authors like to do their work in solitude and take their pleasure in the company that will distract them least from their serious business; but epicene authors like to huddle together and imagine plots and betrayals. So Mr. Connolly sees recent literary history, not in terms of various people employing and exploring their talents in their own ways, but as a series of "movements," sappings, bombings and encirclements, of party racketeering and jerrymandering. It is the Irish in him perhaps. Thus he sees his own career, which some of us might envy and all of us honour, as a struggle against intrigue and repression; for this reason he gives us, in the last section of his book, a closely documented history of his own adolescence. It is a Buchmanite exercise whose publication may fulfil some purgative requirement of his own; it is highly embarrassing to the reader and it is, in the last analysis, unnecessary, for there was nothing the least peculiar about Mr. Connolly's early environment. Among his own family he saw something of rich and poor; he went to a typical private school and to Eton; there he was at great pains to secure election to a club for which he had not the proper qualifications of membership. Over a thousand boys had just the same education as Mr. Connolly and none have grown up at all like him. He has temporarily fallen for the tedious old Pavlov mischief which has done so much to stultify his chief butt, Mr. Aldous Huxley. Mr. Connolly had an easy and agreeable upbringing as far as outward circumstances go; the fact that he was and is unhappy comes from other causes; and he is confident that everyone else is equally discontented.

He is divided in his mind. On one hand he sees English life as a secure, hierarchic organization, with, at the top, a glittering world where the artist should by right preen himself. An artist should have ease and appreciation; he should travel and dine well and be continuously in and out of love. On the other hand, he sees English life as rotten and tottering; the physical and moral dangers so imminent and appalling that the artist can only hope for a complete change for his life to be possible; a change which Mr. Connolly inclines to think may be for the worse. He seems to have two peevish spirits whispering into either ear. One complaining that the bedroom in which he awakes is an ugly contrast to the splendid dining-room where he was entertained the previous evening;

the other saying that the names have been made up for the firing squads; he must shoot first if he does not want to be shot. And it is into the claws of this latter bogey that Mr. Connolly finally surrenders himself; the cold, dank pits of politics into which all his young friends have gone tobogganing; the fear of Fascism, that is the new fear of Hell to the new Quakers. It is indeed a sorry end to so much talent; the most insidious of all the enemies of promise. But it is reasonable to hope that it is not Mr. Connolly's end; that one day he will escape from the café chatter, meet some of the people, whom he now fears as traitors, who are engaged in the practical work of government and think out for himself what Fascism means. It is a growth of certain peculiar soils; principally it needs two things – a frightened middle class who see themselves in danger of extinction in a proletarian State, and some indignant patriots who believe that their country, through internal dissension, is becoming bullied by the rest of the world. In England we had something like a Fascist movement in 1926, when the middle classes broke the General Strike. We have a middle class that is uniquely apt for strenuous physical adventures, amenable to discipline, bursting with *esprit de corps*, and a great fund of patriotism which has escaped serious indignation for some time only because it has been combined with incurious self-confidence. It is quite certain that England would become Fascist before it became Communist; it is quite unlikely to become either; but if anything is calculated to provoke the development which none desire, and Mr. Connolly dreads almost neurotically, it is the behaviour of his hysterical young friends of the Communist Party.

Palinurus in Never-Never Land

OR, THE "HORIZON" BLUE-PRINT OF CHAOS

Fitting neatly the pockets of battle-dress trousers and gas-mask haversack, read in tents and lorries and radio-haunted Nissen huts, passed from waif to waif in transit camps and field hospitals, the monthly magazine, *Horizon*, came to represent to countless soldiers the world of culture which they had left. Many of the contributions, it is true, were non-

Tablet, 27 July 1946, p. 46. This is a response to "Editor's Comment", *Horizon*, June 1946, pp. 365–66.

sensical, but of gentle, civilian nonsense which contrasted sweetly with the harsh nonsense of regimental orders and ABCA. With the armistice the influence of the magazine has spread abroad, where the intellectuals look to England, as in our troubles we English looked to Bloomsbury, as the still unliberated fortress of the mind. Somewhere, we believed, in the minds of the editors of *Horizon* there existed a free and wise society of which we were all members.

Horizon seemed little concerned with politics, and it was not until the eve of the General Election that its editor disconcerted his readers by suddenly exhorting them to vote Socialist. Now, in the June issue, he is more explicit and, under ten headings, offers us the first ground plans of the estate he has been preparing for us. It is a somewhat baffling document.

The first "major indication of a civilized community" is the abolition of the death penalty. When I consider how small, even in the most savagely popular regimes, has been the actual number of people executed, and of that number how many have been the most illustrious of their time, and how painless, dignified and well-prepared is the gallows compared with the various forms in which death awaits us, it has, I confess, seemed to me one of the least of the terrors of the century of the common man.

That it is not mere squeamishness about the taking of life which makes Palinurus – if I may without offence so personify the mind of *Horizon* – put this first of his postulates, is shown by the next two : "2. Model prisons (criminals can be rehabilitated). 3. No slums. (The material conditions which produce crime need not exist.)" I think the implication of these three demands is plain. The civil Government has no authority to *punish* at all. Human wickedness is predestined by economic conditions. Man is naturally virtuous and perfectible. It is the function of the State to perfect him. This is familiar ground. I would dispute his assumptions and conclusions in detail, but the purpose of this enquiry is merely to examine Palinurus's ideal world, not to oppose it with another. So far I do not think I misinterpret him, but his fourth "major indication of a civilized community" does not admit such easy comprehension.

"4. Light and heat supplied free, like water and air. Clothing, nourishment, privacy and medical attention almost free. Transport as near as possible within the reach of all." What is one to say to this? That air is not "supplied" and that water is rarely free; that nothing is "free" which requires the services of others and nothing is "almost free" unless there is a depressed class who labour for almost nothing? That transport of all kinds has always, everywhere, been "as near as possible" within the reach of all?

The basic question, I think, is : free for whom? For everyone or only for Palinurus and his friends? Is he proposing the creation of a privileged class of himself and "Scottie" Wilson and other artists who should be warmed and illuminated by the rest of the community, whose tailors and doctors will delight to reduce their bills for the honour of serving them? If this is the suggestion I do not see how it differs from the wish to enjoy a large private fortune. It is probable, on the other hand, that he means "free for all," in which case he is using "free" in a very loose, modern way to mean that the amenities he claims should be distributed by the State without direct cash payment. In fact, of course, the price would not be lower, for the consumer would be purchasing these commodities indirectly with their cost enhanced by an increased service of middle-men. It would in theory be possible to create a society in which, instead of money, amenities were given to reward work, and it would be possible in such a State to allow literary critics special advantages. That Palinurus has some such ideal in mind, appears in his fifth, succinct demand : "Vocations for all, not just work."

If Palinurus believed, as he plainly does not, in an all-wise God who has a particular task for each individual soul, which the individual is free to accept or decline at will, and whose ultimate destiny is determined by his response to God's vocation, then this demand would be wholly intelligible. But, if not God, who is to do the calling? Plainly the State, and Palinurus is using a word of nobler antecedents to describe the modern principle of "direction of labour." Someone must be called or directed to stoke Palinurus's central heating, to run the electric light plant and to make him his new winter overcoat. But a tiny doubt rises; can Palinurus be absolutely sure that he would find himself "called" to edit *Horizon*? It is just conceivable that he would find himself down a mine, and we should all be greatly the losers. It is to be noted, too, that the State given such enormous responsibilities has been disarmed from all disciplinary powers. Those who are deaf to its "call" can only be "rehabilitated" by psychiatrists, not punished. In the next, more diffuse, demand Palinurus goes further in condemning his functionaries to impotence.

"6. Full toleration of opinion. No censorship of written or spoken words, no tapping of telephones, opening of letters, compiling of dossiers. Special clinics for those who do compile them. No passports, identity cards or money-visas. All travel encouraged." Wretched functionaries! They are forbidden to keep any record of the millions of men and women whom it is their duty to control. If they attempt to do so they are packed off to the clinical prisons, which, one way or another, it seems, will house half the population. Even there they cannot be sure of rehabilitation, for the psychiatrists "called" to attend them are at the same time being encouraged to travel all over the place under assumed names.

The seventh demand is not worth quoting at length. It merely requires that there shall be no "harsh and antiquated" punishments for offences against modesty and sexual morality. Since "rehabilitation" has already been made the only penal sanction, this clause seems redundant. The eighth, however, is extremely odd and intriguing : "8. The acquisition of property to be recognized as an instinct which is, like the wish to excel, beneficial in moderation, but no one to own more property than he can see, nor the lives of other people, including children – and no children to be rich, which means also that no one would be the poorer for having them."

With the best will in the world I cannot conceive that this means anything at all. Is it to be taken literally? That real estate is to be bounded by the horizon from some given view-point? Or does it mean that personal property can only exist in visible and tangible objects? That a man may own a mountain of gold but not the copyright of a novel? Does Palinurus merely forbid domestic slavery and the *patria potestas*, or does he also deny the authority of a ship's captain over his crew? And who is to own babies, if not their parents? Presumably State hostels, but are the matrons of these hostels to be sent to clinics if they keep dossiers of their little charges? Does he merely forbid minors the unrestricted use of their inheritance (as is the universal custom) or does he forbid parents the right to use their property, however plainly visible, for their children's welfare? May man keep a mistress in luxury but not a daughter? Does Palinurus really suppose that parents will feel themselves the richer for having children over whom they have no authority and for whom they can provide no benefits?

"9. A passionate curiosity about art, science and the purpose of life . . . and a desire to preserve architecture, natural beauty and wild life." This seems to me to smack more of the American woman's lecture club than of the civilized community, but I can well believe that there might be some rather anxious curiosity about the purpose of life in Palinurus's Utopia. In passing, how does he propose to preserve wild life when he has stirred up the proletarian anthill and set everyone travelling everywhere? Presumably by the "calling" of a vast army of game wardens. Bird's-nesters sent for rehabilitation to the model prisons.

Tenth, last and funniest : "No discrimination against colour, race or creed." These would have been encouraging words if they had come at the head. Unhappily we have read the preceding nine proposals. We live under a regime which not only discriminates against, but makes it an avowed purpose to exterminate, the nobility, gentry, yeomanry, burgesses and vagabonds, and to produce the modern two-class State of officials and proletariat. It would have been a heartening spectacle to see Palinurus, alone among the Socialists, demanding the preservation of all the threatened classes, but he has given us a glimpse of his ideal State which makes this final cry of defiance sound hollow.

The significant feature of the Palinurus plan is that none of it makes any sense at all. It has been a hobby among literary men for centuries to describe ideal, theoretical States. There have been numberless ingenious contrivances, some so coherent that it seemed only pure mischance which made them remain mere works of reason and imagination without concrete form. It has been Palinurus's achievement to produce a plan so full of internal contradictions that it epitomizes the confusion of all his contemporaries. This plan is not the babbling of a secondary-school girl at a Youth Rally but the written words of the mature and respected leader of the English intellectuals. It is reassuring to know that the revelation came to him in what he, less than poetically, describes as "a lyric contribution to the poetry of motion" – the new cocktail bar of the Golden Arrow train.

Our Guest of Dishonour

Mr. Eden has invited his great new friend Broz to stay with us. We shall be expected to line the streets and foot the bill for the triumphal progress.

Who is this man? He will come under the latest, and perhaps the last, of many aliases as Marshal Tito, the name and title conferred on him by the Russians. "Tito" was simply his Comintern code-word. Marshal was a rank of the Red Army unknown in Yugoslavia. He held Stalin's commision and Stalin sent him his marshal's cap. I well remember the day Tito first wore it on the Island of Vis, where in August 1944 he was living under the protection of our Fleet and Air Force. It was not a well-made cap by English standards. It was not becoming by any standard. But Tito waddled about the island as proud as a dog with two tails because it came like a halo from his Russian heaven.

He was busy then, as now, in the work for which he has a peculiar aptitude – hoodwinking the British. The Germans were then in retreat from the Balkans. Their only use for Yugoslavia was an escape route. The partisans lurked in the hills and forests and left the main roads to the Germans. They had two civil wars on their hands – against the Serbian

Sunday Express, 30 November 1952, p. 1.

royalists and the Croat nationalists. *Tito's job was to persuade us to arm him for these wars under pretence of fighting the Germans. He succeeded.*

As soon as the Red Army invaded from Bulgaria he flew to join it without a word to our headquarters. Thenceforward he refused all co-operation with the West and set himself to impose on his decimated and distracted people a Communist regime with all the familiar, sickening concomitants of secret police and judicial murder. Now he is at it again, and again he is succeeding. The only difference between the Tito of 1944 and 1952 is that he has sought to postpone the fate which devours each Communist hero in turn, by the desperate step of quarrelling with Stalin.

Politicians cannot be squeamish about their business associates. We do not look to them for an example of fastidious moral rectitude. All we ask is common-sense experience of the world. Do they really suppose that Tito, who has betrayed in turn emperor, king, friends, and finally his one consistent loyalty to Stalin, will prove a trustworthy friend to *them*? Apparently, in their naive vanity, they do. They are sending him huge subsidies. It is our money, but it is their political reputations that are at hazard.

We might have rested content to watch the gamble and penalise the losers, but they go too far in bringing him here as an honoured guest because, though the politicians seem oblivious of the fact, there is a loyal multitude of her Majesty's subjects who recognise in him one of the six or seven most deadly and most powerful enemies of all they hold holy. Tito is seeking to extirpate Christianity in Yugoslavia. Make no mistake about it. He is not squabbling with the Vatican about rights and privileges. Orthodox as well as Catholics are doomed if his rule continues. He has not, except in early days when partisan bands roamed the country murdering priests at will, used the same sensational violence as his Hungarian neighbours. *But the aim is identical, as logically it must be in a regime which boasts itself as the only true model Leninist State.*

Some churches are still open and some priests are still at their altars. A few old peasants may be allowed to die in peace. But the younger generation are being driven from their faith with all the specialised mechanism of modern statesmanship. Details of the persecution have been reported from time to time, not very prominently, in the national Press. They follow the pattern – prohibition of religious teaching in schools, compulsory anti-religious teaching, prohibition of religious teaching in the home and in church, except during the actual Mass, crushing financial levies, closing the seminaries and theological faculties at the universities and so on. In the last few weeks a new resolution has been written into the constitution forbidding any member of the governing party to practise any religion at all.

The significant feature of the story is that these measures have been intensified during the last three months, the very period of English Conservative courtship. The Government must suppose that their supporters are ignorant of all this – or are they really unaware that England is still largely a Christian country? In hundreds of thousands of homes the fully documented history of the persecution has been followed with anger in the religious Press. It is not merely the ten per cent Roman Catholic population of the country who are outraged at the prospect of Tito's visit, but zealous churchmen of every denomination.

Our leaders are properly cautious of offending religious and racial minorities. Mr. Eden would not invite the country to feast and flatter a notorious Jew-baiter. Only when Christianity is at stake do our leaders show bland indifference. If they are really indifferent let them shorten their speeches and say frankly : "We see nothing abhorrent in the methods and aims of Communist rule. It is only Russia we are scared of. We will make every effort to strengthen any Communist dictator and arm him to impose his tyranny, provided only that he is temporarily estranged from Stalin. We welcome the transformation of great territories of Christendom into atheist police States. We despise the Christian peoples who look to us for sympathy and we despise the Christian voters at home, who, anyway, break about even at the polls."

Is that really what is in their minds?

No doubt, if Tito comes, a crowd will assemble, as it will for any notoriety, and no doubt there will be some cheering. *But let Mr. Eden not think that his guest is welcome. We are not given to breaking windows and throwing stink-bombs, we English Christians. We refuse to learn the ugly modern lesson that nothing succeeds except conspiracy and violence.* No doubt the deplorable event will pass off without Mr Eden's guest being aware that numberless heads are bowed in national dishonour and in prayer for the frustration of all his ambitions.

Awake My Soul! It is a Lord

'I'm not on business. I'm a member of the House of Lords.' These moving and rather mysterious words were uttered on my doorstep the other evening and recorded by the leading literary critic of the Beaverbrook press.

Spectator, 8 July 1955, pp. 36–37.

They have haunted me, waking and sleeping, ever since. I am sometimes accused of a partiality for lords; whatever touches them, it is hinted, vicariously touches me. Certainly the nobleman who tried to insinuate himself into my house half an hour before dinner that evening, has become a nine days' obsession.

Does anyone, I wonder, remember *Young England*, the drama of more than twenty years ago, which was taken up as an esoteric joke, soon became a popular saturnalia, but never failed to enchant? Here across the years came an authentic echo of that production; and the speaker, too, bald and overgrown though he was, had all the artless bearing of that inimitable troop of Boy Scouts.

But to explain his presence. The popular papers, I conceive, are fitfully and uneasily aware that there are spheres of English life in which they hold a negligible influence. The fifty or sixty thousand people in this country who alone support the Arts, do not go to Lord Beaverbrook's critics for guidance. So it is that artists of all kinds form part of the battle-training of green reporters. 'Don't lounge about the office, lad,' the editors say, 'sit up and insult an artist.' Rather frequently writers, among others, are troubled by the telephone asking for interviews. When these are refused, the journalist goes to what in a newspaper office is lightly called 'the library,' takes the file of his predecessors' misstatements, copies it out, adds a few of his own, and no one suffers except the readers of the popular press, who must, I should think, be getting bored with the recitation of old, false anecdotes. That is the normal routine – unless there is a lord handy, who is not subject to the conventions of the trade.

On the morning of the visit my wife said : 'An *Express* reporter and a lord wanted to come and see you this afternoon.'

'You told them not to?'

'Of course.'

'What lord?'

'Noel someone.'

'Has Noël Coward got a peerage? I'd like to see him.'

'No, it wasn't anyone I had heard of.'

There, I supposed, the matter ended. But that evening, just as I was going to prepare myself for dinner, I heard an altercation at the front door. My poor wife, weary from the hay-field, was being kept from her bath by a forbidding pair.

The lady of the party, Miss Spain, has recorded in two columns their day's doings. They were on what she called a 'pilgrimage.' This took them, uninvited, to tea with the Poet Laureate. 'Lord Noel-Buxton just walked into the house,' she writes, while she trampled the hay. The poet was 'silent, dreaming back in the past,' thinking, no doubt, that in all his years before the mast he had never met such tough customers. He gave them oat-cake. Then he brightened, 'his blue eyes danced.' The old 'darling' had thought of a way out. He urged them on to me. ' "See you? Of course he'll see you." ' On they came to the village where I live which, curiously, they found to be a 'straggly collection of prefabricated houses' (there is not one in the place), and entered the pub, where they got into talk with its rustic patrons. I have since made inquiries and learn that they somehow gave the impression that they were touts for television. Members of the village band sought to interest them in their music, and the cordiality, thus mistakenly engendered, emboldened the two pilgrims. They attempted to effect an entry into my house and wrangled until I dismissed them in terms intelligible even to them.

Lord Noel-Buxton seems to have been unaware of having done anything odd. 'Oh, Nancy, do stop!' he is said to have cried, when I went out to see that they were not slipping round to suck up to the cook. 'He's coming to apologise.'

A faulty appreciation.

What, I have been asking myself ever since, was Lord Noel-Buxton's part in the escapade? He is not, I have established, on the pay-roll of the *Daily Express*. All he seems to have got out of it is a jaunt in a motorcar, an oat-cake and a novel he can hardly hope to understand. Who, in the popular phrase, does he think he is?

Well, I looked him up and find that he is the second generation of one of Ramsay MacDonald's creation. To the student of social stratification this is significant. Is there, in our midst, unregarded, a new social subclass? The men who bought peerages from Lloyd George believed they were founding aristocratic houses, and there was, indeed, then a reasonable supposition that a generation or two of inherited wealth might refine the descendants of the gross originators. But the men who were put into ermine by MacDonald believed that the order they were entering was doomed. That statesman's bizarre appointments in the Church of England are eliminated by time, but the Upper House stands and the peerages he created survive. Are there, I wonder, many such orphans of the storm which blew itself out? Here, at any rate, was one specimen in full plumage on my doorstep.

I asked a secretarial agency, who sometimes helps me, to find out something about him. All they could say was that he is not strong, poor fellow, and was invalided out of the Territorial Army at the beginning of the war. Now, when he is not on a literary pilgrimage, he appears to spend much time paddling in rivers.

He clearly cannot have met many other lords. Students of *Punch* know that from the Eighties of the past century until the Thirties of this there was a standing joke about the distressed descendants of Crusaders who were reduced to retail trade. Now the thing is commonplace; not perhaps at the Co-operative Stores where, presumably, Lord Noel-Buxton does his shopping; but it is hard to believe that nowhere in the purlieus of the Upper House has he ever been approached with an advantageous offer of wine or clothing. But we must believe it. 'I'm not on business. I'm a member of the House of Lords.' The two ideas, in the mind of this naive nobleman, are axiomatically irreconcilable.

We have many sorts of lord in our country : lords haughty, who think that commoners all seek their acquaintance and must be kept at a distance; lords affable, who like mixing with their fellow-men of all degrees and know the conventions of good society by which introductions are effected; lords lavish and leisurely and dead-broke lords eager to earn an honest living. In Lord Noel-Buxton we see the lord predatory. He appears to think that his barony gives him the right to a seat at the dinner-table in any private house in the kingdom.

Fear of this lord is clearly the beginning of wisdom.

Anything Wrong with Priestley?

In the *New Statesman* of August 31 Mr. J. B. Priestley published an article entitled 'What was wrong with Pinfold?' 'Pinfold,' I should explain, is the name I gave to the leading character of my last book, a confessedly autobiographical novel which had already been reviewed (very civilly) in the literary columns of that curiously two-faced magazine. The contrast is notorious between the Jekyll of culture, wit and ingenious competitions and the Hyde of querulous atheism and economics which prefaces it. Mr. Priestley's article appeared in Hyde's section. He is not concerned to help me with my writing, as he is so well qualified to do, but to admonish me about the state of my soul, a subject on which I cannot allow him complete mastership. With 'Let Pinfold take warning' he proclaims in prophetic tones, and with the added authority of some tags from Jung, that I shall soon go permanently off my rocker. The symptoms are that I try to combine two incompatible roles, those of the artist and the Catholic country gentleman.

Which of those dangers to the artistic life, I wonder, does he regard as the more deadly. Not living in the country, surely? Unless I am misinformed Mr. Priestley was at my age a landed proprietor on a scale by which my own modest holding is a peasant's patch.

Catholicism? It is true that my Church imposes certain restrictions which Mr. Priestley might find irksome, but he must have observed that a very large number of his fellow writers profess a creed and attempt to follow a moral law which are either Roman Catholic or, from a Jungian point of view, are almost identical. Mr. T. S. Eliot, Dame Edith Sitwell, Mr. Betjeman, Mr. Graham Greene, Miss Rose Macaulay – the list is illustrious and long. Are they all heading for the bin?

No, what gets Mr. Priestley's goat (supposing he allows such a deleterious animal in his lush pastures) is my attempt to behave like a gentleman. Mr. Priestley has often hinted at a distaste for the upper classes but, having early adopted the *persona* of a generous-hearted, genial fellow, he has only once, I think, attempted to portray them. On that occasion, of which more later, he showed a rather remote acquaintance, like Dickens in creating Sir Mulberry Hawke. It is the strain of minding his manners that is driving poor Pinfold cuckoo. 'He must,' writes Mr. Priestley, 'be at all times the man of ideas, the intellectual, the artist, even if he is asked to resign from Bellamy's Club' (a fictitious institution that occurs in some of my books). Mr. Priestley's clubs must be much stricter than mine. Where I belong I never heard of the committee inquiring into the members' 'ideas.' It is true that we are forbidden to cheat at cards or strike the servants, but for the life of me I can't see anything particularly artistic in either of those activities.

Naturally I hunger for Mr. Priestley's good opinion and would like to keep my sanity for a few more years. I am an old dog to learn new tricks but I dare say I could be taught an accent at a school of elocution. I should not find it beyond me to behave like a cad on occasions – there are several shining examples in the literary world. My hair grows strongly still; I could wear it long. I could hire a Teddyboy suit and lark about the dance halls with a bicycle chain. But would this satisfy Mr. Priestley? Would he not be quick to detect and denounce this new *persona*? 'There was Waugh,' he would say, 'a man of humane education and accustomed to polite society. Tried to pass as Redbrick. No wonder he's in the padded cell.'

I do not flatter myself that Mr. Priestley's solicitude springs solely from love of me. What, I think, really troubles him is that by my manner of life I am letting down the side, all eleven of them whoever they are whom Mr. Priestley captains. 'If authors and artists in this country,' he writes, 'are not only officially regarded without favour but even singled out for unjust treatment – as I for one believe – then the Pinfolds are partly to blame. They not only do not support their profession; they go over to the enemy.'

I say, Priestley old man, are you sure you are feeling all right? Any Voices? I mean to say! No narcotics or brandy in your case, I know, but when a chap starts talking about 'the enemy' and believing, for one, that he is singled out for unjust treatment, isn't it time he consulted his Jungian about his *anima*? Who is persecuting poor Mr. Priestley? Mr. Macmillan does not ask him to breakfast as Gladstone might have done. His income, like everyone else's, is confiscated and 'redistributed' in the Welfare State. Tennyson's life was made hideous by importunate admirers; Mr. Priestley can walk down Piccadilly with a poppy or a lily, but he will be unmolested by the mob who pursue television performers. Is this what Mr. Priestley means by unjust treatment? Pinfold, he says, is vainly waiting for a message from Bonnie Prince Charlie. Is it possible that Mr. Priestley is awaiting a summons to Windsor from Queen Victoria?

Mr. Priestley is an older, richer, more popular man than I, but I cannot forbear saying: 'Let him take warning.' He has had some sharp disappointments in the last twelve years; perhaps he would call them 'traumas.' The voices he hears, like Pinfold's, may be those of a wildly distorted conscience. There was, indeed, a *trahison des clercs* some twenty years back which has left the literary world much discredited. It was then that the astute foresaw the social revolution and knew who would emerge top dog. They went to great lengths to suck up to the lower classes or, as they called it, to 'identify themselves with the workers.' Few excelled Mr. Priestley in his zeal for social justice. It is instructive to re-read his powerful novel *Blackout in Gretley*, which was written at a very dark time in the war when national unity was of vital importance. Its simple theme is that the English upper classes were in conspiracy to keep the workers in subjection even at the cost of national defeat. The villain, Tarlington, is everything deplorable, a man of good family and of smart appearance, a Conservative, the director of an engineering works, a courageous officer in 1914 – and, of course, a German spy. *Blackout in Gretley* is like *The Hill* in reverse; all morals derive from social origin. The police are a fine body of men but the Chief Constables are Fascist beasts. Two attractive women in the same fast set are equally suspect; but one turns out to have been a disorderly waitress before her respectable marriage; she has a heart of gold. The other is the niece of Vice-Admiral Sir Johnson Fund-Tapley and, of course, a traitor. Only two workers show moral delinquency; of these one turns out to be a German officer in disguise; the other, and more wicked, is – a Roman Catholic. Even the bad food at the hotel is ascribed to the fact that it is managed by a retired officer. 'This country has the choice during the next two years,' a virtuous character says, 'of coming fully to life and beginning all over again or of rapidly decaying and dying on the same old feet. It can only accomplish the first by taking a firm grip on about fifty thousand important, influential gentlemanly persons and telling them firmly to shut up and do nothing if they don't want to be put to doing some most unpleasant work.'

Came the dawn. Mr. Priestley was disappointed. No concentration camp was made for the upper classes. Nor have the triumphant workers shown themselves generous or discerning patrons of the arts. Gratitude, perhaps, is not one of their salient virtues. When they feel the need for a little aesthetic pleasure they do not queue at the experimental theatre; they pile into charabancs and tramp round the nearest collection of heirlooms and family portraits; quite enough to inflame the naked artist with an itch of persecution mania.

Aspirations of a Mugwump

I hope to see the Conservative Party return with a substantial majority. I have bitter memories of the Attlee-Cripps régime when the kingdom seemed to be under enemy occupation. I recognise that individually some of the Liberal candidates are more worthy than many of the Conservatives, but any advantage to them can only produce deplorable instability. I have met, seen or heard very few leading politicians; of those I know the Conservatives seem altogether more competent than their opponents.

I have never voted in a parliamentary election. I shall not vote this year. I shall never vote unless a moral or religious issue is involved (e.g., the suppression of Catholic schools). Great Britain is not a democracy. All authority emanates from the Crown. Judges, Anglican bishops, soldiers, sailors, ambassadors, the Poet Laureate, the postman and especially Ministers exist by the royal will. In the last three hundred years, particularly in the last hundred, the Crown has adopted what seems to me a very hazardous process of choosing advisers: popular election. Many great evils have resulted but the expectation of a change of method in my lifetime is pure fantasy.

Crowned heads proverbially lie uneasy. By usurping sovereignty the peoples of many civilised nations have incurred a restless and frustrated sense of responsibility which interferes with their proper work of earning their living and educating their children. If I voted for the Conservative

Spectator, 2 October 1959, p. 435. Contribution to a symposium of election comments.

Party and they were elected, I should feel that I was morally inculpated in their follies – such as their choice of Regius professors; if they failed, I should have made submission to Socialist oppression by admitting the validity of popular election. I do not aspire to advise my Sovereign in her choice of servants.

Commentary for The Private Man

The following pages comprise a deeply felt and plainly worded Call to Order by an American who represents no political party or organization. He is, as his title defines him, a 'private man'; one accustomed to authority and responsibility and imbued with the traditions of his native New England. He is disquieted at the influences which he sees as predominant in many quarters of his own country and of her European allies and his aim, like the younger Cato's, is to recall his contemporaries to the fading virtues of their ancestors. He is making a personal act of protest, and, to that extent, I must dissociate myself from him in the way that editors disclaim responsibility for the opinions of their correspondents. I lack first hand knowledge of the social, economic and political conditions of America; I sometimes dissent from the conclusions he makes from his observations in England; the History, from which he draws his illustrations, is not precisely the History I was taught, either in conspectus or in detail; but I gladly accept the invitation to write this preface because the problems which the author raises are those which vex Conservatives all over the world.

More than sixty years ago, in what seemed the height of the capitalist era, King Edward VII startled a Mansion House Banquet by quoting: 'We are all Socialists nowadays'. Now, when socialism under one guise or another is spreading everywhere, it is not altogether extravagant to say: 'We are all Conservatives'. Progress, as it has been understood since the eighteenth century, has proved a disappointment. For every gain there has been a compensating, or even preponderating, loss. Former 'progressives' suspect that they have gained all that is attainable and are in danger of losing it, while others believe that for a century the 'spirit of the age' has been moving in a wrong direction. Christendom, the West,

T. A. McInerny, *The Private Man*, New York, 1962, pp. vii-xiv.

the Free World – call it what you will – is on the defensive; its division from the opposed Communist world is absolute. There is now no place for the honest dupes of 1930s and '40s. We know what Communism is and either accept or reject it in its totality. This is a wholesome clarification. We know that the qualities we value are not natural gifts but human achievements which must be preserved with effort and sacrifice. This was recognized in the 1950s. But now, in the present decade, many are conscious of a new danger. In war, it is notorious, opponents soon forget the cause of their quarrel, continue the fight for the sake of fighting and in the process assume a resemblance to what they abhorred. We are all Conservatives but what exactly are we striving to conserve? Looking over our shoulders from the ramparts do we see the unconquered citadel already in decay? This, if I read Mr. McInerny rightly, is his central theme, the exploration of which takes him to the roots of human society.

Civilization is, under God, the free association of free men. Man is born in a family and by nature should be fed and taught in a family until he is of an age to take on the responsibilities of parenthood. A man's true freedom is in direct proportion to his power to control the production of the necessaries of family life. The State is an association of families who by reason of kinship or contiguity find it convenient to share corporate duties. The usurpation by the State of the free man's prerogatives is a universally observable process whether the ostensible form of association is autocracy, as in Hitler's Germany and the 'emergent' peoples of former colonies, oligarchy as in Russia, or a popularly elected President and Congress as in the U.S.A. and, from time to time, in France.

Since the early years of the Industrial Revolution there have been individual prophets who have been dimly aware of this trend to wards servility. Ruskin and William Morris believed it could be averted by Socialism; Belloc and Chesterton, by Distributism. In both cases there was nostalgia for an idealized Middle Ages. They saw as the great social evil the regimentation of the poor by avaricious employers who were controlled and often capriciously ruined, by the manipulations of international financiers. No one doubts that there were evils crying for correction, but the great private fortunes accumulated at the cost of human hardship were not all squandered in private indulgence but found their way into benevolent endowments and fructified all over the world in new enterprises. Moreover the physical hardships of the Victorian miner or factory-hand were not more severe than those of the peasant. The evil was primarily moral : the loss of independence and self-respect in the new industrial connurbations. The new Gradgrind is the State and, unlike Gradgrind, the State does not make a fortune.

Mr. McInerny does not speak of the abstract 'State'. He prefers to speak of the 'Public Man'. In England we see our enemy not in the flamboyant politician but in the anonymous and invisible bureaucrat, but conditions are similar. In both our countries it is the policy of governments to diminish the stature of the private man. They threaten to treat all men as the capitalists of the last century treated their newly-urbanised dependents.

Theoretically there is a vast difference between the United States and the United Kingdom. My country is not a democracy. It is a monarchy, aided by two houses of parliament, one of which, of lesser importance, is predominantly hereditary and therefore richly representative of the 'private man' in all his idiosyncrasies. The United States are the first child of the Revolution which destroyed France; there all authority comes from below. In my country the Crown is the consecrated fount of honour, the head of an established Church, the source of legal, naval, military and diplomatic appointments, the redresser of grievances and the punisher of crime. A loyal subject may cast his vote for a candidate to the House of Commons under the pretence that he is tendering the monarch humble advice in the choice of counsellors. Power is delegated from above, not from below – in theory. But in practice we suffer most of the ills of oppression by the majority that Mr. McInerny deplores in his own country. The majority, the public man, the common man, the State, the spirit of the age – the many headed, many named monster knows that the strongest force opposed to him is property. Our great-grandparents used to speak of a modest inherited fortune as 'an independence'. Property enabled a man to perform unremunerative public services, to practise the arts, to defy his rulers. The State destroys private property in three ways; first, by literally robbing the widow and orphan by confiscating bequests; secondly, and more insidiously, by so taxing earned incomes that saving is impossible – in most trades and professions in most countries a man is allowed to enjoy a considerable part of his earnings if he squanders it on travel and entertaining; thrift alone is penalised; thirdly, the State has the power to debase the coinage, a process euphemistically called 'inflation' which in simple terms means paying the majority more than they earn.

It has often been pointed out that Liberty and Equality are irreconcilable conceptions. The three historic catch-words of the Revolution which still stand inscribed on the public buildings of France suffered in esteem in the aftermath of the Second War. To the soldiers of the victorious armies 'Liberation' meant theft – 'I've just liberated a case of brandy'; 'Fraternity' meant fornication – 'Going fratting tonight?'; while-Equality meant for the civilian the ration-book and uniform want. Men are not naturally equal and can only seem so when enslaved. In antiquity even the slaves were able to exercise their varying superiorities.

By introducing a uniform system of education and by seeking to make it universal and compulsory, the State is attempting to minimise natural superiorities. The precocious child is regarded as a problem and his development is, when possible, stunted. The child from a quiet and studious home is seen to have an advantage over his fellows whose parents are rowdy and illiterate; work out of school hours is therefore discouraged. Even examinations, thought by the progressives of the last century to be a defence against privilege, are now denounced in the consultations of school-teachers as introducing an unhealthy spirit of competition into education. In most modern states the governments aspire to destroy the independent schools, which notoriously foster individuality and responsibility.

It would be paranoiac to suppose that there is an organized conspiracy. The 'spirit of the age' is observed in action, but no doubt many public men and bureaucrats are consciously aware that their tasks would be easier if mankind lost its diversity and became wholly docile in accepting what is represented to it as its own good, and when, as constantly happens, a decision has to be made between the opposed claims of liberty and equality, their choice instinctively favours equality. But in this the rulers betray themselves.

When a servile state has been achieved and man has 'nothing to lose but his chains', there is a fatal weakness from without and from within. Men will only fight for what they love. The more uprooted they are from their essential loyalties, the more the control of their own lives and families and the pride in their possessions are taken from them – so much the more readily will they fall victim to attack from nations which have not been so enervated.

Moreover the more pusillanimous they grow in defending their private lives, the more capricious will they become in their choice of rulers. When the State – the public man – claims credit for all benefits, it must accept responsibility for all misfortunes. A people who have forfeited their privacy will easily succumb to rogues and charlatans who promise a change of condition. They will know they have been cheated and turn on any surviving minorities that are pointed out to them as the origins of their malaise. Revolution and persecution will follow their odious course.

The State (ideally, we believe) is the free association of free men. Man develops his highest natural faculties in society. Men are distinguished by the variety and degree of their natural faculties. Therefore the proper structure of a healthy state is pyramidical. The organic life of society should be a continuous process of evolving an aristocracy. In a healthy society there should be no impassable barriers of hereditary caste keeping down the individual; recruitment into the aristocracy should be fostered; nor should there be rigid privilege which preserves in authority men who prove themselves unfit for it; but, by and large, the most valuable possession of any nation is an accepted system of classes, each of which has its proper function and dignity. At the head – I am not sure that McInerny would agree with me in this particular – is the fount of honour and justice; below that men and women who hold office from above and are the custodians of tradition, morality and grace; when occasion arises ready for sacrifice but protected from the infection of corruption and ambition by hereditary possession; the nourishers of the arts, the censors of manners. Below that the classes of industry and scholarship, trained from the nursery in habits of probity. Below that manual labourers proud of their skills and bound to those above them by common allegiance to the monarch. In general a man is best fitted to the tasks he has seen his father perform.

Neither Mr. McInerny nor I can hope to see such a state in its completeness – it has never existed in history nor ever will; but both our nations are yearly drifting further from this ideal. It is not enough to say: 'this is the spirit of the age' and to deplore it, for the spirit of the age is the spirits of those who compose it and the stronger the expressions of dissent from prevailing fashion, the higher the possibility of diverting it from its ruinous course.

5

Catholic

In middle life Waugh acquired a reputation for a narrow religious outlook and a bitter style of controversy. When two of his more notorious battles, with Professor Hugh Trevor-Roper in the *New Statesman*, were virtually restricted to pedantries and abuse, he began to emerge more a bigot than the gallant champion of the Counter-Reformation martyrs he hoped, and to some extent deserved, to be. Letters and reviews in the *Spectator*, the favourite reading matter of Church of England clergymen, provoked floods of protest concluding "Hang the trumpet on the wall, And study Waugh no more," and "I do not like this Holy Waugh". The review of Professor Laski's *Faith, Reason, and Civilization*, "Marxism, the Opiate of the People", is much more impressive. Dealing with a literary text and a contemporary problem, Waugh was able to display his debating ability to advantage.

In his final years, attacks on *aggiornamento* brought Waugh some standing as a Conservative spokesman. This was not an altogether surprising development. He had opposed common prayer between Catholics and Protestants in *The Times* as early as 1948. In 1960 he had referred to the meeting between the Pope and the Archbishop of Canterbury in such terms that the *Daily Mail* relegated his article to its Northern and Irish editions. "Changes in the Church" was a later contribution, a letter in Waugh's idiosyncratic fighting style which brought a little realism into the euphoria of the time, and drew attention to the existence of a Conservative viewpoint when it was almost swamped.

Other aspects of Waugh's religious journalism are now more illuminating to the lay reader. Converted to Catholicism in 1930, he made it plain in "Come Inside" that English Catholic liturgy, architecture, and culture seemed to him inferior to those of the Anglican Church. Hostility to gimcrack devotions, to credulity about miracles, and to domineering clergy found expression in various letters and in "The American Epoch in the Catholic Church". (The Wandering Jew episode in *Helena* gives vivid fictional form to his dislike of commercialized piety, while *Ronald Knox* is highly critical of clerical shortcomings.) Attacks on censorship of books and films (the criticism of the Hays Office in "Why Hollywood is a Term of Disparagement", in Chapter One, is one of many examples of this) and articles defending Christian marriage but recommending that the State should sanction divorce were out of harmony with his Church's official policy. At a time when the Catholic Church was inordinately given to self-praise and demanded unreasonable public conformity from its members Waugh's independence was healthy.

He also made positive contributions. "St. Helena Empress" announces a theme prominent in *Helena* and *Sword of Honour*, that salvation arises from an individual's acceptance of the particular task God calls him to fulfil. "Mgr. Knox at 4 a.m." and "Edith Stein" make a more profound point. Waugh reacted against twentieth-century scepticism by adopting the dogmas of his faith in an extremely literal way. Sometimes he went too far, as in "Felix Culpa?," his otherwise moving review of *The Heart of the Matter*. There, from the viewpoint of a "rule of thumb" Catholic, he makes explicit judgments about imponderable human motives. He relished putting forward the stark alternatives of Heaven and Hell, as in "Half in Love with Easeful Death". There was, however, an altogether more attractive side to this literalness – a hard-won vision of Christianity in its simplest and most basic terms. Sceptical, melancholic to the point of being suicidal, inclined to malice, Waugh had no natural aptitude for Faith, Hope, or Charity. He was pre-eminently Mgr. Knox's soul tempted to despair of being a Christian, one for whom it was nearly always 4 a.m. But like Edith Stein he searched for the truth in a thorough and practical way, disciplining his intelligence to disregard the ambiguities of speculative theology and the humanly unattractive aspects of the Church. He arrived at the blunt facts on which Christianity is founded – the death and resurrection of Christ, and accepted as a logical consequence of those facts the "machinery of salvation" embodied in the Christian Church. He may or may not have been mistaken in what he accepted as fact; it is impossible not to admire the discipline and strength of purpose which enabled him to defy the temper of the times and his natural inclinations in order to follow the truth as he understood it.

Come Inside

I was born in England in 1903 with a strong hereditary predisposition toward the Established Church. My family tree burgeons on every twig with Anglican clergymen. My father was what was called a "sound churchman"; that is to say, he attended church regularly and led an exemplary life. He had no interest in theology. He had no interest in politics but always voted Tory as his father and grandfather had done. In the same spirit he was punctilious in his religious duties.

At the age of ten I composed a long and tedious poem about Purgatory in the metre of *Hiawatha* and to the dismay of my parents, who held a just estimate of my character, expressed my intention of becoming a clergyman. The enthusiasm which my little school-fellows devoted to birds' eggs and model trains I turned on church affairs and spoke glibly of chasubles and Erastianism. I was accordingly sent to the school which was reputed to have the strongest ecclesiastical bent. At the age of sixteen I formally notified the school chaplain that there was no God. At the age of twenty-six I was received into the Catholic Church to which all subsequent experience has served to confirm my loyalty.

I am now invited to explain these vagaries.

First, of my early religiosity. I am reluctant to deny all reality to that precocious enthusiasm, but it was in the main a hobby like the birds' eggs and model trains of my school-fellows. The appeal was part hereditary and part aesthetic. Many are drawn in this way throughout their lives. In my case it was a concomitant of puberty. But those of my readers outside England should understand that the aesthetic appeal of the Church of England is unique and peculiar to those islands. Elsewhere a first interest in the Catholic Church is often kindled in the convert's imagination by the splendours of her worship in contrast with the bleakness and meanness of the Protestant sects. In England the pull is all the other way. The medieval cathedrals and churches, the rich ceremonies that surround the monarchy, the historic titles of Canterbury and York, the social organization of the country parishes, the traditional culture of Oxford and Cambridge, the liturgy composed in the heyday of English prose

The Road to Damascus, ed. John A. O'Brien, London, 1949, pp. 10–16.

style – all these are the property of the Church of England, while Catholics meet in modern buildings, often of deplorable design, and are usually served by simple Irish missionaries.

The shallowness of my early piety is shown by the ease with which I abandoned it. There are, of course, countless Catholics who, for a part of their lives at least, lose their faith, but it is always after a bitter struggle – usually a moral struggle. I shed my inherited faith as lightheartedly as though it had been an outgrown coat. The circumstances were these : During the first World War many university dons patriotically volunteered to release young schoolmasters to serve in the army. Among these there came to my school a leading Oxford theologian, now a bishop. This learned and devout man inadvertently made me an atheist. He explained to his divinity class that none of the books of the Bible were by their supposed authors; he invited us to speculate, in the manner of the fourth century, on the nature of Christ. When he had removed the inherited axioms of my faith I found myself quite unable to follow him in the higher flights of logic by which he reconciled his own scepticism with his position as a clergyman.

At the same time I read Pope's *Essay on Man*; the notes led me to Leibnitz and I began an unguided and half-comprehended study of metaphysics. I advanced far enough to be thoroughly muddled about the nature of cognition. It seemed simplest to abandon the quest and assume that man was incapable of knowing anything. I have no doubt I was a prig and a bore but I think that if I had been a Catholic boy at a Catholic school I should have found among its teaching orders someone patient enough to examine with me my callow presumption. Also, if I had been fortified by the sacraments, I should have valued my faith too highly to abandon it so capriciously. At my school I was quite correctly regarded as "going through a phase" normal to all clever boys, and left to find my own way home.

The next ten years of my life are material more suitable to the novelist than the essayist. Those who have read my works will perhaps understand the character of the world into which I exuberantly launched myself. Ten years of that world sufficed to show me that life there, or anywhere, was unintelligible and unendurable without God. The conclusion was obvious; the question now arises : Why Rome? A Catholic who loses his faith and rediscovers the need of it returns inevitably to the church he left. Why did not I?

Here, I think, the European has some slight advantage in particular over the American. It is possible, I conceive, for a man to grow up in parts of the United States without ever being really aware of the Church's unique position. He sees Catholics as one out of a number of admirable societies, each claiming his allegiance. That is not possible for a European. England was Catholic for nine hundred years, then Protestant for three hundred, then agnostic for a century. The Catholic structure still lies lightly buried beneath every phase of English life; history, topography, law, archaeology everywhere reveal Catholic origins. Foreign travel anywhere reveals the local, temporary character of the heresies and schisms and the universal, eternal character of the Church. It was self-evident to me that no heresy or schism could be right and the Church wrong. It was possible that all were wrong, that the whole Christian revelation was an imposture or a misconception. But if the Christian revelation was true, then the Church was the society founded by Christ and all other bodies were only good so far as they had salvaged something from the wrecks of the Great Schism and the Reformation. This proposition seemed so plain to me that it admitted of no discussion. It only remained to examine the historical and philosophic grounds for supposing the Christian revelation to be genuine. I was fortunate enough to be introduced to a brilliant and holy priest who undertook to prove this to me, and so on firm intellectual conviction but with little emotion I was admitted into the Church.

My life since then has been an endless delighted tour of discovery in the huge territory of which I was made free. I have heard it said that some converts in later life look back rather wistfuliy to the fervour of their first months of faith. With me it is quite the opposite. I look back aghast at the presumption with which I thought myself suitable for reception and with wonder at the trust of the priest who saw the possibility of growth in such a dry soul.

From time to time friends outside the Church consult me. They are attracted by certain features, repelled or puzzled by others. To them I can only say, from my own experience : "Come inside. You cannot know what the Church is like from outside. However learned you are in theology, nothing you know amounts to anything in comparison with the knowledge of the simplest actual member of the Communion of Saints."

Marxism, the Opiate of the People

It is a sad reflexion on our times that a man bearing the once honorific title of Professor should find it necessary to explain the inadequacy of his

Review of *Faith, Reason, and Civilization*, by Harold Laski, *Tablet*, 22 April 1944, p. 200.

published work by pleading the conflicting claims of his duty as a citizen; sad, not that he should be preoccupied by his duties in this national crisis, but that he should think it better to write badly than not to write at all. For this is a deplorably shoddy piece of work; there is, I think, no literary vice that is not exemplified in it, and had we not the Professor's assurance that it is "essentially an essay, nothing more," we might well take it for something much less – a hotch-potch of miscellaneous papers written at various times for various readers; only thus, it would have been charitable to think, could a writer of Professor Laski's long experience have produced a work so diffuse, repetitive and contradictory. It is a pity he did not take more trouble; six weeks' hard work could have put the thing into shape. Instead he lays himself open to the charge of being a literary Mrs. Jellaby, who is too busy planning great economic changes to plan a pamphlet; so set on preaching the dignity of labour that he shirks his own work. And that is a pity because his argument is of some topical interest.

The argument so far as I can claim to have followed it successfully through the hairpin bends and blind alleys in which it abounds, is this: Youth is being driven dumbly to the slaughter in a quarrel not of its making, for ends it does not understand; the rest of the community, on the other hand, is for the first time finding self-fulfilment in self-sacrifice for the common good. The unique felicity of this situation we owe to the spread of an interest in the Natural Sciences. At this stage (chapter VI) there follows a train of reasoning which merits full analysis: All good comes from natural science, says the Professor; natural science must be taught; the State is the teacher; but mere instruction is not enough; the seed must must fall on a prepared soil; the child from an impoverished home cannot hope to be a scientist; therefore it is the duty of the State to ensure a home for each of its subjects where science can flourish, i.e. one of physical comfort and security. But there is also something requisite besides refrigerators and pensions – "values"; the "values" of the past are dead; they are not to be found in art because Mr. T. S. Eliot is not understood by manual labourers and James Joyce is understood by nobody. "Values" can only be found now in Soviet Russia; the battle of Stalingrad proves it; all is not perfect in Russia, but there is no alternative source.

I do not think I am misinterpreting the Professor; if I am it is his own fault, for the argument has had to be traced through a multitude of digressions, which consist, for the most part, in a restatement of the conventional, socialist interpretation of history.

In a brief review it is best to disregard the digressions and concentrate on the argument. One may ask whether it is not odd that the spontaneous ebullition of self-fulfilment which the Professor finds on all sides should coincide with a system of legal compulsion unparalleled in English history; one may ask "Is heroic military defence really conclusive evidence that the defenders have superior 'values' to the attackers? If so, what about the Alcazar at Toledo, or the ruins of Cassino?"; one may ask "Does religion not offer 'values'?" and to this one gets an answer; in fact one gets two.

First, the Professor says religion is no good because it does not look like being immediately, universally acceptable. In his own sense that is a satisfactory answer. I, personally, do not believe that there will be universal peace and good will until the world is converted to Christianity and brought under Christ's Vicar; whether that ever comes about is not ordained, but depends on human free-will. It may well be that the Church will remain for ever an underground movement and that the Second Coming will find it still in a minority. Certainly I am one with the Professor in seeing no human probability of universal conversion in the next few thousand years. And the Professor must have a quick answer to reassure anxious pupils that they can safely concentrate on their books, and, if successful in attracting the notice of their superiors, expect influential positions, without the fear of being directed summarily into the mines or the Army Pay Corps. Looking about for a magic word to pacify the class, the Professor plumps for "Stalin."

But he does not leave it there. By a train of associations which does more credit to his zeal as a fire-watcher (or whatever citizen occupation has lately given him this self-fulfilment) than to his historical acumen, he traces Decay of civilization – Rome – rise of Christianity = Decay of capitalism – Russia – rise of Marxism; and throughout this book pursues the analogy until he almost seems seeking to convince us of an identity. It is therefore important to know what the Professor understands by this word, "Christianity," which he uses with such assurance.

It was, he tells us, founded by a man whom the New Testament "clearly" represents as "one figure, however mighty, in the long record of Hebrew prophets, like Amos or Hosea." This, it is notable, he has learned from the New Testament itself, not from one of Mr. Gollancz's popular tracts. Now the claim of a man to be God is stupendous and, it may well seem, preposterous. Such a man might be a lunatic or a charlatan, or, just conceivably, God; what he could not be is a prophet like Amos or Hosea. This prophet, according to the Professor, "protested passionately against the class-divisions of society," "but had no very deep concern with a workaday world." In that he conforms to a type that has become common enough in modern politics, but where does the Professor find him in the Gospels? Our Lord's reproaches to the scribes and pharisees were directed not at their privileged position but at their betrayal of the trust which justified the privileges, and as for the "workaday world," what does he imagine was the life of the carpenter's shop at

Nazareth? How could Our Lord show deeper concern for the workaday world than by living in it for half a normal lifetime, and then dying for it?

The religion founded by this stage creature of Professor Laski's musings over the stirrup-pump was confronted with a problem, and found an answer. "The problem," he writes – not even, it is worth remarking, "one of the numerous problems" – but "*The* problem that Christianity sought to solve was to reconcile the existence of the poverty of the poor with a State power which safeguarded the riches of the wealthy." Whom did this problem obsess? Not the Fathers, if one can judge by their writings. Many highly complex and recondite problems seem to have vexed them, but this one, *the* one, scarcely at all. Who then? The answer is as surprising as anything else in Professor Laski's exposition of our Faith; it was the altar boys. "A poor handful of brave acolytes" are cited as the original trustees of 'values.' How well one can see these precocious children clustered round the sacristy door. "It's all very well for *him* to worry about the Dual Nature; what we want is to reconcile the existence of the poverty of the poor...."

The question thus posed had already been answered. "The central faith of the Gospels," says the Professor – again note the pedagogic self-assurance; not "an arguable corollary to the Faith," but the Central Faith of the Gospels – "is" – guess what – "that where the claim of son upon parents or brother upon brother, is set in terms of the view that proximity of relationship means that one's property is proportionately available to one's kin also, the family becomes the nurse of avarice and narrowness, a hindrance, rather than a help, to fraternity in the commonwealth."

Imagine the scene on that first Easter morning; the little group of dismayed disciples, in the upper room, behind the barred doors; day breaking; the messenger hot-foot from the sepulchre; "Good news! Good news!"; they crowd round and there, for the first time, hear the great message that is to shake the earth, "When the claim of son upon parents or brother upon brother is set in terms of the view . . ." Thomas can't believe it. Then the thing is confirmed in flesh and blood and fire, and the disciples set out to the uttermost parts of the earth to carry the good news and die for it. ". . . that proximity of relationship means that one's property is proportionately available . . ."

There we have Professor Laski's idea of our Church; there his portrait of its Founder; there the problem; there his somewhat disconcerting solution. And when we have learned all this the Professor lets us into another secret, suddenly and quite casually after we have puzzled our way through 117 pages. "What it is not seriously open to a scholar to deny is that there is no more ground for accepting the validity of the postulates upon which the Churches build their rights than there is for accepting those of Mohammedanism and Buddhism." Shake off the superfluous negatives, translate his horrible jargon into English, and read, "Scholars have conclusively proved that the claims of Christianity are as false as those of Mohammedanism and Buddhism."

Really, he might have told us this earlier. If the whole thing has been proved a fraud, it doesn't matter what it was all about – not enough anyway to compensate for the pain of reading Professor Laski's prose. It was all a fraud, it seems, put about by the rich Romans, as a means of keeping the poor in their place. Has the whole of our reading of this tract been wasted? Not entirely I think, for, although Professor Laski's views on Christianity are of no possible interest to christians, he may yet be studied as a guide to contemporary politics. Perhaps there is a little kernel of wisdom hidden in the husk.

The Professor thinks there is an analogy between Christianity and Marxism. We see what he means by Christianity; what then does he think of Marxism? That it was once a secret whispered in upper rooms by humble, hopeful people; that it has become the official creed of a great empire; that an astute government has succeeded in so impressing a people with this creed that they willingly endure long toil, hard living, constant supervision, ruthless punishment, recurrent tragedy; that the latest imposture is more grossly impudent than its predecessor, Christianity, for the latter said, "Ye will be happy hereafter," and cannot be proved wrong (until Professor Laski's scholars get to work) while the former says "My dear comrades, you may not realize it, but you *are* happy at this moment"; that Marxism is the new opium of the people – is this what the Professor means? I doubt it, but it is what he comes very near saying in these muddled pages.

Half in Love With Easeful Death

AN EXAMINATION OF CALIFORNIAN BURIAL CUSTOMS

In a thousand years or so, when the first archaeologists from beyond the date-line unload their boat on the sands of Southern California, they will find much the same scene as confronted the Franciscan Missionaries. A dry landscape will extend from the ocean to the mountains. Bel Air and

Tablet, 18 October 1947, pp. 246–48.

Beverly Hills will lie naked save for scrub and cactus, all their flimsy multitude of architectural styles turned long ago to dust, while the horned toad and the turkey buzzard leave their faint imprint on the dunes that will drift on Sunset Boulevard.

For Los Angeles, when its brief history comes to an end, will fall swiftly and silently. Too far dispersed for effective bombardment, too unimportant strategically for the use of expensive atomic devices, it will be destroyed by drought. Its water comes 250 miles from the Colorado River. A handful of parachutists or partisans anywhere along that vital aqueduct can make the coastal strip uninhabitable. Bones will whiten along the Santa Fé trail as the great recession struggles Eastwards. Nature will re-assert herself and the seasons gently obliterate the vast, deserted suburb. Its history will pass from memory to legend until, centuries later, as we have supposed, the archæologists prick their ears at the cryptic references in the texts of the twentieth century to a cult which one flourished on this forgotten strand; of the idol Oscar – sexless image of infertility – of the great Star Goddesses who were once noisily worshipped there in a Holy Wood.

Without the testimony of tombs the science of archæology could barely exist, and it will be a commonplace among the scholars of 2947 that the great cultural decline of the twentieth century was first evident in the grave-yard. The wish to furnish the dead with magnificent habitations, to make an enduring record of their virtues and victories, to honour them and edify their descendants, raised all the great monuments of antiquity, the pyramids, the Taj Mahal, St. Peter's at Rome, and was the mainspring of all the visual arts. It died, mysteriously and suddenly, at the end of the nineteenth century. England, once very rich in sepulchral statuary, commemorated her fallen soldiers of the First World War by a simple inscription in the floor of an Abbey built nine centuries earlier to shelter the remains of a Saxon king. Rich patrons of art who in an earlier century would have spent the last decade of their lives in planning their own elaborate obsequies, deposed that their ashes should be broadcast from aeroplanes. The more practical Germans sent their corpses to the soap boiler. Only the primitive heathens of Russia observed a once-universal tradition in their shrine to Lenin.

All this will be a commonplace in the schools of 2947. The discoveries, therefore, of the Holy Wood Archæological Expedition will be revolutionary, for when they have excavated and catalogued, and speculated hopelessly about the meaning of, a temple designed in the shape of a Derby hat and a concrete pavement covered with diverse monopedic prints, and have surveyed the featureless ruins of the great film studios, their steps will inevitably tend northward to what was once Glendale, and there they will encounter, on a gentle slope among embosoming hills, mellowed but still firm-rooted as the rocks, something to confound all the accepted generalizations, a necropolis of the age of the Pharaohs, created in the middle of the impious twentieth century, the vast structure of Forest Lawn Memorial Park.

We can touch hands across the millennium with these discoverers, for it is in the same mood of incredulous awe that the visitor of our own age must approach this stupendous property. Visitors, indeed, flock there – in twice the numbers that frequent the Metropolitan Museum in New York – and with good reason, for there are many splendid collections of Art elsewhere but Forest Lawn is entirely unique. Behind the largest wrought-iron gates in the world lie 300 acres of park-land, judiciously planted with evergreen (for no plant which sheds its leaf has a place there). The lawns, watered and drained by 80 miles of pipe, do not at first betray their solemn purpose. Even the names given to their various sections – Eventide, Babyland, Graceland, Inspiration Slope, Slumberland, Sweet Memories, Vesperland, Dawn of Tomorrow – are none of them specifically suggestive of the grave-yard. The visitor is soothed by countless radios concealed about the vegetation, which ceaselessly discourse the 'Hindu Lovesong' and other popular melodies, and the amplified twittering of caged birds. It is only when he leaves the $7\frac{1}{2}$ miles of paved roadway that he becomes aware of the thousands of little bronze plates which lie in the grass. Commenting on this peculiarity in the *Art Guide of Forest Lawn with Interpretations* Mr. Bruce Barton, author of *What can a man believe?* says : 'The cemeteries of the world cry out man's utter hopelessness in the face of death. Their symbols are pagan and pessimistic . . . Here sorrow sees no ghastly monuments, but only life and hope.' The Christian visitor might here remark that by far the commonest feature of other grave-yards is still the Cross, a symbol in which previous generations have found more Life and Hope than in the most elaborately watered evergreen shrub. This reproach will soon be removed in Forest Lawn's own grand way by a new acquisition, a prodigious canvas of the Crucifixion which took thirty years of the Polish painter, Jan Styka's life to complete; it will require a vast new building to house it. A miniature, 1/49th of the area of the original, now occupies one whole side of the largest hall in Forest Lawn and an explanatory speech has been recorded for the gramophone, identifying the hundreds of figures which in the original abound in life size. The canvas has had an unhappy history. Shipped to the U.S.A. in 1904 for the St. Louis Exhibition, it was impounded for excise dues and sold, without profit to the artist, to its importer, who was, however, unable to find a pavilion large enough to house it. Since then it has lain about in warehouses, a prey to 'silver fish,' and has been shown only once, in the Chicago Opera House, where it filled the entire stage and extended far into the auditorium. Soon it will form a suitable addition to the wonders of Forest Lawn.

These can be only briefly indicated in an essay of this length. There is the largest assembly of marble statuary in the United States, mostly secular in character, animals, children and even sculptured toys predominating; some of it erotic, and some of it enigmatically allegorical. There is also what is claimed to be the finest collection of stained glass in America, the glory of which is 'The Last Supper' in the Court of Honour; the original by Leonardo da Vinci has here, in the words of *Pictorial Forest Lawn*, been 'recreated in vibrant, glowing and indestructible colours.'

There are gardens and terraces, and a huge range of buildings, the most prominent of which is the rather Italian Mausoleum. There in marble fronted tiers lie the coffins, gallery after gallery of them, surrounded by statuary and stained glass. Each niche bears a bronze plaque with the inmate's name, sometimes in magnified counterfeit of his signature. Each has a pair of bronze vases which a modest investment can keep perpetually replenished with fresh flowers. Adjacent lies the Columbarium, where stand urns of ashes from the Crematory. There is the Tudor-style Administration Building, the Mortuary (Tudor exterior, Georgian interior) and the more functional Crematory. All are designed to defy the operations of time; they are in 'Class A steel and concrete,' proof against fire and earthquake. The Mausoleum alone, we are told, contains enough steel and concrete for a sixty storey office building, and its foundations penetrate thirty-three feet into solid rock.

The Memorial Court of Honour is the crowning achievement of this group. 'Beneath the rare marbles of its floor are crypts which money cannot purchase, reserved as gifts of honoured interment for Americans whose lives shall have been crowned with genius.' There have so far been two recipients of this gift, Gutzon Borglum, the first sculptor in history to employ dynamite instead of the chisel, and Mrs. Carrie Jacobs-Bond, author and composer of 'The End of a Perfect Day,' at whose funeral last year, which cost 25,000 dollars, Dr. Eaton, the Chairman of Forest Lawn, pronounced the solemn words : 'By the authority vested in me by the Council of Regents, I do herewith pronounce Carrie Jacobs-Bond an immortal of the Memorial Court of Honour.'

There is at the highest point a water-tower named 'The Tower of Legends,' where at the dawn of Easter Sunday a number of white doves are liberated in the presence of a huge concourse whose singing is broadcast 'from coast to coast.' Of this building 'a noted art authority' has remarked : 'It depicts, more truly than any structure I have ever seen, real American architecture. It deserves the attention of the world' (*Art Guide*). But this precious edifice, alas, is due for demolition and will soon give place to the non-sectarian, Bishopless 'Cathedral' which is to house Jan Styka's masterpiece and provide in its shade fresh galleries of urns and coffins.

There are already three non-sectarian churches, 'The Little Church of the Flowers,' 'The Wee Kirk o' the Heather' and 'The Church of the Recessional.' The first is, with modifications, a replica of Stoke Poges Church where Gray wrote his *Elegy*; the second a reconstruction of the ruins of a chapel at Glencairn, Dumfriesshire where Annie Laurie worshipped; the third, again with modifications, is a replica of the parish church of Rottingdean in Sussex where Rudyard Kipling is claimed by Dr. Eaton to have been inspired – by heaven knows what aberration of oratory from the pulpit so artlessly reproduced – to write *Kim*. The American visitor may well be surprised at the overwhelmingly British character of these places of worship in a State which has never enjoyed the blessings of British rule and is now inhabited by the most cosmopolitan people in the United States. The British visitor is surprised also at the modifications.

It is odd to find a church dedicated to Kipling, whose religion was highly idiosyncratic. The building is used not only for funerals but for weddings and christenings. Its courtyard is used for betrothals; there is a stone ring, named by Dr. Eaton the ring of Aldyth, through which the young lover is invited to clasp hands and swear fidelity to what Kipling described as 'a rag and a bone and hank of hair.' Round the courtyard are incised the texts of *Recessional*, *If*, and *When earth's last picture is painted*. The interior of St Margaret's, Rottingdean, is not particularly remarkable among the many ancient parish churches of England, but the architects of Forest Lawn have used their ingenuity to enliven it. One aisle has been constructed of glass instead of stone, and filled with pot-plants and caged canaries; a chapel, hidden in what is no doubt thought to be devotional half-darkness, is illuminated by a spotlit painting of Bougereau's entitled 'Song of the Angels'; in a kind of sacristry relics of the patron saint are exposed to veneration. They are not what ecclesiastics call 'major relics'; some photographs by the Topical Press, a rifle scoresheet signed by the poet, the photostatic copy of a letter to Sir Roderick Jones expressing Kipling's hope of attending a christening, a copy of Lady Jones's popular novel, *National Velvet*, an oleograph text from a nearby cottage; and so forth.

What will the archæologists of 2947 make of all this and of the countless other rareties of the place? What webs of conjecture will be spun by the professors of Comparative Religion? We know with what confidence they define the intimate beliefs of remote ages. They flourished in the nineteenth century. Then G. K. Chesterton, in a masterly book, sadly neglected in Europe but honoured in the U.S.A. – *The Everlasting Man*

– gently exposed their fatuity. But they will flourish again, for it is a brand of scholarship well suited to dreamy natures who are not troubled by the itch of precise thought. What will the professors of the future make of Forest Lawn? What do we make of it ourselves? Here is the thing, under our noses, a first class anthropological puzzle of our own period and neighbourhood. What does it mean?

First, of course, it is self-evidently a successful commercial undertaking. The works of sculpture enhance the value of the grave sites; the unification in a single business of all the allied crafts of undertaking is practical and, I believe, unique. But all this is the least interesting feature.

Secondly, the Park is a monument to local tradition. Europeans, whose traditions are measured in centuries, are wrong to suppose that American traditions, because they are a matter of decades, are the less powerful. They are a recent, swift and wiry growth. Southern California has developed a local character which is unique in the United States. The territory was won by military conquest less than a century ago. In the generations that followed the Spanish culture was obliterated, and survives today only in reconstructions. The main immigrations took place in living memory, and still continue. In 1930 it was calculated that of the million and a quarter inhabitants of Los Angeles half had arrived in the previous five years; only one tenth could claim longer than fifteen years' standing. In the last seventeen years the balance has changed still more in the newcomers' favour. Of this vast influx the rich came first. There was no pioneer period in which hungry young people won a living from the land. Elderly people from the East and Middle West brought their money with them to enjoy it in the sunshine, and they set up a tradition of leisure which is apparent today in the pathological sloth of the hotel servants and the aimless, genial coffee-house chatter which the Film Executives call 'conferences.'

It is not the leisure of Palm Beach and Monte Carlo where busy men go for a holiday. It is the leisure of those whose work is done. Here on the ultimate, sunset-shore they warm their old bodies and believe themselves alive, opening their scaly eyes two or three times a day to browse on salads and fruits. They have long forgotten the lands that gave them birth and the arts and trades they once practised. Here you find, forgetful and forgotten, men and women you supposed to be long dead, editors of defunct newspapers, playwrights and artists who were once the glory of long-demolished theatres, and round them congregate the priests of countless preposterous cults to soothe them into the cocoon-state in which they will slough their old bodies. The ideal is to shade off, so finely that it becomes imperceptible, the moment of transition, and it is to this process that Forest Lawn is the most conspicuous monument.

Dr. Eaton has set up his Credo at the entrance. 'I believe in a happy

Eternal Life,' he says. 'I believe those of us left behind should be glad in the certain belief that those gone before have entered into that happier Life.' This theme is repeated on Coleus Terrace : 'Be happy because they for whom you mourn are happy – far happier than ever before.' And again in Vesperland : '. . . Happy because Forest Lawn has eradicated the old customs of Death and depicts Life not Death.'

The implication of these texts is clear. Forest Lawn has consciously turned its back on the 'old customs of death,' the grim traditional alternatives of Heaven and Hell, and promises immediate eternal happiness for all its inmates. Similar claims are made for other holy places – the Ganges, Debra Lebanos in Abyssinia, and so on. Some of the simpler crusaders probably believed that they would go straight to Heaven if they died in the Holy Land. But there is a catch in most of these dispensations, a sincere repentance, sometimes an arduous pilgrimage, sometimes a monastic rule in the closing years. Dr. Eaton is the first man to offer eternal salvation at an inclusive charge as part of his undertaking service.

There is a vital theological point on which Dr. Eaton gives no *ex cathedra* definition. Does burial in Forest Lawn itself sanctify, or is sanctity the necessary qualification for admission? Discrimination is exercised. There is no room for the negro or the Chinaman, however devout; avowed atheists are welcome, but notorious ill-doers are not. Al Capone, for example, had he applied, would have been excluded, although he died fortified by the last rites of his Church. 'Fatty' Arbuckle was refused burial, because, although acquitted by three juries of the crime imputed to him by rumour, he had been found guilty, twenty years or so earlier, of giving a rowdy party. Suicides, on the other hand, who, in 'the old customs of death' would lie at a crossroads, impaled, come in considerable numbers and, often, particularly in cases of hanging, present peculiar problems to the embalmer.

Embalming is so widely practised in California that many believe it to be a legal obligation. At Forest Lawn the bodies lie in state, sometimes on sofas, sometimes in open coffins, in apartments furnished like those of a luxurious hotel, and named 'Slumber Rooms.' Here the bereaved see them for the last time, fresh from the final beauty parlour, looking rather smaller than in life and much more dandified. There is a hint of the bassinette about these coffins, with their linings of quilted and padded satin and their frilled silk pillows. There is more than a hint, indeed, throughout Forest Lawn that death is a form of infancy, a Wordsworthian return to innocence. 'I am the Spirit of Forest Lawn,' wrote K. C. Beaton, in less than Wordsworthian phrase : 'I speak in the language of the Duck Baby,* happy childhood at play.' We are very far here from the traditional

---

* A bronze figure by Edith Barrett Parsons representing a laughing nude child with poultry. It inspired Leo Robinson's poem "After the lights went out".

conception of an adult soul naked at the judgment seat and a body turning to corruption. There is usually a marble skeleton lurking somewhere
among the marble draperies and quartered escutcheons of the tombs of
the high renaissance; often you find, gruesomely portrayed, the corpse half
decayed with marble worms writhing in the marble adipocere. These
macabre achievements were done with a simple moral purpose – to remind a highly civilized people that beauty was skin deep and pomp was
mortal. In those realistic times Hell waited for the wicked and a long
purgation for all but the saints, but Heaven, if at last attained, was a
place of perfect knowledge. In Forest Lawn, as the builder claims, these
old values are reversed. The body does not decay; it lives on, more chic
in death than ever before, in its indestructible class A steel and concrete
shelf; the soul goes straight from the Slumber Room to Paradise, where
it enjoys an endless infancy – one of a great Caucasian nursery-party
where Knights of Pythias toddle on chubby unsteady legs beside a Borglum whose baby-fingers could never direct a pneumatic drill and a Carrie
Jacobs-Bond whose artless ditties are for the Duck Baby alone.

That, I think, is the message. To those of us too old-fashioned to listen
respectfully, there is the hope that we may find ourselves, one day beyond
time, standing at the balustrade of Heaven among the unrecognizably
grown-up denizens of Forest Lawn, and, leaning there beside them,
amicably gaze down on Southern California, and share with them the
huge joke of what the Professors of Anthropology will make of it all.

Felix Culpa?

Of Mr. Graham Greene alone among contemporary writers one can say
without affectation that his breaking silence with a new serious novel is
a literary "event." It is eight years since the publication of *The Power
and the Glory*. During that time he has remained inconspicuous and his
reputation has grown huge. We have had leisure to re-read his earlier
books and to appreciate the gravity and intensity which underlie their
severe modern surface. More than this, the spirit of the time has begun
to catch up with them.

Review of *The Heart of the Matter*, by Graham Greene, *Commonweal*, 16 July
1948, pp. 322–25.

The artist, however aloof he holds himself, is always and specially the creature of the *zeitgeist;* however formally antique his tastes, he is in spite of himself in the advance guard. Men of affairs stumble far behind.

In the last twenty-five years the artist's interest has moved from sociology to eschatology. Out of hearing, out of sight, politicians and journalists and popular preachers exhort him to sing the splendours of high wages and sanitation. His eyes are on the Four Last Things, and so mountainous are the disappointments of recent history that there are already signs of a popular breakaway to join him, of a stampede to the heights.

I find the question most commonly asked by the agnostic is not : "Do you believe in the authenticity of the Holy House at Loreto?" or "Do you think an individual can justly inherit a right to the labour of another?" but "Do you believe in Hell?"

Mr. Greene has long shown an absorbing curiosity in the subject. In *Brighton Rock* he ingeniously gave life to a theological abstraction. We are often told : "The Church does not teach that any man is damned. We only know that Hell exists for those who deserve it. Perhaps it is now empty and will remain so for all eternity." This was not the sentiment of earlier and healthier ages. The Last Judgment above the medieval door showed the lost and the saved as fairly equally divided; the path to salvation as exceedingly narrow and beset with booby-traps; the reek of brimstone was everywhere. Mr. Greene challenged the soft modern mood by creating a completely damnable youth. Pinkie of *Brighton Rock* is the ideal examinee for entry to Hell. He gets a pure alpha on every paper. His story is a brilliant and appalling imaginative achievement but falls short of the real hell-fire sermon by its very completeness. We leave our seats edified but smug. However vile we are, we are better than Pinkie. The warning of the preacher was that one unrepented slip obliterated the accumulated merits of a lifetime's struggle to be good. *Brighton Rock* might be taken to mean that one has to be as wicked as Pinkie before one runs into serious danger.

Mr. Greene's latest book, *The Heart of the Matter*, should be read as the complement of *Brighton Rock*. It poses a vastly more subtle problem. Its hero speaks of the Church as "knowing all the answers," but his life and death comprise a problem to which the answer is in the mind of God alone, the reconciliation of perfect justice with perfect mercy. It is a book which only a Catholic could write and only a Catholic can understand. I mean that only a Catholic can understand the nature of the problem. Many Catholics, I am sure, will gravely misunderstand it, particularly in the United States of America, where its selection as the Book of the Month will bring it to a much larger public than can profitably read it. There are loyal Catholics here and in America who think it the function of the Catholic writer to produce only advertising brochures setting out in attractive terms the advantages of Church membership. To them this profoundly reverent book will seem a scandal. For it not only portrays Catholics as unlikeable human beings but shows them as tortured by their Faith. It will be the object of controversy and perhaps even of condemnation. Thousands of heathen will read it with innocent excitement, quite unaware that they are intruding among the innermost mysteries of faith. There is a third class who will see what this book intends and yet be troubled by doubt of its theological propriety.

Mr. Greene divides his fiction into "Novels" and "Entertainments." Superficially there is no great difference between the two categories. There is no Ruth Draper switch from comic to pathetic. "Novels" and "Entertainments" are both written in the same grim style, both deal mainly with charmless characters, both have a structure of sound, exciting plot. You cannot tell from the skeleton whether the man was baptized or not. And that is the difference; the "Novels" have been baptized, held deep under in the waters of life. The author has said : "These characters are not my creation but God's. They have an eternal destiny. They are not merely playing a part for the reader's amusement. They are souls whom Christ died to save." This, I think, explains his preoccupation with the charmless. The children of Adam are not a race of noble savages who need only a divine spark to perfect them. They are aboriginally corrupt. Their tiny relative advantages of intelligence and taste and good looks and good manners are quite insignificant. The compassion and condescension of the Word becoming flesh are glorified in the depths.

As I have said above, the style of writing is grim. It is not a specifically literary style at all. The words are functional, devoid of sensuous attraction, of ancestry and of independent life. Literary stylists regard language as intrinsically precious and its proper use as a worthy and pleasant task. A polyglot could read Mr. Greene, lay him aside, retain a sharp memory of all he said and yet, I think, entirely forget what tongue he was using. The words are simply mathematical signs for his thought. Moreover, no relation is established between writer and reader. The reader has not had a conversation with a third party such as he enjoys with Sterne or Thackeray. Nor is there within the structure of the story an observer through whom the events are recorded and the emotions transmitted. It is as though out of an infinite length of film, sequences had been cut which, assembled, comprise an experience which is the reader's alone, without any correspondence to the experience of the protagonists. The writer has become director and producer. Indeed, the affinity to the film is everywhere apparent. It is the camera's eye which moves from the hotel balcony to the street below, picks out the policeman, follows him to his office, moves about the room from the handcuffs on the wall to the broken rosary in the drawer, recording significant detail. It is the modern way of telling a story. In Elizabethan drama one can usually discern an artistic sense formed on the dumb-show and the masque. In Henry James's novels scene after scene evolves as though on the stage of a drawing-room comedy. Now it is the cinema which has taught a new habit of narrative. Perhaps it is the only contribution the cinema is destined to make to the arts.

There is no technical trick about good story-telling in this or any other manner. All depends on the natural qualities of the narrator's mind, whether or no he sees events in a necessary sequence. Mr. Greene is a story-teller of genius. Born in another age, he would still be spinning yarns. His particular habits are accidental. The plot of *The Heart of the Matter* might well have been used by M. Simenon or Mr. Somerset Maugham.

The scene is a West African port in war time. It has affinities with the Brighton of *Brighton Rock*, parasitic, cosmopolitan, corrupt. The population are all strangers, British officials, detribalized natives, immigrant West Indian Negroes, Asiatics, Syrians. There are poisonous gossip at the club and voodoo bottles on the wharf, intrigues for administrative posts, intrigues to monopolize the illicit diamond trade. The hero, Scobie, is deputy-commissioner of police, one of the oldest inhabitants among the white officials; he has a compassionate liking for the place and the people. He is honest and unpopular and, when the story begins, he has been passed over for promotion. His wife Louise is also unpopular, for other reasons. She is neurotic and pretentious. Their only child died at school in England. Both are Catholic. His failure to get made commissioner is the final humiliation. She whines and nags to escape to South Africa. Two hundred pounds are needed to send her. Husband and wife are found together in the depths of distress.

The illegal export of diamonds is prevalent, both as industrial stones for the benefit of the enemy and gems for private investment. Scobie's police are entirely ineffective in stopping it, although it is notorious that two Syrians, Tallit and Yusef, are competitors for the monopoly. A police-spy is sent from England to investigate. He falls in love with Louise. Scobie, in order to fulfil his promise to get Louise out of the country, borrows money from Yusef. As a result of this association he is involved in an attempt to "frame" Tallit. The police-spy animated by hate and jealousy is on his heels. Meanwhile survivors from a torpedoed ship are brought across from French territory, among them an English bride widowed in the sinking. She and Scobie fall in love and she becomes his mistress. Yusef secures evidence of the intrigue and blackmails Scobie into definitely criminal participation in his trade. His association with Yusef culminates in the murder of Ali, Scobie's supposedly devoted native servant, whom he now suspects of giving information to the police-spy. Louise returns. Unable to abandon either woman, inextricably involved in crime, hunted by his enemy, Scobie takes poison; his women become listlessly acquiescent to other suitors.

These are the bare bones of the story, the ground plan on which almost any kind of building might be erected. The art of story-telling has little to do with the choice of plot. One can imagine the dreariest kind of film – (Miss Bacall's pretty head lolling on the stretcher) – accurately constructed to these specifications. Mr. Greene, as his admirers would expect, makes of his material a precise and plausible drama. His technical mastery has never been better manifested than in his statement of the scene – the sweat and infection, the ill-built town, which is beautiful for a few minutes at sundown, the brothel where all men are equal, the vultures, the priest who, when he laughed "swung his great empty-sounding bell to and fro, Ho, ho, ho, like a leper proclaiming his misery," the snobbery of the second-class public schools, the law which all can evade, the ever-present haunting underworld of gossip, spying, bribery, violence and betrayal. There are incidents of the highest imaginative power – Scobie at the bedside of a dying child, improvising his tale of the Bantus. It is so well done that one forgets the doer. The characters are real people whose moral and spiritual predicament is our own because they are part of our personal experience.

As I have suggested above, Scobie is the complement of Pinkie. Both believe in damnation and believe themselves damned. Both die in mortal sin as defined by moral theologians. The conclusion of the book is the reflection that no one knows the secrets of the human heart or the nature of God's mercy. It is improper to speculate on another's damnation. Nevertheless the reader is haunted by the question: Is Scobie damned? One does not really worry very much about whether Becky Sharp or Fagin is damned. It is the central question of *The Heart of the Matter*.* I believe that Mr. Greene thinks him a saint. Perhaps I am wrong in this, but in any case Mr. Greene's opinion on that matter is of no more value than the reader's. Scobie is not Mr. Greene's creature, devised to illustrate a thesis. He is a man of independent soul. Can one separate his moral from his spiritual state? Both are complex and ambiguous.

* In a letter dated 11 August 1948 about a French translation of this review, Waugh asked A. D. Peters to delete the passage: "I believe that Mr Greene thinks him a saint . . . a man of independent soul"; and to substitute for it, "Several critics have taken Scobie to be a saint." Waugh continued: "You might make a note of this correction in case anyone else ever wants to reprint the review – as I should very much like them to do." A letter to the *Tablet*, 17 July 1948, p. 41, also indicates the need for this correction. Ed.

First, there is his professional delinquency. In the first pages he appears as an Aristides, disliked for his rectitude; by the end of the book he has become a criminal. There is nothing inevitable in his decline. He compromises himself first in order to get his wife's passage money. She is in a deplorable nervous condition; perhaps, even, her reason is in danger. He is full of compassion. But she is making his own life intolerable; he wants her out of the way for his own peace. As things turn out the trip to South Africa was quite unnecessary. Providence had its own cure ready if he had only waited. He gets the commissionership in the end, which was ostensibly all that Louise wanted. But behind that again lies the deeper cause of her melancholy, that Scobie no longer loves her in the way that would gratify her vanity. And behind the betrayal of his official trust lies the futility of his official position. The law he administers has little connection with morals or justice. It is all a matter of regulations – a Portuguese sea-captain's right to correspond with his daughter in Germany, the right of a tenant to divide and sub-let her hut, the right of a merchant to provide out of his own property for the security of his family. He knows that his subordinates are corrupt and can do nothing about it. Whom or what has he in fact betrayed, except his own pride?

Secondly, there is his adultery. His affection for the waif cast up on the beach is at first compassionate and protective; it becomes carnal. Why? He is an elderly man long schooled in chastity. There is another suitor of Helen Rolt, Bagster the Air Force philanderer. It is Bagster's prowling round the bungalow which precipitates the change of relationship. It is Bagster in the background who makes him persevere in adultery when his wife's return affords a convenient occasion for parting. Bagster is a promiscuous cad. Helen must be saved from Bagster. Why? Scobie arrogates to himself the prerogations of providence. He presumes that an illicit relation with himself is better than an illicit relation with Bagster. But why, in fact, need it have been illicit? She might marry Bagster.

Thirdly there is the murder of Ali. We do not know whether Ali was betraying him. If he had not been a smuggler and an adulterer there would have been nothing to betray. Ali dies to emphasize the culpability of these sins.

Fourthly there are the sacrilegious communions which Louise forces upon him; and fifthly, his suicide, a re-statement of that blasphemy in other terms. He dies believing himself damned but also in an obscure way – at least in a way that is obscure to me – believing that he is offering his damnation as a loving sacrifice for others.

We are told that he is actuated throughout by the love of God. A love, it is true, that falls short of trust, but a love, we must suppose, which sanctifies his sins. That is the heart of the matter. Is such a sacrifice feasible? To me the idea is totally unintelligible, but it is not unfamiliar.

Did the Quietists not speak in something like these terms? I ask in all humility whether nowadays logical rule-of-thumb Catholics are not a little too humble towards the mystics. We are inclined to say: "Ah, that is mysticism. I'm quite out of my depth there," as though the subject were higher mathematics, while in fact our whole Faith is essentially mystical. We may well fight shy of discussing ecstatic states of prayer with which we have no acquaintance, but sacrilege and suicide are acts of which we are perfectly capable. To me the idea of willing my own damnation for the love of God is either a very loose poetical expression or a mad blasphemy, for the God who accepted that sacrifice could be neither just nor lovable.

Mr. Greene has put a quotation from Péguy at the beginning of the book *"Le pécheur est au coeur même de chrétienté . . . Nul n'est aussi compétent que le pécheur en matière de chrétienté. Nul, si ce n'est le saint,"* and it seems to me probable that it was in his mind to illustrate the *"Nouveau Théologien"* from which it is taken, just as in *Brighton Rock* he illustrates the Penny Catechism. The theme of that remarkable essay is that Christianity is a city to which a bad citizen belongs and the good stranger does not. Péguy describes the Church, very beautifully, as a chain of saints and sinners with clasped fingers, pulling one another up to Jesus. But there are also passages which, if read literally, are grossly exorbitant. Péguy was not three years a convert when he wrote it, and he was not in communion with the Church. He daily saw men and women, who seemed to him lacking his own intense spirituality, trooping up to the altar rails while he was obliged to stay in his place excommunicate. The *"Nouveau Théologien"* is his meditation on his predicament. He feels there is a city of which he is a true citizen, but it is not the community of conventional practising Catholics, who are not, in his odd, often repeated phrase, *"compétent en matière de chrétienté."* He feels a kinship with the saints that these conventional church-goers do not know and in his strange, narrow, brooding mind he makes the preposterous deduction that this very true and strong bond is made, not by his faith and love, but by his sins. *"Littéralement,"* he writes, *"celui qui est pécheur, celui qui commet un péché est déjà chrétien, est en cela même chrétien. On pourrait presque dire est un bon chrétien." "Littéralement"?*: what is the precise force of that passage? Much depends on it. Does "literally" mean that any and every sinner is by virtue of his sin a Christian? Was Yusef a sinner and therefore Christian? No, because Péguy has already stated that strangers outside the chain of clasped hands cannot commit sin at all. Is Yusef damned? Can a sinner by this definition never be damned? The argument works in a circle of undefined terms. And what of the *"presque"*? How does one "almost" say something? Is one prevented by the fear of shocking others or the realization at the last moment that what one was going to say does not in fact make sense? In that case why record it? Why 'almost" say it? This is not a matter of quibbling. If Péguy is saying anything at all, he is saying something very startling and something which people seem to find increasingly important. Mr. Greene has removed the argument from Péguy's mumbled version and re-stated it in brilliantly plain human terms; and it is there, at the heart of the matter, that the literary critic must resign his judgment to the theologian.

The American Epoch in the Catholic Church

"A.D. or B.C. ?" How often among the monuments of the Old World, the dazed sight-seer asks this question, interrupting the guide's flow of dates! How often he wearily leaves it unasked! A.D. 100 or 100 B.C.; a span of two centuries; what does that matter, one way or the other, compared with the huge, crowded interval between then and now?

For most people the birth of Christ is a chronological device, used beyond the bounds of Christendom in Delhi and Telaviv and Moscow; a date-line as arbitrary as the meridian of Greenwich. It is not even accurate, for Christ was born four or five years before the traditional date. From time to time politicians have sought to impose an exploit of their own – the first French Republic, the Fascist March on Rome – as a more notable event from which to number the years. The old calendar came back for reasons of convenience rather than piety. But the Christian, when he dates his letters from the Year of Our Lord, is affirming his Faith. He is placing the Incarnation where for him it must always stand, in the centre of human history. Before that Year of Grace man lived in the mists, haunted by ancestral memories of a lost Eden, taught enigmatically by hints and portents, punished by awful dooms. The Incarnation restored order. In place of his bloody guilt-offerings man was given a single, complete expiation; in place of his magic, the sacramental system, a regular service of communication with the supernatural; in place of his mystery-cults, an open, divinely constituted human society in which to live and multiply. All his history from then onwards, seen through

Month, November 1949, pp. 293–308. First printed *Life* (Chicago), 19 September 1949.

Christian eyes, all the migrations of peoples and the rise and fall of empires, comprise merely a succession of moods and phases in the life of that society, the Church Christ founded.

In this deep perspective it seems that in every age some one branch of the Church, racial, cultural or national, bears peculiar responsibilities towards the whole. Vitality mysteriously waxes and wanes among the peoples. Again and again Christianity seems dying at its centre. Always Providence has another people quietly maturing to relieve the decadent of their burden. To a Christian of the fourth century the seat of authority at Rome must have seemed almost on the frontier; France, Spain and Germany were crude, missionary countries while all that was subtle and gracious in the Faith flourished in the Southern and Eastern Mediterranean. For him it was barely possible to conceive of a Church which had lost Constantinople, Alexandria and Carthage. To Louis XIV the Faith of those places belong to remote history. He could not think of Christendom without France. Yet in less than a century France was officially atheist. Challoner, the saintly Catholic leader of eighteenth-century England, would have thought it a preposterous forecast that the grandchildren of his dim, disheartened little flock would see the bishops restored and the religious orders flourishing in every county. So the battle continues, one that can never be lost and may never be won until the Last Trump. No loss is impossible, no loss irretrievable, no loss – not Rome itself – mortal. It may well be that Catholics of to-day, in their own life-time, may have to make enormous adjustments in their conception of the temporal nature of the Church. Many indeed are already doing so, and in the process turning their regard with hope and curiosity to the New World, where, it seems, Providence is schooling and strengthening a people for the historic destiny long borne by Europe.

Hope and curiosity. At first sight hope is subdued by many features of American history and psychology. Indeed, it could be quite plausibly argued that the people of the United States were resolutely anti-Catholic. Although most of the great adventures of exploration in the new continent were made by Catholic missionaries, the first colonists (everywhere except in Maryland) were Protestants whose chief complaint against their mother country was that she retained too much traditional character in her Established Church. School textbooks do not make much of the fact, which research abundantly proves, that it was the Quebec Act tolerating Popery in Canada, quite as much as the Stamp Act and the Tea Duties, which rendered George III intolerable to the colonists. The Constitution-makers little thought that in separating Church and State they were laying their country open to the prodigious Catholic growth of the nineteenth century, and in recent months the Supreme Court has shown in the McCollum case, that the phrase may be interpreted to the Church's injury. In foreign policy, when religious questions were involved, America has usually supported the anti-Catholic side, particularly where she is most powerful, in Mexico. President Wilson did nothing to oppose the disastrous anti-Catholic prejudices of the peace-makers of 1919.

Moreover the individual qualities that are regarded as particularly characteristic of Americans, their endemic revolt against traditional authority, their respect for success and sheer activity, their belief that progress is beneficent, their welcome of novelties, their suspicion of titles and uniforms and ceremonies, their dislike of dogmas that divide good citizens and their love of the generalities which unite them, their resentment of discipline – all these and others are unsympathetic to the habits of the Church. Mr. Geoffrey Gorer has discerned deep in the American soul a psychopathic antagonism to paternity and all its symbols; Catholics call both their priests and their God, "Father." The language of the Church is largely that of the Court; her liturgy was composed in lands where the honorific titles of Royalty were accepted naturally and it abounds in phrases which sound strange on republican and democratic lips. Many pages could be filled with instances of this kind, proving on paper very cogently that America can never play an important part in the life of the Church. It would be a fatuous exercise, for already at this moment Catholics are the largest religious body in the United States, the richest and in certain ways the most lively branch of the Catholic Church in the world.

Fifty years ago it even looked as though America might soon become predominantly Catholic. That hope, or fear, is now remote. Immigration from Catholic Europe has dwindled, peasant stock has lost its fertility in the cities, conversions barely keep pace with apostasies. Humanly speaking it is now certain that the Church is stabilized as a minority, the most important in the country, but subject to both the advantages and disadvantages of an unprivileged position. There is a paradox inherent in all her history that the Church, designed in her nature to be universal, remains everywhere a minority. We are inclined to think that from the age of Constantine to that of Luther there was a single, consistently triumphant, universally respected authority and to wonder why, in fact, she made such poor use of her opportunities. In fact, of course, the Church has always been at grips with enemies inside or outside her body, has never enjoyed that serene rule her constitution expects, has repeatedly suffered disasters from which it seemed barely possible she would recover. Her position in America cannot be understood unless her previous history is kept always in mind. From time to time, from place to place she has been in hiding; and she has been on the throne. In America her problems are less simple. There she is firmly grounded in a neutral, secular state.

The United States does not form part of Christendom in the traditional sense of the word. She is the child of late eighteenth-century "enlightenment" and the liberalism of her founders has persisted through all the changes of her history and penetrated into every part of her life. Separation of Church and State was an essential dogma. Government, whatever its form, was looked upon as the captain of a liner, whose concern is purely with navigation. He holds his command ultimately from the passengers. Under his immediate authority the public rooms of his ship are used for religious assemblies of all kinds, while in the bar anyone may quietly blaspheme. That is the ideal relationship between ruler and ruled, between the individual *qua* citizen and the individual *qua* immortal soul, as conceived by doctrinaire liberals of the period when the United States were founded. Men required and tolerated very little from their government. The realm of "private life" was large and inviolable. And the division of Church and State is feasible only under those conditions. To-day in most nations the analogy between State and ship has broken down. In some places the Captain has developed the mentality of Bligh of the *Bounty*; in others the passengers have been more or less willingly pressed into the crew; all are continuously occupied in keeping the ship running; the voyage is no longer a means to an end but an end in itself. As the State, whether it consist of the will of the majority or the power of a clique, usurps more and more of the individual's "private life," the more prominent become the discrepancies between the secular and the religious philosophies, for many things are convenient to the ruler which are not healthy for the soul.

The tragic fate of Europe is witness to the failure of secular states. But America through the unique circumstances of her growth has so far been proof against this decay and is thus the centre of hope even for those who are most critical of her idiosyncrasies.

These idiosyncrasies are now the object of boundless curiosity. A generation ago they caused mild amusement as the eccentricities of a likeable but remote people. To-day they are studied as portents of the development of the whole Western world. Catholics in particular study them, for it is a necessary consequence of the universality of the Church that she should develop marked superficial variations in her different branches. The Mass as offered in, say, St. Patrick's in New York or in a Tyrolean village or a Franciscan mission in Africa, is barely recognizable by the uninitiated as the same sacrifice. Mr. Aldous Huxley, no fool, writes in *Ends and Means*: "Christianity, like Hinduism or Buddhism, is not one religion but several. A Christian Church in Southern Spain or Mexico or Sicily is singularly like a Hindu temple. The eye is delighted by the same gaudy colours, the same tripe-like decorations, the same gesticulatory statues; the nose inhales the same intoxicating smells; the ear and, along with it, the understanding are lulled by the drone of the same incomprehensible incantations, roused by the same loud impressive music. At the other end of the scale, consider the chapel of a Cistercian monastery and the meditation hall of a community of Zen Buddhists. They are equally bare. . . . Here are two distinct religions for two distinct kinds of human beings." Only a very learned man can be quite as hopelessly and articulately wrong as that. Any altar-boy could tell him that the "incantations" of the Mass are identical whether in Guadelupe or Gethsemani, Ky, and are comprehensible or not simply so far as one understands Latin. Cistercian incense smells the same as Jesuit. There is high farce in his picture of a home-sick Andalusian in India frequenting the rites of Juggernaut in preference to the more severe devotions of the mission church. But it is palpably true that each culture gives an idiosyncratic local flavour to its church.

We differ most, perhaps, in our notions of reverence. I have seen a procession of the Blessed Sacrament in Spain which the people applauded by exploding fire-crackers under the feet of the clergy. It was done with genuine devotion, but to a Northern mind the effect was disconcerting. In the same way it strikes Europeans as odd that Americans find the voices of film stars on the radio an aid to saying the rosary. American manufacturers of "religious goods" offer many ingenious novelties, including a "rosary aid," which records each "Ave" on a dial with a sharp click, and a plastic crucifix which, I was assured, had the advantage that you could "throw it on the ground and stamp on it." But I remembered that in France I had seen children eating ginger-bread Madonnas. All these observations add to the charm of travel. But there is also "flavour" of a more philosophic kind.

Europeans are very anxious to catch the American flavour for they believe that for two or three generations it will predominate. They ask countless questions about it and get some very misleading answers, for one can find instances to give colour to almost any generalization. I saw both in London and Chicago the Italian film *Paisa*, one incident of which portrays, with fewer anomalies than usual, the life of a small Franciscan community in a remote mountain district. Three American chaplains arrive there and are warmly welcomed. It transpires that only one is Catholic, the other two being respectively a Protestant and a Jew. The friars are disconcerted and impose a fast on themselves for the conversion of their two non-Catholic guests. In London the audience was mainly non-Catholic, but its sympathy was plainly with the friars. In Chicago the audience was composed mainly of Italian speakers, presumably Catholics of a sort, and to them the friars seemed purely comic. It would be easy to generalize from this contrast that American Catholics care little for doctrinal niceties or the ascetic life; that they exalt the natural virtues above the supernatural, and considered good fellowship and material generosity the true ends of man. That is, in fact, just the kind of generalization which is current in Europe. Yet at that very time Boston was being torn by theological controversy, a contumacious Irish priest proclaiming damnation on all heretics and the authorities reaffirming the possibility of salvation outside the Church in the orthodox terms, which are generous but strict. And all over the country monks and nuns were quietly going about their business of the Opus Dei, singing their office and living by medieval rules, in just the fashion which excited laughter in a Chicago theatre.

The two chief impressions which I brought home from America were, first, that there is as great variety there between the outward forms of Catholicism as can be found in Europe, and secondly that Catholicism is not something alien and opposed to the American spirit but an essential part of it.

To enlarge on these two propositions. In vast areas of what is now the United States Catholicism was in colonial times the established religion. It was loosely established and in most of those areas now survives mainly in picturesque, ruined or restored, missions. Only two States can be said to have a strong, continuous Catholic tradition – Louisiana and Maryland. In the first of these the Church has never known persecution or even discouragement, and over a length of time that is not an entirely healthy condition. Catholics need to be reminded every few generations that theirs is a challenging creed. In no European country have the faithful been subject to so enervating a toleration as have the inhabitants of New Orleans. It is therefore not surprising that they take their faith easily and sentimentally, with some scepticism among the rich and some superstition among the poor, of the kind that was found in France before the Revolution. It is one of the Devil's devices to persuade people that their religion is so much "in their bones" that they do not have to bother; that it is in rather poor taste to talk too much about it. Marital confusions, the material advantages of secular education, the mere lassitude induced by the climate, keep many from practising their religion. There is a strange shrine there, unrecognized by the clergy, where the decoration and forms of prayer are Catholic, to which the coloured people resort for cures and favours. There is witchcraft in New Orleans, as there was at the court of Mme. de Montespan. Yet it was there that I saw one of the most moving sights of my tour. Ash Wednesday; warm rain falling in streets unsightly with the draggled survivals of carnival. The Roosevelt Hotel overflowing with crapulous tourists planning their return journeys. How many of them knew anything about Lent? But across the way the Jesuit Church was teeming with life all day long; a continuous, dense crowd of all colours and conditions moving up to the altar rails and returning with their foreheads signed with ash. And the old grim message was being repeated over each penitent: "Dust thou art and unto dust shalt thou return." One grows parched for that straight style of speech in the desert of modern euphemisms, where the halt and lame are dubbed "handicapped"; the hungry, "under-privileged"; the mad, "emotionally disturbed." Here it was, plainly stated, quietly accepted, and all that day, all over that light-hearted city, one encountered the little black smudge on the forehead which sealed us members of a great brotherhood who can both rejoice and recognize the limits of rejoicing.

The history of Maryland has been different. Catholicism was never established there as an official religion as it was in the French and Spanish colonies. The State was founded by Catholics as a place where they could practise their religion in peace, side by side with Protestants. The peace was soon broken and the Church persecuted and subdued. But it survived and emerged at the Declaration of Independence in much the same temper as in England at the Catholic Emancipation Act. The old Catholic families of Baltimore have much in common with the old Catholic families of Lancashire. The countryside round Leonardstown has the same tradition of Jesuit missionaries moving in disguise from family to family, celebrating Mass in remote plantations, inculcating the same austere devotional habits, the same tenacious, unobtrusive fidelity. That peninsula between Chesapeake Bay and the Potomac is one of the most fascinating areas for the Catholic visitor, and one of the things which inspires him most is the heroic fidelity of the negro Catholics. The Church has not always been a kind mother to them. Everywhere in the South Catholic planters brought their slaves to the sacraments, but in the bitter years after the Reconstruction few whites, priests or laity, recognized any special obligation towards them. Often they could only practise their religion at the cost of much humiliation. Some drifted from the Church to preposterous sects or reverted to paganism, but many families remained steadfast. Theirs was a sharper test than the white Catholics had earlier undergone, for here the persecutors were fellow-members in the Household of the Faith. But, supernaturally, they knew the character of the Church better than their clergy. To-day all this is fast changing. Catholics are everywhere leading the movement to make amends and in another generation, no doubt, those scandals will seem to belong to the distant past. But in the effort to forget them, honour must never be neglected to those thousands of coloured Catholics who so accurately traced their Master's road amid insult and injury.

Except in Louisiana and Maryland Catholics form a negligible part of the *haute bourgeoisie* of the Country Clubs and Social Registers. Most of them, Irish apart, grew up to the sound of foreign languages spoken by parents or grandparents in the home. Some, in the South-West, are survivors of Spanish colonization; most descend from the great waves of immigration from Central and Southern Europe. To the newly arrived immigrant his church is especially dear. It unites him in prayer and association with the home he has left; it is a social centre where he meets his own kind; it is a refuge full of familiar things in a bewildering new world. But the second and third generations have no tender memories of Europe. They have been reared on tales of the oppression and squalor from which their parents courageously rescued them. They want to be purely American and they develop a raw and rather guilty resentment against the Old World which I think, explains the loud Sicilian laughter I heard in the Chicago cinema. There is a temptation to identify the Church with their inferior station; to associate it with the smell of garlic and olive oil and grandfather muttering over the foreign language newspaper; to think of it as something to be discarded, as they rise in the social scale, as they discard their accents and surnames. Some, of course, do so. It is rare to find formal apostates, but occasionally parents who have ceased to care about their religion have their children brought up by Episcopalian or Baptist, in the belief that it gives them a better start in life and that, anyway, it is the child's business to choose for himself later on. But not often : it is one of the prime achievements of the American Catholic clergy that they have reconciled those first stirrings of a new loyalty with the ancestral faith, and Europeans should remember the problem that had to be solved before they look askance at the cruder expressions of nationalism which get quoted.

The Irish, on the other hand, present a precisely contrasting problem. They have never suffered a prick of shame in avowing their origins. Indeed, the further they move in time and place from their homeland the louder they sing about it. Should they ever return they would be shocked by the cynicism of their Dublin cousins. The problem with the Irish is to guard them from the huge presumption of treating the Universal Church as a friendly association of their own, and that problem has not been solved. In New York on St. Patrick's day, among the green carnations first invented by the Irishman, Oscar Wilde, for quite another significance; in Boston on any day of the year; the stranger might well suppose that Catholicism was a tribal cult. Only when he comes to study American hagiology does he learn that other races have their share in Pentecost. To the European it seems that the Irish have been led to betray their manifest historical destiny. When Englishmen in the last century founded a review which was to be for Catholics what the *Edinburgh Review* was for rationalists, they called it the *Dublin Review*. When there was a project for a national Catholic University, Newman went to Ireland. Had Ireland remained in the United Kingdom, Dublin would today be one of the great religious capitals of the world where Catholics from all over the British Empire resorted for education and leadership. That splendid hope was defeated by the politicians. What Europe lost, America has gained. The historic destiny of the Irish is being fulfilled on the other side of the Atlantic, where they have settled in their millions, bringing with them all their ancient grudges and the melancholy of the bogs, but, also, their hard, ancient wisdom. They alone of the newcomers are never for a moment taken in by the multifarious frauds of modernity. They have been changed from peasants and soldiers into townsmen. They have learned some of the superficial habits of "good citizenship," but at heart they remain the same adroit and joyless race that broke the hearts of all who ever tried to help them.

It is one of the functions of an upper class to remind the clergy of the true balance between their spiritual and their temporal positions. In most Catholic communities in the United States, so far as there is an upper class at all, the clergy themselves comprise it. From one year to another they never meet anyone better informed or more elegant than themselves. The deference with which they are treated on purely social occasions would tend to spoil all but the most heroic humility.

The presbyteries of Mr. Harry Sylvester's *Moon Gaffney* and Mr. J. F. Powers' *Prince of Darkness* are not mere literary inventions. Reading those admirable stories one can understand why there is often a distinct whiff of anti-clericalism where Irish priests are in power. They are faithful and chaste and, in youth at any rate, industrious, but many live out their lives in a painful state of transition; they have lost their ancestral simplicity without yet acquiring a modest carriage of their superior learning or, more important, delicacy in their human relations, or imagination, or agility of mind. To them, however, and to the Germans, must go the main credit for the construction of the Church in America. Without them the more sensitive Latins and Slavs would have at first huddled together in obscure congregations, then dispersed and perhaps have been lost to the Faith. The Irish with their truculence and practical good sense have built and paid for the churches, opening new parishes as fast as the population grew; they have staffed the active religious orders and have created a national system of Catholic education.

This last achievement is, indeed, something entirely unique. Without help from the State – indeed in direct competition with it – the poor of the nation have covered their land with schools, colleges and universities, boldly asserting the principle that nothing less than an entire Christian education is necessary to produce Christians. For the Faith is not a mere matter of learning a few prayers and pious stories in the home. It is a complete culture infusing all human knowledge. It is no doubt true that some branches of specialized scholarship can best be learned in the vastly richer, secular institutions. The Catholic colleges do not set themselves the aims of Harvard or Oxford or the Sorbonne. Their object is to transform a proletariat into a bourgeoisie; to produce a faithful laity, qualified to take its part in the general life of the nation; and in this way they are manifestly successful. Their students are not, in the main, drawn from scholarly homes. Many of them handle the English language uneasily. The teaching faculties are still dependent on European recruits for many of the refinements of learning. But, when all this is said, the Englishman, who can boast no single institution of higher Catholic education and is obliged to frequent universities that are Anglican in formation and agnostic in temper, can only applaud what American Catholics have done in the last hundred years. It is a very great thing that young men who are going out to be dentists or salesmen should have a grounding of formal logic and Christian ethics. "Prove syllogistically that natural rights exist" : "Give the fundamental reason why usury is wrong" : "What is the difference between soul and mind?" : "Give and explain a definition of Sacrifice" : These are questions chosen almost at random from the examination papers of a Jesuit College. I have heard it said that American adolescents tend to "learn the answers" parrotwise without much speculation. This was not the impression I formed in talking with them, but even if it were so, they have learned something which most Europeans ignore. It is a great gain, while the memory is active, to store up formulas. Experience will give them life and later, when he is confronted with a problem, phrases from his college days will come into a man's mind with sudden vivid importance. I noticed this enormous advantage which religiously educated American adults enjoy over their more learned fellows from the secular universities. With the latter, when discussion became general, one got the impression that outside their particular subjects everything was shapeless and meaningless. Nuclear fission threatens material progress; they apprehend this and are at once in despair. What are they here for if not to participate in a benevolent scheme of evolution? It is a question which only the God-fearing can answer. The Catholic remembers the phrases of his youth, which at the time, perhaps, seemed a mere combination of words to be memorized for the satisfaction of an examiner, and suddenly the words have topical significance. He can tap at will the inexhaustible sources of theology.

This fine work of education is, at the moment, somewhat precarious. In America, as elsewhere, the independent schools are in the position of a poker-player among men much richer than himself who are continually raising the stakes. The apparatus of education is becoming exorbitantly expensive. The Catholic colleges cannot long hope to compete with the State in providing the engines of modern Physical Science. There is, moreover, a powerful group in the nation who openly aspire to uniformity as to something good in itself. I met many anxious Catholic educationalists, but I left with confidence that those who have achieved such stupendous feats in the recent past will somehow triumph over their enemies.

There is no doubt that the Catholic colleges maintain a remarkably high standard of duty and piety. The holy places of Notre Dame are crowded before a football match. The number and frequency of communions are startling to a European and dispose of the charge of Jansenism often loosely preferred against the Irish clergy. The habit thus inculcated often continues through life as any visitor to any church can recognize. The quantity is there. No one can judge the quality. Every soul in his traffic with God has his own secrets. A youth who is inarticulate in conversation may well be eloquent in prayer. It would be an intolerable impertinence to attempt to judge. What is plain to the observer is that throughout the nation the altar rails are everywhere crowded. It is normally from just such a deep soil of popular devotion that the fine flowers of the Faith grow. The Church does not exist in order to produce elegant preachers or imaginative writers or artists or philosophers. It exists to produce saints. God alone knows his own. Without doubt lives of deep unobtrusive sanctity are being lived in all parts of the United States, but it is true that the American Church up to the present time has produced few illustrious heroes or heroines. Archbishop Cicognani in his *Sanctity in America* lately collected thirty-five brief biographies of men and women of eminent holiness who worked in the United States. Of these, thirty-one were foreign-born and foreign-educated. Of the four natives none, it may be noted, were of Irish extraction. Two, Catherine Tekakwitha, the Indian, and Mother Elizabeth Ann Seton, the Foundress of the Sisters of Charity, were converts. Bishop Richard Miles, the Dominican of Tennessee, was a zealous and devoted pastor and administrator. Sister Miriam Teresa Demjanovich was training to be a teacher. None were pure contemplatives.

The contemplative life is, of course, only one form of the Christian life. It is a matter of observation, however, that the health of religion in any place and age may be fairly judged by the number of contemplative vocations. Until recent years America has a poor record in this matter, but lately there are signs of change. The case of Thomas Merton has aroused wide interest but he is merely one, unusually articulate, representative of a wide and healthy movement. New Trappist houses are being established, postulants for Carmel exceed the accommodation. Man is made for the knowledge of God and for no other purpose. Where that purpose is recognized there will always be found many who seek Him in the cloisters, from which Grace spreads to an entire people.

The Church and the world need monks and nuns more than they need writers. These merely decorate. The Church can get along very well without them. If they appear, it is a natural growth. They are not much in evidence in America at the moment, and the well-meant attempts to produce them artifically by special courses of study seem to me unlikely to succeed. A more fruitful source of such luxuries is the variety of interests which Catholics have quite recently developed – the small magazines devoted to the liturgy, to social studies, to the translation and explanation of foreign literature and so forth; the works, for example, of John and Mary Ryan in Boston, of John Pick in Milwaukee, of *Commonweal* in New York, of the Sheil School in Chicago. There is a fermentation everywhere.

I mentioned a second conclusion: that Catholicism is part of the American spirit. I do not mean that it lacks enemies. Recently there was an attempt, which very nearly succeeded, to ban specifically Christian Christmas Carols from the State schools in New York. The shops all over the country seek to substitute Santa Claus and his reindeer for the Christchild. I witnessed, early in Lent, the arrival at a railway station of an "Easter Bunny", attended by brass band and a posse of police. Just as the early Christians adopted the pagan festivals and consecrated them, so everywhere, but particularly in the United States, pagan commerce is seeking to adopt and desecrate the feasts of the Church. And wherever the matter is one for public authority, the State is "neutral" – a euphemism for "unchristian."

I mean that "Americanism" is the complex of what all Americans consider the good life and that in this complex Christianity, and preeminently Catholicism, is the redeeming part. Unhappily "Americanism" has come to mean for most of the world what a few, very vociferous, far from typical, Americans wish to make it. The peoples of other continents look to America half in hope and half in alarm. They see that their own future is inextricably involved with it and their judgment is based on what they see in the cinema, what they read in the popular magazines, what they hear from the loudest advertiser. Gratitude for the enormous material benefits received is tempered with distaste for what they believe is the spiritual poverty of the benefactor. It is only when one travels in America that one realizes that most Americans either share this distaste or are genuinely unaware of the kind of false impression which interested parties have conspired to spread.

The Christian believes that he was created to know, love and serve God in this world and to be happy with him in the next. That is the sole reason for his existence. "Good citizenship," properly understood, is a necessary by-product of this essential task, but more and more the phrase has come to mean mere amenability to the demands of the government. At present the State makes few exorbitant demands in America, but there are many Americans, resolutely opposed to the mechanisms of Communism and Fascism, who yet exalt this limited conception of "good-citizenship" as the highest virtue, and regard the creation of a homogeneous society as the first end of statesmanship. In this popular, neutral opinion Catholics, Protestants, Jews, atheists, theosophists and all the strange sects of the nation differ only in the rites they practise, or do not practise, in certain buildings for an hour or two a week. This is pure make-believe. They differ hugely in morals, social custom, and philosophy of life – in fact in all the things they value most highly. The neutral, secular state can only function justly by keeping itself within strict limits. It is not for a foreigner to predict how long the government of the United States will resist the prevalent temptation to encroachment. He merely notes admiringly and gratefully that hitherto the temptations have been largely resisted, and also that the constitutional separation of Church and State does not, when temptation offers, guarantee the continued welfare of any particular, minority, religious body.

The Catholic holds certain territories that he can never surrender to the temporal power. He hopes that in his time there will be no invasion, but he knows that the history of his Church is one of conflict. If his rulers force him to choose between them and his Faith, in the last resort he must choose his Faith. And because in his heart he knows this, he tends to be conspicuously loyal whenever he can be so with a clear conscience. Bossuet could write without embarrassment : *"Le Roi, Jésus-Christ et l'Eglise, Dieu en ces trois noms."* Similarly many American prelates speak as though they believed that representative, majority government were of divine institution, and the lay American Catholic insists more emphatically on his "Americanism" than do Protestants or atheists of, perhaps, longer American ancestry.

There is a purely American "way of life" led by every good American Christian that is point-for-point opposed to the publicized and largely fictitious "way of life" dreaded in Europe and Asia. And that, by the Grace of God, is the "way of life" that will prevail.

St. Helena Empress

We are advised to meditate on the lives of the saints, but this precept originated in the ages when meditation was a more precise and arduous activity than we are tempted to think it to-day. Heavy apparatus has been at work in the last hundred years to enervate and stultify the imaginative faculties. First, realistic novels and plays, then the cinema have made the urban mentality increasingly subject to suggestion so that it now lapses effortlessly into a trance-like escape from its condition. It is said that great popularity in fiction and film is only attained by works into which readers and audience can transpose themselves and be vicariously endangered, loved and applauded. This kind of reverie is not meditation, even when its objects are worthy of high devotion. It may do little harm, perhaps even some little good, to fall day-dreaming and play the parts of Sir Thomas More, King Lewis IX or Father Damien. There are evident dangers in identifying ourselves with Saint Francis or Saint John of the Cross. We can invoke the help of the saints and study the workings of God in them, but if we delude ourselves that we are walking in their shoes, seeing through their eyes and thinking with their minds, we lose sight of the one certain course of our salvation. There is only one saint that Bridget Hogan can actually become, Saint Bridget Hogan, and that saint she *must* become, here or in the fires of purgatory, if she is to enter heaven. She cannot slip through in fancy-dress, made up as Joan of Arc.

For this reason it is well to pay particular attention to the saints about whom our information is incomplete. There are names in the calendar about which we know nothing at all except those names, and then sometimes in a form that would puzzle their contemporaries. There are others about whom, humanly speaking, we know almost everything, who have left us a conspectus of their minds in their own writings, who were accompanied through life by pious biographers recording every movement and saying, who were conspicuous in the history of their times so that we can see them from all sides as they impressed friends and opponents. And mid-way between these two groups are the saints who are remembered

Month, January 1952, pp. 7–11.

for a single act. To this class Helena eminently belongs. In extreme old age, as Empress Dowager, she made a journey into one part of her son's immense dominions, to Jerusalem. From that journey spring the relics of the True Cross that are venerated everywhere in Christendom. That is what we know; most else is surmise.

Helena was at a time, literally, the most important woman in the world, yet we know next to nothing about her. Two places claim to be her birthplace: Colchester in England and Drepanum, a seaside resort, now quite vanished, in Turkey. The evidence for neither is so strong that Englishman or Turk need abandon his pretension. She was probably of modest rank, not servile, not illustrious. Constantius married her early in his rise to power and abandoned her later for a royal match. She may have been brought up at one of the post-stables on an Imperial trunk road and have there attracted Constantius's attention on one of his official journeys. Or she may, conceivably, have been what legend makes her, the daughter of a British chief. She bore one son, Constantine the Great, probably at Nish in Serbia. After her divorce she settled at Trier (Trèves) where the Cathedral probably stands on the foundations of her palace. Almost certainly it was there that she became Christian. Lactantius, who was tutor to her grandson Crispus, may have helped instruct her. At the very end of her life she suddenly emerged for her great adventure. She died at Constantinople and her body was thereupon or later moved to Rome. Her tomb never became a great centre of pilgrimage. She, herself, seems never to have attracted great personal devotion; but she was a popular saint. Numberless churches are dedicated to her; numberless girls baptized with her name; she appears everywhere in painting, sculpture and mosaic. She has fitted, in a homely and substantial way, into the family life of Christendom.

There is little of heroism or genius in any of this. We can assume that she was devout, chaste, munificent; a thoroughly good woman in an age when palaces were mostly occupied by the wicked; but she lived grandly and comfortably whereas most of the saints in every age have accepted poverty as the condition of their calling. We know of no suffering of hers, physical, spiritual or mental, beyond the normal bereavements, disappointments and infirmities which we all expect to bear. Yet she lived in an age when Christians had often to choose between flight, apostasy or brutal punishment. Where, one may ask, lies her sanctity? Where the particular lesson for us who live in such very different circumstances?

For the world of Constantine, as we catch glimpses of it, is utterly remote from ours. There are certain superficial similarities. Poetry was dead and prose dying. Architecture had lapsed into the horny hands of engineers. Sculpture had fallen so low that in all his empire Constantine could not find a mason capable of decorating his triumphal arch and preferred instead to rob the two-hundred-year-old arch of Trajan. An enormous bureaucracy was virtually sovereign, controlling taxation on the sources of wealth, for the pleasure of city mobs and for the defence of frontiers more and more dangerously pressed by barbarians from the East. The civilized world was obliged to find a new capital. All this seems familiar but for the event of supreme importance, the victory of Christianity, we can find no counterpart in contemporary history. We cannot by any effort of the imagination share the emotions of Lactantius or Macarius. Helena, more than anyone, stands in the heart of that mystery.

She might claim, like that other, less prudent queen : "In my end is my beginning." But for her final, triumphant journey she would have no fame. We should think of her, if at all, as we think of Constantine; someone who neatly made the best of both worlds. The strong purpose of her pilgrimage shed a new and happier light on the long years of uneventful retirement showing us that it was by an act of will, grounded in patience and humility, that she accepted her position. Or rather, her positions. We do not know in exactly what state Constantius found her. She certainly did not choose him for his hopes of power. Those hopes, indeed, proved her undoing and dismissed her, divorced, into exile. In a court full of intrigue and murder she formed no party, took no steps against her rival, but quietly accepted her disgrace. Constantine rose to power, proclaimed her empress, struck coins in her honour, opened the whole imperial treasury for her use. And she accepted that too. Only in her religious practices did she maintain her private station, slipping in to mass at Rome among the crowd, helping with the housework at the convent on Mount Sion. She accepted the fact that God had His own use for her. Others faced the lions in the circus; others lived in caves in the desert. She was to be St. Helena Empress, not St. Helena Martyr or St. Helena Anchorite. She accepted a state of life full of dangers to the soul in which many foundered, and she remained fixed in her purpose until at last it seemed God had no other need of her except to continue to the end, a kind old lady. Then came her call to a single peculiar act of service, something unattempted before and unrepeatable – the finding of the True Cross.

We have no absolute certainty that she found it. The old sneer, that there was enough "wood of the cross" to build a ship, though still repeated, has long been nullified. All the splinters and shavings venerated everywhere have been patiently measured and found to comprise a volume far short of a cross. We know that most of these fragments have a plain pedigree back to the early fourth century. But there is no guarantee which would satisfy an antiquary, of the authenticity of Helena's discovery. If she found the True Cross, it was by direct supernatural aid, not by archaeological reasoning. That, from the first, was its patent of title. There are certain elements about the surviving relics which are so odd that they seem to preclude the possibility of imposture. The "Label," for example – the inscription *Jesus of Nazareth, King of the Jews* – now preserved in Santa Croce seems the most unlikely product of a forger's art. And who would have tried to cheat her? Not St. Macarius certainly. But it *is* nevertheless possible that Helena was tricked, or that she and her companions mistook casual baulks of timber, builders' waste long buried, for the wood they sought; that the Label, somehow, got added to her treasure later. Even so her enterprise was something life-bringing.

It is not fantastic to claim that her discovery entitles her to a place in the Doctorate of the Church, for she was not merely adding one more stupendous trophy to the hoard of relics which were everywhere being unearthed and enshrined. She was asserting in sensational form a dogma that was in danger of neglect. Power was shifting. In the academies of the Eastern and South-Eastern Mediterranean sharp, sly minds were everywhere looking for phrases and analogies to reconcile the new, blunt creed for which men had died, with the ancient speculations which had beguiled their minds, and with the occult rites which had for generations spiced their logic.

Another phase of existence which select souls enjoyed when the body was shed; a priesthood; a sacramental system, even in certain details of eating, anointing and washing – all these had already a shadowy place in fashionable thought. Everything about the new religion was capable of interpretation, could be refined and diminished; everything except the unreasonable assertion that God became man and died on the Cross; not a myth or an allegory; true God, truly incarnate, tortured to death at a particular moment in time, at a particular geographical place, as a matter of plain historical fact. This was the stumbling block in Carthage, Alexandria, Ephesus and Athens, and at this all the talents of the time went to work, to reduce, hide and eliminate.

Constantine was no match for them. Schooled on battle fields and in diplomatic conferences, where retreat was often the highest strategy, where truth was a compromise between irreconcilable opposites; busy with all the affairs of state; unused to the technical terms of philosophy; Constantine not yet baptized, still fuddled perhaps by dreams of Alexander, not quite sure that he was not himself divine, not himself the incarnation of the Supreme Being of whom Jove and Jehovah were alike imperfect emanations; Constantine was quite out of his depth. The situation of the Church was more perilous, though few saw it, than in the days of persecution. And at that crisis suddenly emerged God-sent from luxurious retirement in the far north, a lonely, resolute old woman with a single concrete, practical task clear before her; to turn the eyes of the world back to the planks of wood on which their salvation hung.

That was Helena's achievement, and for us who, whatever our difficulties, are no longer troubled by those particular philosophic confusions that clouded the fourth century, it has the refreshing quality that we cannot hope to imitate it. The Cross is very plain for us to-day; plainer perhaps than for many centuries. What we can learn from Helena is something about the workings of God; that He wants a different thing from each of us, laborious or easy, conspicuous or quite private, but something which only we can do and for which we were each created.

Mgr. Knox at 4 a.m.

Most mature writers employ a single idiosyncratic recognisable style. Not so Mgr. Knox. If one had to name the single characteristic of his genius that sets him furthest apart, it would not be his humour or wit or scholarship, or subtlety – though of course he has all these qualities in pre-eminent abundance – but his versatility. In his translation of the Vulgate he exhibits a vast variety; compare his treatment of narrative, poetry and exhortation. Look beyond that great work and compare *Let Dons Delight, Broadcast Minds, The Mass in Slow Motion, Enthusiasm;* each a notable literary achievement in an entirely distinct *genre.* No major writer in our history has ever shown such an extent of accomplishment. Certain minor writers with little to say have shown skill in pastiche, but here we are dealing with a profound, learned and original mind. Is there anywhere in all this dazzling display a quintessential Knox? One can only offer a personal opinion. One admirer at least finds him in the quiet little Oxford conferences, begun when he was chaplain and continued since then as a regular guest.

The Oxford of Mgr. Knox's chaplaincy was the perplexed generation of the 1930s. Logical Positivism and Communism were the fashion. In that decade two great men living within a few yards of one another, Father Martin D'Arcy, S.J., and Mgr. Knox, were providentially raised as defenders of the Faith. There is quite a different University today with quite different problems which are being bravely handled by their suc-

Review of *The Hidden Stream*, by Ronald Knox, *Duckett's Register*, December 1952, pp. 153–54.

cessors. It is neither invidious nor sentimental to look back on that decade as a golden age of Oxford Catholicism.

Mgr. Knox's purpose in these sermons was not primarily to attract converts or to awaken the adolescent conscience. He speaks to young people who have grown up in Catholic homes and at Catholic schools and have, most of them, had little previous contact with unbelievers. His task is to equip them to meet arguments against the Faith which they have never heard before and to ensure that the simple dogmatic and apologetic instruction of their youth keeps pace with the Philosophy and History Schools which are mostly directed by unsympathetic minds.

In *Soft Garments*, the previous series, he took his charges methodically through the curriculum of Faith restating and revivifying the definitions in colloquial terms, with brilliantly apt local illustrations.

In *The Hidden Stream* he follows something of the same plan but in this series he has come closer to his hearers. Although a visitor from outside he seems to be more intimate than before. He is sharing his own difficulties – the fidgeting doubts that disturb the early hours of the light sleeper – and explaining how he allays them until dawn comes and with it the daily sacrifice that dispels them. The group of problems to which he reverts so often that they can be said to comprise a central theme, deal with the inexplicable interdependence of mind and matter, body and soul. Do modern undergraduates worry much about these deep mysteries? If not, they should. Outwardly their preoccupations today seem largely practical – good works, social order, participation in the politics of the time, the observation of the moral law, resistance to Communism, the cultivation of tolerance. All necessary and admirable. But perhaps more of them than appears have their black moments when the enthusiasm of the rally has worn off, when the phrase "social justice" seems estranged from the salvation of the soul. In what Mgr. Knox calls "the 4 a.m." mood a sense of futility creeps in, a suspicion that the Christian system does not really hang together, that there are flaws in the logic, and adroit shifting about between natural causes, revelation and authority, that there are too many unresolved contradictions. And there are some, perhaps many, to whom it is nearly always 4 a.m. To this mood with its temptation to despair, Mgr. Knox talks with unfailing kindness and solace. He is not concerned here to demolish, as he has so brilliantly done in the past, false opinions. He is restoring and creating confidence.

Fortunate young people to hear that comforting voice! But it is not for them alone. Those who have left their formal education far behind them will find huge solace in reading and re-reading this book. It should be at every bedside, ready to be opened at 4 a.m.

Changes in the Church
QUESTIONS FOR THE 'PROGRESSIVES'

Sir, – Like all editors you justly claim that you are not responsible for the opinions of your correspondents and claim credit for establishing an open "forum".

On the other hand you write of "exploding renewal" and "manifest dynamism of the Holy Spirit", thus seeming to sympathise with the Northern innovators who wish to change the outward aspect of the Church.

I think you injure your cause when week by week you publish (to me) fatuous and outrageous proposals by irresponsible people.

Father John Sheerin is neither fatuous nor outrageous but I find him a little smug. If I read him correctly he is pleading for magnanimity towards defeated opponents.

The old (and young) buffers should not be reprobated. They have been imperfectly "instructed". The "progressive" should ask the "conservative with consummate courtesy" to re-examine his position.

I cannot claim consummate courtesy but may I, with round politeness, suggest that the progressives should re-examine their own? Were *they* perfectly instructed? Did they find the discipline of their seminaries rather irksome? Did they think they were wasting time on the Latin which they found uncongenial?

Do they want to marry and beget other little progressives? Do they, like the present Pope, think Italian literature a more enjoyable pursuit than apologetics?

The distinction between Catholicism and *Romanita* has already been stressed in the American journal *Commonweal.* Of course it is possible to have the Faith without *Romanita* and to have *Romanita* without the Faith, but as a matter of recorded history the two have kept very close. "Peter has spoken" remains the guarantee of orthodoxy.

It is surely (?), a journalistic trick to write of "the Johannine era". Pope John was a pious and attractive man. Many of the innovations, which many of us find so obnoxious, were introduced by Pius XII.

Catholic Herald, 7 August 1964, p. 4.

Pope John's life at Bergamo, Rome, in the Levant, at Paris and Venice was lived with very meagre association with Protestants until, in his extreme old age, he found himself visited by polite clergymen of various sects whom he greeted, as he did with the Russian atheists, with "consummate courtesy".

I do not believe he had any conception of the true character of modern Protestantism. I quote from an article in *Time* magazine of 10th July :

"The one persuasive way of referring to Jesus today is as a 'remarkably free man'. After the Resurrection the disciples suddenly possessed some of the unique and 'contagious' freedom that Jesus had. In telling the story of Jesus of Nazareth, therefore, they told it as the story of the free man who had set them free . . . He who says 'Jesus is love' says that Jesus' freedom has been contagious . . . Van Buren concludes that Christianity will have to strip itself of its supernatural elements . . . just as alchemy had to abandon its mystical overtones to become the useful science of Chemistry."

These words are not those of a Californian crank but of a clergyman of the "Episcopal Church" of America, who derive what Orders they have from the Archbishop of Canterbury. I am sure that such questions were not raised on the much publicised meeting of the Archbishop and Pope John.

Father Sheerin suggests that Catholic Conservatism is the product of the defensive policy necessary in the last century against the nationalistic-masonic-secularism of the time. I would ask him to consider that the function of the Church in every age has been conservative – to transmit undiminished and uncontaminated the creed inherited from its predecessors.

Not "is this fashionable notion one that we should accept?" but "is this dogma (a subject on which we agree) the Faith as we received it?" has been the question (as far as I know) at all General Councils. I have seen no evidence that Pope Paul had anything else in mind when he summoned the present Council.

Conservatism is not a new influence in the Church. It is not the heresies of the sixteenth and seventeenth century, the agnosticism of the eighteenth century, the atheism of the nineteenth and twentieth centuries, that have been the foes of the Faith turning her from serene supremacy to sharp controversy.

Throughout her entire life the Church has been at active war with enemies from without and traitors from within. The war against Communism in our own age is acute but it is mild compared with those fought and often won by our predecessors.

Finally, a word about liturgy. It is natural to the Germans to make a row. The torchlit, vociferous assemblies of the Hitler Youth expressed a national passion. It is well that this should be canalised into the life of the Church. But it is essentially un-English.

We seek no "Sieg Heils". We pray in silence. "Participation" in the Mass does not mean hearing our own voices. It means God hearing our voices. Only He knows who is "participating" at Mass. I believe, to compare small things with great, that I "participate" in a work of art when I study it and love it silently. No need to shout.

Anyone who has taken part in a play knows that he can rant on the stage with his mind elsewhere. If the Germans want to be noisy, let them. But why should they disturb our devotions?

"Diversity" is deemed by the Progressives as one of their aims against the stifling *Romanita*. May they allow it to English Catholics.

I am now old but I was young when I was received into the Church. I was not at all attracted by the splendour of her great ceremonies – which the Protestants could well counterfeit. Of the extraneous attractions of the Church which most drew me was the spectacle of the priest and his server at low Mass, stumping up to the altar without a glance to discover how many or how few he had in his congregation; a craftsman and his apprentice; a man with a job which he alone was qualified to do.

That is the Mass I have grown to know and love. By all means let the rowdy have their "dialogues", but let us who value silence not be completely forgotten.

Your obedient servant,

Evelyn Waugh

Edith Stein

Last year a little book named *Waiting on God* attracted great attention inside and outside the Church. It comprised a selection from the writings of a young, highly intelligent French Jewess, Simone Weil, who died in

Reviews of *Waiting on God*, by Simone Weil, and *Edith Stein*, by Sister Teresia de Spiritu Sancto, O.D.C. (Posselt), *Catholic Mother*, Christmas 1952, pp. 6–7. Lady Lothian, who edited the *Catholic Mother* in 1952, writes: "Evelyn Waugh wrote the enclosed at my request to help *me* pursue research into the attitudes towards Christianity of women who were highly respected as philosophers. I asked if I might publish it. He was kind enough to agree although it had been written for private information only." Ed.

England in 1943. The most interesting pages were taken from her letters to a French Dominican priest, whose answers are lacking. In them Mlle. Weil professes an ardent love for the proletariat and a zeal for self-sacrifice, which she attempted to put into action by taking employment first in a factory and later at the Headquarters of the Free French in London; she was consumptive and hastened her death by going short of food in sympathy for her countrymen under the occupation. She seemed to accept the main truths of Christianity, but died unbaptized leaving a copious apologia which can be reduced to two themes : a distaste for the exclusive and authoritative tone of the Church and for the unworthiness of some of its members and a conviction that God would tell her as He had St. Paul in an unmistakable and personal way when He required her submission. Some readers, among them the present writer, are unable to silence the suspicion that this apologia could be starkly summarized : "The Church isn't quite good enough for *Me*, but, of course, if God really insists . . ."

At almost the same time there appeared another book, *Edith Stein* by Sister Teresia de Spiritu Sancto, O.D.C. (Discalced Carmelite). It is the biography, or rather the first sketch for a biography, of a highly intelligent German Jewess, who was known for the last eight years of her life as Sister Teresia Benedicta a Cruce, O.D.C. It has been admirably compiled from her own and her friends' accounts and reveals a life which has remarkable similarities to Mlle. Weil's and still more remarkable contrasts. It might be a useful exercise to make a line for line comparison between the two women, but it is an ungracious habit to praise one thing while disparaging another. Suffice to say that those who have been dismayed by the vogue of Mlle. Weil may find a prompt restorative in Edith Stein.

She was born at Breslau on October 12th, 1891, the youngest of seven children who were left fatherless when Edith was three years old. Thenceforward the mother assumed control of the family and the family business – the masculine occupation of timber merchant – and managed it prosperously until the early '30s when industry was breaking down throughout Germany. The matriarch was devoutly and rigidly orthodox in religion. The children were in various degrees infected by the scepticism of their period, Edith most of all. From the moment she began to think until her twenty-second year she was dogmatically atheist. There was nothing recognizably Jewish in her appearance but she was Jewish at heart and even after her conversion to Christianity she could happily pray beside her mother in the synagogue.

The early chapters of the book give a charming picture of German Jewry in its heyday under the Empire, the period of Edith's adolescence. The Steins were well-to-do, living in solid, unostentatious comfort, patriotic – indeed thoroughly Prussian – in sympathies, highly respectful of the *Kultur* which their race had done so much to establish. They associated only with Jews, chiefly with their own kin, but they regarded themselves as being as German as the junkers. They were a distinct part of the nation, Jewish Germans rather than German Jews, with little sympathy for Zionism or international socialism; the antithesis of the Nazi bogey. This was the world, now vanished without trace, in which Edith grew up.

She was a bright, pretty, affectionate child; the only fault imputed to her was excessive ambition. German education under the Kaiser was formidably efficient. She set all her precocious intellect and energies into surmounting its various grades and was brilliantly successful. At adolescence she was possessed by what is described as a thirst for knowledge, but which is perhaps better called a thirst for truth. All her intellectual force was early canalised into philosophy and she began her search of the Universities for a master who would show her the way of truth; the quest which found its final satisfaction in Carmel.

At Göttingen she found a group of students and teachers gathered round Edmund Husserl, whose writing she already knew. Their philosophical system is called the Phenomenological School. Edith soon established herself in the inner circle of disciples both by her quick comprehension and her original speculations, and in 1916 when he was appointed Professor at Freiburg, the master summoned Edith to be his personal assistant. In order to accept this post she left the Red Cross in which she had devotedly served since the outbreak of war. But first she had another task. At Göttingen Husserl had for his colleague Adolph Reinach, an apostate Lutheran who returned to his faith while in the army. Reinach was killed and Edith accepted the task of arranging his manuscript writings. She was now 26 years old but had never given any thought to Christianity. The phenomenologists had broken down her crude rationalism; many of them had begun to move towards Catholicism, but it had not occurred to Edith to examine the credentials of the Church. Reinach had stated shortly before his death that he would teach philosophy in future only as a means of leading men to God. No doubt among the papers which Edith now perused, there were indications of this change of heart, but what impressed her was the behaviour of his widow. Edith could see nothing but absolute loss in the premature end of a brilliant academic career. Frau Reinach (who later became a Catholic) accepted it with resignation and hope and for the first time Edith encountered Christian Faith in action; she noted the phenomenon in her accurate mind.

After the war, in a vastly changed world, the German Universities made an attempt to re-establish the old life. Edith became "Fräulein

Doktor" with a growing reputation as a philosopher but the slim, simple appearance of a young girl; she wrote a thesis on the Soul which was a plain acknowledgement of the religious basis of life. Some of her friends supposed her to be already a Christian. But her conversion was delayed until she chose at random from the shelf of a friend St. Teresa of Avila's *Life* of herself. Edith read the book straight through and concluded: "That is the Truth". She then set about instructing herself in the practical, thorough way in which she did everything. She bought a catechism and a missal and studied them. Then for the first time in her life she went to Mass and understood every phrase and gesture. After Mass she followed the priest to the presbytery and asked for baptism.

"Who has instructed you and for how long?" "Test my knowledge". The subsequent discussion ranged over the whole field of Catholic theology. Edith's answers were satisfactory and she was baptized on New Year's Day, 1922. There can have been few conversions so cool and impersonal. Contrast it with Pascal's. But this was no mere intellectual acceptance of a philosophical system. It was the start of a new life of devotion and prayer.

The effects of this huge change on Edith's mother, sisters and friends, the transition of the popular lecturer to Carmelite nun with the first turbulence of the German disaster in the background, are briefly but beautifully told. As the Nazis came to power, Edith was moved, as was hoped for her safety, to a sister house in Holland. The Nazis came there too. Sister Teresia Benedicta a Cruce went calmly about her duties. Permission was sought and obtained too late, to transfer her to safety to Switzerland.

On Sunday, 26th July, 1942, the Archbishop of Utrecht issued a pastoral condemning the persecution of the Jews. Retribution was immediate. All Catholic priests and religious with Jewish connections were rounded up by the S.S. On August 1st, Edith was arrested and driven off with the other victims of the Terror; somewhere, quite soon probably, she was killed in one of the extermination camps in the East. Attempts have been made to sift the various conflicting reports of people who saw her or thought they saw her during her last journey. Nothing is certain except the fact of her death. She disappeared bodily in the total, hellish darkness.

Her spirit shines out, very clear and lonely; a brilliant intelligence; a pure, disciplined will; a single motive power, the Grace of God. The circumstances of her death touch us for they lie at the heart of contemporary disaster. The aimless, impersonal wickedness which could drag a victim from the holy silence of Carmel and drive her, stripped and crowded, to the gas chamber and the furnace, still lurks in the darkness.

But Edith's death is perhaps an irrelevant horror. Her life was completed in Carmel. She did not sit, waiting on God. She went out alone and by the God-given light of her intelligence and strength of purpose, she found Him.